THISTLE AND ROSE

To four teachers :

ANDREW J. MURRAY

JOHN MACLEAN

IAIN CRICHTON SMITH

and MACK ROSENTHAL

CONTENTS

Thistle and Rose

THE PARADOXICAL VISION

"Scotland seems a colder and quieter place, since Christopher Murray Grieve died in the first hour of Saturday morning." So ran the editorial in *The Scotsman* on the eleventh of September 1978.

And beyond Scotland—in America, in Russia, in India, in Greece, in Canada, in Africa—there were those who noted his passing and who felt his loss.

The genius of Hugh MacDiarmid was no longer in doubt. ("One of the great European poets of this century," proclaimed the same *Scotsman* editorial). In the last decade his poetry had finally been receiving appropriate attention and acclaim, and his death called forth an outpouring of appreciation and reverence—ironically of the type often satirized by MacDiarmid himself in his attacks on the Burns cult.

The man whose finest work dates from the 1920's had had to wait half a century for the recognition he deserved. And he must have watched, with some amusement, from his cottage in Biggar, as the seventies produced their bumper crop of MacDiarmid interest and scholarship. Never had his work been so available. Never had so many critics turned in his direction.

1970 saw the publication of *The Penguin Book of Scottish Verse* and *The Penguin Book of Socialist Verse,* each of which reserved a prominent place for MacDiarmid. 1971's vintage was equally impressive: the republication of *A Drunk Man Looks at the Thistle,* and numerous articles in reputable magazines and journals.[1] And subsequent years have given us the *Hugh MacDiarmid Anthology,* edited by Michael Grieve and Alexander Scott, and the very fine *Illustrated Biography,* compiled and published by Gordon Wright to mark the eighty-fifth birthday. When MacDiarmid died, a two-volume *Complete Poems* was in press. (An authorized biography is already under way).

All this activity would not have been possible without the American publication in 1962 of the first *Collected Poems*. This volume, edited by M. L. Rosenthal in collaboration with the poet, marked a turning point in MacDiarmid studies. For the first time, readers throughout the world could gain easy access to the best of the poetry, including the early work in Lallans[2] which had long been out of print.

But while the 1962 *Collected Poems* marked the beginning of MacDiarmid's worldwide reputation, the sixties in general were a turbulent era. The need to propagandize MacDiarmid's work and to make up for decades of neglect resulted in sudden outpourings of extravagant praise of an almost religious fervour: "Dunbar, Burns and MacDiarmid are the great Scottish trio. Let pedants wrangle over which of these deserves the precedence; there can be little doubt that MacDiarmid is the greatest miracle."[3] MacDiarmid's own passions, always extreme, have proved contagious, evoking wonder or wrath, but rarely indifference. During the sixties bitter feuds and wild cries of plagiarism balanced the uncritical worship of MacDiarmid's work. Duncan Glen's historical approach in *Hugh MacDiarmid and the Scottish Renaissance* and Kenneth Buthlay's brave but limited attempt to deal critically with the total work in *Hugh MacDiarmid*, both published in 1964, are important beginnings. Amidst all the excitement, propaganda, and brouhaha, these quietly valuable studies are exceptional, as is M. L. Rosenthal's suggestion that he is "probably the least known of poets in our language who might conceivably be called 'great'."[4]

I have tried to emulate this voice, letting my passions respond to the poetry, but calling frequently on steadying reason to avoid embroilment in issues other than the poetry—my central issue. By examining the poems chronologically and sympathetically and by exploring the relationship between language, formal dynamics, image, and theme, I have tried to discover the essence of MacDiarmid's vision and poetry, the peculiar combination of qualities that make up his greatness, and the characteristics of his highly individual contribution to the poetry of this century.

Essentially MacDiarmid is a poet of paradox. The guiding impetus behind all his poetry and all his prose consists of an attempt to bring together under the aegis of paradox "contraries" or disparate elements. His poetic role is to bring unity, to make possible a synthesis, and to bridge an otherwise unbridgeable abyss; and this he achieves through the use of paradox. Characteristically the form that this paradox takes is an attempt to return to pre-Fall Eden in order to reach future paradise. By going back into the past, one reaches the future and thereby effects a synthesis of past, present, and future, moving from time into the timeless world of paradox: "In my end is my beginning," or, as the paradox manifests itself in MacDiarmid's poetry, "In my beginning is my end."

When one recognizes this basic and central paradox, the other paradoxical elements seem almost logical. His return to Lallans and then to Gaelic in an attempt to bring Scottish poetry into line with the most modern developments in European poetry is a manifestation of his paradoxical belief that by returning to an Ur-culture or Ur-language one can reach a future paradise. (Lallans often sounds more ancient than the language of *Beowulf,* and the Gaels pride themselves on speaking the language spoken in the Garden of Eden). The Lawrentian theme of a primal life-force with which modern man has lost touch and with which he must re-establish contact appears frequently in MacDiarmid's poems—another version of the basic paradox. His Scottish Nationalism is yet another version. By becoming more national, one becomes more international. By freeing the essential Scottish spirit, bound in captivity by England's domination (a second Fall), he hopes to lead Scotland into a new world of "unity in diversity." Similarly MacDiarmid's Marxism with its emphasis on roots, on the necessity of freeing the essential spirit of man, bound in captivity by Capitalism's domination (another Fall), runs along the same paradoxical lines. Significantly his favourite quotation from Lenin, one that pops up over and over again in his prose writings, emphasizes the importance of repossessing the past:

> . . . we must utilize every moment in which we are free from war that we may learn, and *learn from the bottom up.* . . . It would be a very serious mistake to suppose that one can become a Communist without making one's own the treasures of human knowledge. . . . Communism becomes an empty phrase, a mere facade, and the Communist a mere bluffer, if he has not worked over in his consciousness the whole inheritance of human knowledge . . . made his own, and worked over anew, all that was of value in the more than two thousand years of development of human thought.[5]

All these elements combine into a peculiar Scottish-Marxist-Christian-pagan-Lawrentian amalgam. Everywhere MacDiarmid turns, he sees with Blake's "double vision," the vision of paradox that unites contraries, and it is this vision that makes possible the strange amalgam. This "double vision" stands behind all his work and makes sense out of what would otherwise seem nonsense. Here is the informing spirt. The return to an Eden-like past in order to reach paradise is the central and essential ingredient. MacDiarmid seems to apply the visions of Rousseau and Wordsworth ("The child is father of the man") to every imaginable context.

In a recent interview with Duncan Glen, MacDiarmid talked of his name-changing from "Christopher" (Christ-bearer) to "Hugh" which "in the old Gothic is 'divine wisdom'," and in the process revealed his central belief in the unifying virtue of paradox:

GLEN: It is what you really believe in?
MACD: Yes.
GLEN: This eternal flame. Is that a fair statement?
MACD: Yes, yes, I think so.
GLEN: You said it was unchanging somewhere. This is a mystical thought. . . . I know you always knock me for saying mysticism but . . .
MACD: Change itself is necessarily unchanging, by definition.
GLEN: Yes. The beginning is the end.
MACD: (*with laughter*) Yes. Yes. [6]

The various paradoxes in which MacDiarmid delighted in this interview are typical. The man himself, Christopher Murray Grieve, with his *nom de plume* or *nom de guerre,* as Buthlay has it, presents the critic with a veritable maze of paradoxes. He is a man who insists, to the embarrassment of both the Communist and Scottish Nationalist Parties, on being both a Communist and a Scottish Nationalist, while insisting at the same time that "I must be a Bolshevik / Before the Revolution, but I'll cease to be one quick / When Communism comes to rule the roost." [7] He vigorously attacks the whole Scottish educational system, especially the universities, while at the same time delighting in the approbation of the intellectual establishment: his honorary degree from Edinburgh University, his pride in his professorial acquaintances. While he insists upon the intellectual content of his poetry, its wellsprings are emotional. He is publically a fierce, aggressive, arrogant, and unforgiving figure, while in private the most gentle of men. He thinks of himself as a member of an élite, far removed from the "vast majority o' men," yet insists upon espousing their cause and on identifying his plight with theirs. He is sacrilegious and blasphemous in his attacks on organized Christianity, while insisting both on the Christ-like paradox of the divine in man and on the link between man's potential and Marxism. The insecurity of Christopher Grieve goes hand in hand with the arrogance of Hugh MacDiarmid.

The source of the paradox as it appears both in the man and in the poetry is to be found in Grieve's childhood and in MacDiarmid's treatment of that childhood in his poetry and prose writings. Consequently, I shall concentrate in this chapter on Grieve's childhood and shall delay other biographical details to appropriate chapters. (In Chapter Three, I shall treat the influence of George Ogilvie and the war years, in relation to *Annals of the Five Senses;* in Chapter Five, the effects of his marital troubles upon the paradoxical vision, in relation to *Circumjack*; in Chapter Six, his isolation in the Shetland Islands and the psychic injury of his divorce, in relation to *Stony Limits;* and in Chapter Seven, his political activities, in relation to *First Hymn to Lenin* and *Second Hymn*). Meanwhile I hope to clarify the relationship between Grieve and his childhood and between Grieve and Hugh MacDiarmid, relationships that are central to the paradoxical vision.

MacDiarmid's attitude towards his childhood is certainly as full of paradoxes as his poetry is. It suggests that, just as the child is father of the man, so the young Christopher Grieve is the father of Hugh MacDiarmid. A tension always exists between the idealized version of his childhood presented in his writings and a great unhappiness or insecurity associated with his actual childhood. Here lies the paradigm of the central paradox, the need to repossess the Eden of pre-Fall years as a means of reaching future paradise.

Christopher Murray Grieve was born on 11 August 1892 in Langholm, a Scottish mill town near the English border. He was the first-born son of John Grieve, a rural postman and descendant of mill-workers, and Elizabeth Graham whose ancestors were farmers. Both the Grieves and the Grahams had some connections with literature: an ancestor John Grieve (1781-1836) had been a friend of James Hogg, the Ettrick shepherd, and was himself a poet; William Laidlaw (1780-1845), the amanuensis of Sir Walter Scott, was a distant relative on the Grieve side; John Grieve, Christopher's father, had written some sermons; his mother had produced "some poems (very bad!) . . . before she was married"; and two cousins, John and Robert Laidlaw, had published "poems and sketches and articles of various kinds."[8] Obviously a "literary strain had been struggling to come to something on both my father's side and my mother's for several generations."[9]

In his autobiography *Lucky Poet,* MacDiarmid emphasizes this debt to his ancestors and the fortunate ease of access to the Public Library:

> It was that library, however, that was the great determining factor. My father was a rural postman . . . and we lived in the post office buildings. The library . . . was upstairs. I had constant access to it, and used to fill a big washing-basket with books and bring it downstairs as often as I wanted to. My parents never interfered with or supervised my reading in any way, nor were they ever in the least inclined to deprecate my "wasting all my time reading". There were upwards of twelve thousand books in the library. . . . I certainly read almost every one of them.[10]

The situation sounds idyllic, the perfect breeding ground for a poet. And when MacDiarmid adds to these advantages (hereditary genius, identification with both working and agricultural class, easy access to the works of other writers) an Eden-like background, it would appear that every element in his childhood contributed joyfully and constructively to his development as a poet:

> My boyhood was an incredibly happy one. Langholm was, indeed—and presumably still is—a wonderful place to be a boy in.
>
> Scotland is not generally regarded as a land flowing with milk and honey—and I have lived in diverse parts of it long enough now to know that it is seldom, perhaps, that it presents itself in that guise. Nevertheless, it can do so at times, and probably does so far more frequently than is commonly understood. It certainly did so in my boyhood—with a bountifulness so inexhaustible that it has supplied all my subsequent poetry with a tremendous wealth of sensuous satisfaction, a teeming gratitude of reminiscence, and that I have still an immense reservoir to draw upon. My earliest impressions are of an almost tropical luxuriance of Nature—of great forests, of honey-scented heather hills, and moorlands infinitely rich in little-appreciated beauties of flowering, of animal and insect life, of strange and subtle relationships of water and light. . . .[11]

The "tremendous wealth of sensuous satisfaction" that is such an important element in MacDiarmid's poetry comes obviously from the rich memories of his boyhood and of the Garden of Eden that was Langholm.

But a serpent lurked in the garden even then, despite MacDiarmid's emphasis on the paradisiacal memories, and probably the presence of the serpent has made him a greater poet. His attitude to Langholm is by no means as simple as he would have us believe. In *Lucky Poet* he claims: "There is an old saying—'Out of the World and into Langholm', and throughout my life I have applied it in this way. It has been my touchstone in all creative matters."[12] The serpent's presence can be glimpsed both in the "out of the World" suggestion in this quotation and in the "presumably still is" hesitation in the previous quotation. For one reason or another, Christopher Grieve has *not* gone back· to Langholm, although the imagination of Hugh MacDiarmid has returned to the Langholm of memory, and perhaps of fantasy. (Significantly, the only honour which, to my knowledge, MacDiarmid has refused, has been the Freedom of Langholm).

In the introductory section of *Lucky Poet* MacDiarmid comes as close as he ever does to a confrontation with Grieve's refusal to go back to the "real" Langholm:

In the same poem I speculate as to what had kept me from going back to Langholm (I have not been there for over twenty years, and then it was only for one night; and prior to that I had not seen it for a good few years) and severed all the ties myself between myself and my relative so completely.

> Guid kens it wasna snobbery or hate,
> Selfishness, ingratitude, or chance that reft
> Sae early, sae completely, ties that last
> Maist folk for life—or was't?

Apart from the fact that I have always been extremely chary of intimacy, making many acquaintances but very, very few real friends, the reason was, of course, that by the time I had come to my early teens I had outgrown them completely, lived in a different mental world altogether, and felt that to retain relationships with them would be to foster a kind of infantilism in myself. (No. That's not the real reason, either. I have been friendly enough with any number of people with whom I have no 'community of insight'. It is just an accident that I've never been back to Langolm—it has just never been convenient.)[13]

The indecision, the fluctuation of certainty ("of course," "that's not the real reason''), the quick rejection of the suggestion of ''infantilism,'' and the weak conclusion that it is ''just an accident'' suggest that Grieve is pushing back a recognition of some childhood unhappiness and guilt in order to avoid a confrontation with what I in my ignorance have called the ''serpent.''

There is more evidence in MacDiarmid's own writings that his childhood was not as blissful as he would like to describe it. Twice in *Lucky Poet* he draws attention to his brother and himself being ''jeered at'': once because his parents were ''exceptionally straight-forward and serious-minded people'' while the rest of the community had ''easier standards''; and secondly because he and his brother were kept ''tidier than they were,'' dressed in Highland dress on ''highdays and holidays,'' ''due to my mother, who had genteel ideas,'' the result of this gentility being that ''we were jeered at as 'Mother's angels'.''[14]

The relationship between Grieve's mother, his brother, and himself seems to be crucial here. MacDiarmid recognizes its importance in *Lucky Poet* when he describes his attempt to ''commit my first murder'': ''attempting, in short, to smash in the head of my newly-born brother with a poker, and, when I was disarmed, continuing to insist that, despite that horrible red-faced object, I 'was still Mummy's boy, too'.''[15] This sibling rivalry emerges in another incident described in *Lucky Poet,* an incident that upsets two of the paradisiacal elements insisted upon elsewhere: the impression that Grieve was continually surrounded by the ''tropical luxuriance of nature,'' and the suggestion that his parents had always encouraged his reading, never deprecating his ''wasting all my time reading'':

> . . . relatively I was not an open-air boy. . . . I was probably far more of a house-bird than any of my contemporaries. I preferred to read and write, and my mother was constantly at me for not going out more—like my brother, for example, who was always on our golf-course and earned a good few shillings a week caddying.[16]

The importance of this description emerges in two of the 1927 short stories in Lallans, ''Andy'' and ''Maria.'' In both these stories the envy of a brother who is out on the golf-course earning money, a recognition of manliness, and his mother's admiration, is a crucial element. (Grieve's brother's name was Andrew Graham). In ''Andy'':

> Andy was his mither's Jacob. She thocht he was that manly—aye oot fishin', or caddyin' at the golf-course and makin' money. Nae books

for him—barrin' his schule books, and nae mair o' them than he could
help—and syne he'd to be helped wi' them. Andy—and his
mither—took fu' advantage then o' his superior learnin'. But tho' his
mither wanted Andy to get on, at hert she sympathised wi' his
contempt for book-lear, and tho' she made him help Andy she didna
like him ony the better for bein' able to dae't.[17]

And in "Maria":

It was queer to think his brither was up on the golf course somewhere
caddyin'. He wadna come and sit like this. Nae fear. 'Tam was his
mither's boy.' What gar'd folk say that in sic a way as to mak' ye feel a
wee thing ashamed—as if ye were a kind o' lassie-boy?[18]

The autobiographical elements in "Andy" are reinforced not only by the
parallel sibling rivalry in "Maria," but also by the plot whose origin is
revealed in *Lucky Poet*:

. . . one day . . . my brother and I were angling. He had hooked a trout
and was greatly excited. My father nipped over to advise him in
playing it, but by the time he reached my brother's side the trout had
got off the hook. Instantly there was a tremendous splash; my brother
had plunged into the pool after it.[19]

One can imagine how Grieve's parents must have related this story as
additional proof of Andrew's fearlessness. In "Andy," however, the
Christopher Grieve figure performs the climactic act of heroism: he
plunges in after his brother, rescues him, and catches a fish for good
measure. Significantly he is grateful that he has a witness for his heroic
act:

It 'ud be owre the toon in nae time. He was a hero. It was a guid job
ither folk had seen it tae, or Andy and his mither 'ud hae whittled it
doon to naething.[20]

This basic situation—a sibling and a mother who are in league against
the central character, who "whittle doon to naething" everything he
does, and who make it more and more necessary for the sensitive
dreamer to prove himself, even if this only draws them more closely
together—appears not only in "Andy" and "Maria," but also in "The
Moon through Glass," another 1927 short story in Lallans. Now,
however, the central character is female, and the sibling also female. Not

only is the basic situation very similar, but the central character knows that she'll be "tell't her fingers were a' thooms." She shares this lack of physical coordination and confidence with the central character in "Andy," the boy who is grateful that his father "never lost his temper and said his fingers maun be a' thooms—or no' often."[21] In both cases mother and sibling gang up on the sensitive-dreamer-Grieve-like figure and transform into ridicule any attempt at heroism.

Possibly we may never know the precise dynamics of Grieve's childhood psyche. At least we know that the relationship with his brother was a complex one. And the description of Andy's mind, revealed as he is trying to land his fish, is a prototype for MacDiarmid's disgust and violence in the face of Philistine stupidity:

> Puir Andy, he felt wae [sad] for him—wi' a face like that, makin' a life-or-daith maitter o' something you could buy for tippence for breakfast frae the man that cam' roon wi' the lorry. His face like that was like seein' the flair o' the sea—a'e meenit a' jobblin' waves, and the next—naething but dour black glaur [dark black mud]. He felt he could gang richt through the bottom o' Andy's mind noo to the promised land like the Jews gaen through the Reid Sea; but it was a fell clarty [extremely dirty] road.[22]

The revolting physicality of Andy, his denial of all that is important, and his wasting of time and effort on all the unimportant aspects of life, bespeak a rejection on Grieve's part of all that his mother and brother stood for. His denial shrieks out in his enraged rejection of Andy and all that Andy represents.

It almost appears that Grieve was forced from his earliest childhood into a position of rebellion. Both his parents were "intensely religious," and their social life seems to have consisted of entertaining church-officers and ministers. By linking himself to the "hairy people" of the Borders (ironically as physical as Andy), to the classmate who gave a "very able object-lesson in sexual intercourse on the top of one of the desks with one of our class-mates, a sonsy [buxom] wench," and to his Grieve grandfather who was "drinking blood" (red medicine) in his first memory of him, Christopher Grieve was probably attempting to shock his mother, or the memory of his mother, into recognition of *him:*

> She dealt exclusively in incredible clichés. "Ah! wait till you see the light," she would say to me; or: "You see, you haven't been washed in

the blood of the Lamb yet.'' . . . Though, in fact, it did little or
nothing to spoil our personal relations with each other, there was an
incredible gulf fixed between that humble, devout *little* [my italics]
mother and the son who was to write poems like:

> Hunters were oot on a Scottish hill
> A'e day when the sun stood suddenly still
> At noon, and turned the colour of the port
> —A perfect nuisance, spoilin' their sport,
> Syne it gaed pitch-black a' the gither.
> Isn't that just like our Scottish weather?[23]

Whatever the precise reason, Grieve was pushed into a position where he
felt obliged to shock the bourgeois, cliché-ridden Christianity of his
mother; and from this attempt much of his most powerful poetry seems
to have risen.

The ambiguous relationship to both mother and brother may explain
some of the conflicting approaches to self, both in *Lucky Poet* and in the
poetry. Grieve seems to cry, ''I was no child prodigy; any more than I
have proved a world beater since; indeed, my brother did much better at
school than I did,'' while MacDiarmid sees to it that we learn, ''Here is a
boy who has a great future before him. He is not like other children: I am
certain that he has exceptional gifts.''[24] Grieve's headmaster seems to
speak for MacDiarmid when he prophesies: ''My brother, he said, would
do well, and far better than I in medal competitions and bursary
examinations and the like, but I was 'the one that really mattered if. . . .'
It was a big IF. IF, he said, I did not spoil it all by sheer carelessness.''[25]
The need to prove himself a hero, to outdo, in ways which his mother
and brother would not even think of, both his mother and his brother,
seems to be the impetus behind much of MacDiarmid's poetry. It goes a
long way towards explaining his delight in shocking the bourgeois, his
implacable hatred of the Philistine, and his advocacy of an intellectual
élite. It may also be the wellspring of the disgust-wonder synthesis, the
peculiarly powerful hallmark of his poetry.

A deep insecurity and an overweening arrogance go hand in hand
throughout MacDiarmid's prose writings. Just as he felt obligated to
prove himself and to become world-famous by the time he was thirty (a
plan which the First World War held up), so he continues to impress
upon the public his importance and his acceptance. In the 1965 *The
Company I've Kept,* he writes:

It has been written of me that I 'seemed to have read everything and to know everybody', and there can be no doubt, I think, that the circle of my acquaintanceship is vastly greater than that of most people. Greater—and far more various. There can be few alive who have known and been on friendly terms with W. B. Yeats, T. S. Eliot, and Dylan Thomas, to name only three of the best-known of a multitude of poets I have known. [26]

In one particularly revealing section of *Lucky Poet*, insecurity and arrogance hover over a photograph of the two Grieve brothers and suggest a link with the rivalry issue:

There is an early photograph of my brother and myself—how slight and shy I look; how burly and self-assertive my brother looks in comparison! And even to-day I look timid and modest—who have never known what it was to meet a situation I could not handle, who would be entirely equal to the occasion if I were summoned at a moment's notice to address the House of Commons or the House of Lords, or to lead a Scottish Sinn Fein rising—or, indeed, to deal with any other situation I can imagine. If there was ever a man who was ready, intellectually or physically, to start from any point to any other . . ., that man am I. [27]

The lack of confidence, coupled with a need to prove himself superior, has given us some of MacDiarmid's most interesting poetry. It has pushed him always towards the extreme, the unknown, and the unexplored, because, as he recognizes in a rare moment of insight, there is no competition there. While Grieve's brother might excel in bursary competitions, *he* would avoid competition:

And, indeed, I knew myself. I was fully conscious of my unconquerable aversion from entering into competition with anyone—I was determined to operate only in directions in which there could be no competition, since the whole aim would be the production of work that was *sui generis*. [28]

As a result of this decision, perhaps an inevitable one, MacDiarmid has continually explored new possibilities in poetry: the Lallans lyric that touches eternity, rather than the kailyard; the *Drunk Man* sequence that gave to Scottish literature one of its masterpieces; the Gaelic and "synthetic English" experiments; and the "poetry of fact." Sometimes what he gives is new and exciting, sometimes new and irritating, sometimes new and boring, but he remains throughout faithful to Pound's command, "Make it new."

Much of Grieve's early history is rather mysterious. Some of the facts we have; some we do not. His parents' horror at his announcing that he intended to be a poet led him, upon finishing his high-school education at Langholm Academy, to enter somewhat reluctantly the Broughton Junior Student Centre in Edinburgh with the plan of becoming a teacher. There he came under the influence of George Ogilvie, a fine teacher of English, to whom in later years he was to look for guidance and support. Ogilvie has left an evocative account of the young Grieve, and the details of the portrait support my suggestion that his driving impetus was a need to prove himself:

> I remember vividly Grieve's arrival [on 2nd September 1908] amongst us. I see the little slimly built figure in hodden grey, the small sharp featured face with its piercing eyes, the striking head with its broad brow and great mass of flaxen curly hair. He hailed from Langholm, and had a Border accent you could have cut with a knife. I am afraid some of the city students smiled at first at the newcomer, but he very speedily won their respect. He certainly very quickly established himself in mine. [29]

But what about Grieve's father? His death in 1911 marked a turning point in Grieve's life: "My father died suddenly before I was finished at the Junior Student Centre. I took immediate advantage of the fact to abandon my plans for becoming a teacher." [30] The matter-of-fact way in which MacDiarmid announces this incident in *Lucky Poet* belies the emotional content of the experience entirely, and this emotion makes itself felt in other ways.

Often when he refers to his father's death, he talks about himself as being much younger than in fact he was (eighteen or nineteen): "when I was still a boy," "a laddie when he dee'd," and "when I was a student in my early teens." [31] When he tackles the subject of his father's death in his poems, there is always an awareness of a great gulf between them, an almost impassable distance, and a tentative reaching-out on the part of either father or son: "He looked in vain, and I again"; "the last wild look," "An' I think that mebbe at last I ken / What your look meant then"; "We look upon each ither noo like hills / Across a valley." [32] The distance between father and son is great, increased indeed by Grieve's thinking of himself as a "laddie." Despite all his shortcomings, however, he must try to reach across the abyss. This abyss and the desperately painful attempt to bridge it may well be the matrix for MacDiarmid's constant attempt to synthesize opposites, to bring together elements which are otherwise far apart, and to reach the extreme that makes the paradoxical unity possible.

Whether or not this speculation (and with the scanty evidence in our possession it must remain a speculation) comes close to the truth or not, Grieve's father's death has meant more to him than a handy excuse to leave the teaching profession. The father figure in "Andy" *could* be reached by the Grieve-like son, provided that brother and mother were not present: "He believed he could ha'e explained his feelin's aboot the haill thing in a way his faither 'ud understand—but he haurdly ever saw his faither alane."[33] A link between father and son trembles on the brink of possibility:

> He kent his faither jaloused [suspected] something o' this—but no' juist eneuch. He lookit at him in a queer switherin' way whiles—and syne sided wi' his mither and Andy; it was that muckle easier. But he felt that if he could juist explain things to his faither aince he'd hae nae mair bother.[34]

The "queer switherin' " look that father gives to son unites them for a brief moment. The equivalent in the poetry is the moment of paradoxical vision that brings together elements that would otherwise be far apart. The Fall becomes powerless when vision unites Eden and paradise. With Grieve's father's death, the possibility of bridging the gap between them also dies, but the impetus to bring together, to unite, and to close the gap persists in the poetry of Hugh MacDiarmid.

The trembling moment of vision brings together man and god, beauty and ugliness, life and death, disgust and tenderness, Lenin and Christ, Scotland and the cosmos.

And in the "queer switherin' " movement Christopher Grieve and Hugh MacDiarmid become one.

CHAPTER TWO

'Trembling Sunbeams'

THE VISION AND THE POETRY

The task that faces me—the delineation of the relationship between MacDiarmid's paradoxical vision of synthesis and his poetry—is anything but easy. As MacDiarmid wrote in 1926, "Comprehensibility is error: Art is beyond understanding," and "The ideal observer of art—as against art-at-work—is God, conscious of all that has been and *will* be achieved."[1] While Duncan Glen has given a fine historical account of MacDiarmid's contributions to the Scottish Renaissance and Kenneth Buthlay has done pioneer work in his treatment of the entire opus,[2] no critic has yet produced a sufficiently detailed study of the poetry as a whole. The temptation has always been to concentrate on his Marxism, or his Scottish Nationalism, or his use of Lallans, or his "poetry of fact," or individual lyrics, to the exclusion of a consideration of his poetry as a whole. The Gargantuan size and the chameleon-like movements of the total work are sufficiently daunting. At the very moment when his poetry seems within human grasp, it wriggles away like the most slippery of fish, and the critic wishes more and more that he possessed the qualities of the "ideal observer of art." While I make no claims to be such a divinity, I bring to this study an awareness of my shortcomings, a conviction of the importance of MacDiarmid's poetry, and a gratitude to him for many hours of excited thought, joyful discovery, and the "extension of human consciousness."[3]

The recognition that MacDiarmid's vision is essentially paradoxical is the Ariadne's thread through the labyrinth of his poetry. To the service of this vision he subjects all the other elements in his poetry—language, politics, form, image, myth, theme, and moral standards. He is willing for the sake of this vision to risk boring, or confusing, or infuriating his readers. Everything he writes takes the paradoxical vision as a central point of reference.

Before I attempt to trace in detail the relationship between the vision and the poetry, it will be necessary to identify the major components of the vision, to suggest the basic connections between the vision and the poetry, and to establish some points of reference in the Scottish, Romantic, and modern traditions. This chapter, I hope, will provide the framework for the subsequent detailed study of the poetry.

The paradox that lies at the centre of his work manifests itself in many different ways and absorbs many varied ingredients. One of the most long-lasting influences upon his thought, as Duncan Glen has recently noted,[4] has been his early study of Solovyov, in particular his *La Russie et l'Eglise Universelle*. As early as 1923 he was noting a "Russo-Scottish parallelism" between J. Y. Simpson's *Man and the Attainment of Immortality* and Solovyov's work. Approvingly he draws attention to Simpson's suggestion that "with the origin of man there emerged the possibility of some new relationship, 'a moral linkage' with God; and only in so far as this possibility is realized does man attain the true 'individuality which is immortality'."[5] This "moral linkage" between man and God, a possibility that is inherent in man, provides MacDiarmid with a pattern for his vision of synthesis. Through the paradoxical vision of the poet, man and God meet. Like Solovyov's Sophia, the poet "plays before God, evoking before God images of possible extra-divine existence, shapes of chaotic multiplicity, and reabsorbing them again into herself."[6] Not only does this early and devoted acceptance of Solovyov's theory go a long way towards explaining MacDiarmid's rather idiosyncratic religious impulse, several steps removed from the orthodox Church of Scotland and the religion of his parents, but it also explains much of his fascination with all things Russian. Solovyov has given to the paradoxical vision a link between Scotland and Russia and between man and God.

MacDiarmid's unshakeable belief that poetry provides the "moral linkage" between the human and the divine emerges over and over again in his writing and indicates perhaps that in his own way he is as "devout" and as uncompromising as the "little mother" of his childhood: "As I have said, in one of my poems, I . . . would sacrifice a million people any day for one immortal lyric,"[7] where the horrifying phrase is "any day." The romanticism of this view, coupled with the uncompromising and tough acceptance of the logical consequences and with an aristocratic disgust for what man at present is, gives to his poetry a strange and powerful tension as brute and angel are brought forcibly together under the aegis of paradox. His muse has both a divine halo and feet of clay.

Part of the responsibility for this paradoxical combination (the major source lying in Grieve's psyche and in his reaction to his childhood experiences) belongs to an as yet unrecognized source—namely Ouspensky's *Tertium Organum*. Its influence on MacDiarmid and on his poetry has been enormous. It began early: "A Moment in Eternity," written in 1921,[8] with its Ouspenskian concentration on unity and infinity, indicates that MacDiarmid had already read *Tertium Organum*: the 1926 essay "Art and the Unknown" presents Ouspensky's ideas with very little disguise and no acknowledgement. The essentially paradoxical nature of Ouspensky's theory of a "higher logic" must have fitted naturally and easily into the MacDiarmid paradox:

> *A is both A and Not-A*
> or *Everything is both A and Not-A.*
> or *Everything is All.*[9]

Ouspensky's "logic of the infinite" is the intellectual source of MacDiarmid's paradox.

Ouspensky, however, gives him more than the basic paradox. Solovyov's theory of Sophia gains definition from Ouspensky: man reaches God by the extension of consciousness. MacDiarmid's claim that the "function of art is the extension of human consciousness"[10] comes directly from *Tertium Organum*: "Poetry endeavors to express both music and thought together. The combination of feeling and thought . . . leads to a higher form of psychic life. . . . Art anticipates a psychic evolution and divines its future forms"; "the entire body of teachings of religio-philosophic movements have as their avowed or hidden purpose, *the expansion of consciousness.*"[11]

Probably because of the attraction of his "logic of the infinite," Ouspensky bequeaths to MacDiarmid other related concepts. The importance of art ("the most important of human activities," according to MacDiarmid) had been stressed earlier by Ouspensky: "At the present stage of our development we possess nothing so powerful, as an instrument of knowledge of the world of causes, as art."[12] He is also responsible for MacDiarmid's belief, reinforced by his need to prove himself a hero, in the concept of an intellectual élite: an "infinitesimal minority of the people, " those with higher consciousness who are on their way to a Nietzchean "linkage" with God, "the only real and important evolution for us—the evolution into superman."[13] Accompanying this idea is a vast scorn and distrust of what MacDiarmid calls "the vast majority o' men," and what Ouspensky had viewed as an active threat to evolution: "The enormous majority of the population of this globe is engaged . . . in destroying . . . and falsifying the ideas of the minority. The majority is without ideas."[14] The appeal of this theory to Grieve, an insecure minority faced with the combined forces of mother and brother, must have been irresistible.

Even the concept of the "ideal observer of art . . . conscious of all human experience up to the given moment" in the 1926 "Art and the Unknown" comes from *Tertium Organum,* although this time Ouspensky is quoting Bucke's *Cosmic Consciousness:* "The cosmic vision or the cosmic intuition, from which what may be called the new mind takes its name, is thus seen to be . . . complex and union of all prior thought and experience—just as self-consciousness is the complex and union of all thought and experience prior to it."[15] Here lies the intellectual origin of the basic thrust in MacDiarmid's paradoxical vision—the movement back into the past, the recapturing of the past, in order to reach the future and the "new mind."

His work has proved as faithful to Ouspensky's theories as to Solovyov's. Key concepts ("diversity in unity," "synthesis in differentiation," "unity of all opposites," "wonderment," "the voice of the silence," "the spur of love," "the marvellous and the mystic," and the belief that there can be "nothing dead or mechanical in nature") originate in *Tertium Organum* and remain throughout all his work as a solid core of ideas, major points of reference.[16] The ideas of Solovyov and Ouspensky have proved sufficiently suggestive, paradoxical, and all-embracing for MacDiarmid to build upon them many different kinds of poetry.

Ouspensky had also emphasized both the importance of language and its limitations. He saw language in relation to concepts as a limiting force and recognized the need for a new kind of language to transmit the new concepts.[17] At the same time he looked to the artist as a "clairvoyant . . . a magician [who would possess] the power to make others see that which they do not themselves see, but which he does see."[18] MacDiarmid, in his approach to language, seems to have amalgamated these two ideas with Solovyov. Words become magic, the incantation to summon up the God, the means of achieving the "moral linkage."

As early as 1923 he wrote, "We have been enormously struck by the resemblance—the moral resemblance—between Jamieson's Etymo-logical Dictionary of the Scottish language and James Joyce's

Ulysses,"[19] where the significant link between the two is a *moral* one. He continued: "A *vis comica* that has not yet been liberated lies bound by desuetude and misappreciation in the recesses of the Doric: and its potential uprising would be no less prodigious, uncontrollable, and utterly at variance with conventional morality than was Joyce's tremendous outpouring." This faith in words, this conviction that language holds within its recesses forces capable of unsettling the world, is close to Faustus's discovery in Marlowe's play. Significantly in 1952 MacDiarmid is quoting Blake's "All poets are of the devil's party."[20]

Paradoxically and appropriately, however, they are also members of the divine company: Lucifer before his fall, or Lucifer about to fall, as suggested by the name-changing from the devout "Christopher" to the proud "Hugh" of "divine wisdom." Language links the poet with God.

His delight in language goes far beyond seeing it as an intrinsically important component of the poem, or even recognizing, as Pound did, the relationship between language and society. In *Lucky Poet* MacDiarmid states explicitly the dependent relationship he sees:

> . . . the act of poetry being the reverse of what it is usually thought to be; not an idea gradually shaping itself in words, but deriving entirely from words—and it was in fact (as only my friend F. G. Scott divined) in this way that I wrote all the best of my Scots poems.[21]

Even the use of the word "divined" in this quotation is indicative of the magic relationship he sees between language and poetry. The core of his poetic theory (that man can be united with God, that poetry is the means by which this synthesis can happen, that language is the force that shapes poetry) explains the importance he attaches to the word. Like St John he could cry, "In the beginning was the Word." And through the magic word the paradoxical synthesis is incarnate. All MacDiarmid's rummaging around in dictionaries, his delight in discovering a new or an arcane word, his incantatory catalogues of words, all spring from this belief in the magical, holy, shaping power of language. It has given us some of his best poetry and some of his worst. It has continually led him into both new and ancient areas of consciousness, and it has rarely been satisfied with standard English. Language, like Browning's "sunset touch," can disturb and extend human consciousness. It can force man to "look at things from an unaccustomed angle, see the unfamiliar and unsuspected aspects of all the everyday familiar things that in the sinful arrogance of his individuality he had taken as fixed and fundamental, given and unchanging.''[22] Through language he reaches the paradoxical vision and forms the ''moral linkage'' with God.

Central to his concept of paradoxical synthesis is a belief in the extreme, the extreme without which the paradox could not take shape. Only the élite can reach it; the ''vast majority o' men'' retreat from extremes: ''Heaven an' Hell's no' nice eneuch for some fowk. They want a' sorts o' half-wey hooses to suit their particular requirements.''[23] To MacDiarmid any real progress is impossible if one is not willing to venture beyond the known into the unknown, to dare the extreme in order to make the paradox possible. His belief is essentially Blakean: ''The road to excess leads to the palace of wisdom''; ''If the fool would persist in his folly he would become wise''; ''Without contraries is no progression.''[24] And by becoming more human, by freeing himself from all that binds him, man becomes more like God. On this Blakean attempt to bring together opposites and to achieve a synthesis between man and God, heaven and hell, the past and the future, the particular and the universal, MacDiarmid's poetry rests.

The result of this belief in paradox and in the cultivation of the extreme to make possible a unity is often startling: a weird distortion of size and time (the world like an old white bone, the tears of a child appearing like a second flood, a glass of water containing the universe); or a shocking juxtaposition of tone (gross bawdiness shattering an ambience of wonder). The unexpected bursts into his poetry, reversing direction or changing focus without warning—a movement that forces the reader to take part in the central paradox and to move with it from one extreme to the other. The meeting place of his extremes is often painful, or shocking, or horrifying. In his poetry extremes never meet at the ''still point of the turning world,'' but rather at a moment of tension and movement, whether violent, or trembling, or ''twinklin' and fizzin' wi' fire,'' the human more human, and the inhuman or superhuman more true to its own nature. The satire that springs from his deep disgust with the Yahoos of the world, their physical grossness often as appalling to MacDiarmid as to Swift, counterbalances the Blakean innocence of his vision: ''The new city must be a city of friends and lovers.''[25] From the unexpected synthesis of disgust and wonder his most powerful poetry emerges: the early lyrics, *A Drunk Man Looks at the Thistle*, ''Harry Semen,'' and later poems like ''The Two Parents.'' I can think of no other poet who has so effectively made disgust and wonder touch each other. The combination of these two elements in precarious and dynamic balance is the most exciting and unique feature of his poetry, a manifestation of the central paradox in his vision of man.

Perhaps this paradoxical combination of elements is ultimately of a sexual origin. The combination of disgust and wonder is closer to the most intimate moments in Lawrence's novels or short stories than to anything else. Certainly in the early poems a sexual context is usually present either explicitly or implicitly, with the moment of pure vision emerging orgasmically from the disgust that precedes or surrounds it. For example, the brutal drunkenness of "The Looking Glass" suddenly soars into the pure ecstasy of "The Unknown Goddess":

> But what aboot it—hic—aboot it
> Mony a man's been that afore.
> It's no' a fact that in his lugs   *ears*
> A wund like this need roar! . . .
>
> *I ha'e forekent ye! O I ha'e forekent.*
> *The years forecast your face afore they went.*

This in turn moves to the climactic

> *And generations that I thocht unborn*
> *Hail the strange Goddess frae my hert's-hert torn! . . .*
>
> (p 71)

Immediately the sexual connotations of the vision ("generations that I thocht unborn," and the release of the Goddess "frae my hert's-hert") are converted into unredeemed physical terms as the speaker resumes the tone of disgust he had established in "The Looking Glass": "Or dost thou mak' a thistle o' me, wumman?" Disgust and wonder are continually touching each other, emerging from each other.

Characteristically the moment of vision is concentrated in a trembling or flickering movement: the "yow-trummle" (ewe-tremble) and "chitterin' licht" (shivering light) of "The Watergaw"; the trembling of the moonlight in the thistle's branches in *A Drunk Man;* the "tiny hardly visible trembling of the water. / This is the nearest analogy to the essence of human life" of "The Glass of Pure Water." In this same poem MacDiarmid links this movement with Sacco and Vanzetti in the death cell, with "talking to God," and with the Recording Angel's report on human life: "the subtlest movement—just like that—and no more; / A hundred years of life on the Earth / Summed up, not a detail missed or

wrongly assessed, / In that little inconceivably intricate movement"
(p 470). This "little inconceivably intricate movement" is frequently the
hallmark of his most suggestive poems—the trembling, miraculous
movement of life, seen for an instant in its entirety, perfect in its
paradoxical synthesis of all that is. It suggests, of course, the "queer
switherin' look" that links father and son together in "Andy." And it
also suggests the trembling moment of sexual climax. While the sexual
implications drop away in his poetry of the thirties, the quivering
moments of paradoxical vision remain—as in the "Glass of Pure Water"
section quoted above.

MacDiarmid's development as regards both form and language seem
to be intimately connected with his commitment to paradox. He begins
with the particular and moves towards the universal. In a 1971 interview
with Duncan Glen he replied to a question about his closeness to Eliot
with his "Tradition and the Individual Talent" and to William Carlos
Williams "with his belief in the future of the American idiom," by
moving into a discussion neither about language nor tradition, but about
form in relation to theme: "No. I go much nearer Eliot, of course, than I
do William Carlos Williams, but my man is Pound, definitely. Eliot,
after all, showed a narrowing tendency . . . but Pound opened out all
along the line, took in more and more."[26] The reference is obviously
both to the form of the *Cantos* and to Pound's "horizon after horizon"
approach, in contrast to Eliot's *Four Quartets* with its departure from
the fragmented openness of *The Waste Land* to a concentration on an
ordered and limited unity. Like Pound, MacDiarmid has taken "in more
and more," moving from the short lyric (*Sangschaw* and *Penny Wheep*)
in which he glimpsed eternity in a grain of sand, to the poetic sequence
(*A Drunk Man*) in which grains of sand came together to form a pattern
of eternity, to the enormous Canto-like *Haud Ferrit*, revealed only in
glimpses, which promised to try to collect all the grains of sand in
existence. Originally MacDiarmid focused on a part "unique and
individual," and moved gradually into an attempt to compose a "wider
whole," to use Solovyov's terminology.

In a parallel manner, he has moved from one end of the paradox to the
other in his use of language. The "unique and individual" language
(Lallans) is dropped for the more widely spoken English, and then for
the all-encompassing polyglot of the later poems. The capacity he
admired in Pound, the capacity to "open out all along the line, to take in
more and more," is the capacity that he himself has sought to cultivate.

30

The development has in many ways been unfortunate. When he moved from Lallans to English, his poetry lost more than it gained. The primal power of Lallans defeats translation, and MacDiarmid found no substitute. English with a Scottish accent and an odd word of dialect provided a midway stage, a "hauf-way hoose" that managed to *approach* the guttural, earthy power of Lallans, as no other subsequent language has done. The tone of horrified and horrifying disgust is less violent in standard English or polyglot, and as a result appears in muted form in the later poetry—a Sassoon-like irony, rather than unadulterated disgust. Equally well, as Iain C. Smith has pointed out, the very real tenderness of the early lyrics ("Bonnie Broukit Bairn," for instance) is missing in the later work. Smith suggests that he began as "the poet with both a masculine and feminine sensibility and eventually allowed the masculine elements in himself to dominate his work, thereby . . . becoming less human than he once was."[27] Substituting "intellect" for "masculine sensibility" and "emotion" for "feminine sensibility" (true, I think, to Smith's intent) allows me to accept this description. *Both* the violence and the tenderness present in the early work are diminished in the later poetry. Both the disgust and the wonder are muted. By attempting to "take in more and more," he has lost more and more.

I am tempted to conclude that when Edwin Muir in 1936 suggested that English had become the language of thought and that Lallans had become the language of feeling, he was describing, more accurately than either he or MacDiarmid was aware, the choice made by MacDiarmid in the late twenties and early thirties when he moved from Lallans to English with a Scottish accent and Gaelic quotations, and, after a brief attempt at "synthetic Scots," to standard and "synthetic" English. Because MacDiarmid had gone as far as was possible for him in Lallans, he moved on to new experiments, new languages, new areas of consciousness, and in the process sacrificed what Smith describes as the "hallucinatory" quality of the lyrics, and what I see as a peculiarly pure blending of violence and tenderness.

Similarly with the movement from the lyric to the sequence to the long poem, MacDiarmid has sacrificed the concentrated and intensified power of the lyric and of the effective "hauf-way hoose" sequence to the larger movement and to the more diffuse effect of the long poem without a clear architectonic frame. By "opening up more and more," by being willing to explore every side street, he accepts the hazards of formlessness and lack of intensity. This is not to deny that there are many magnificent passages in the later writings; they *are* there, but they are of a very different nature from his early work, and the moments of intensity are much less frequent. The poet of paradox falls victim to the paradox that less is often more. In his later writing the lack of formal control is usually accompanied by an emotional flatness, a tone often reminiscent of an uninspired lecturer. Severe formal limits and the emotional tension that is released within them make for a much more successful, interesting, dynamic poetry when MacDiarmid is the poet in question, and especially when the language is Lallans.

Without a doubt his early work in Lallans (*Sangschaw, Penny Wheep, A Drunk Man*) presents the vision of paradoxical synthesis in its purest, most dramatic, and moving form. By going back to the Scottish Chaucerians, their language, and their lucid vision, MacDiarmid repossesses in the twentieth century the moment of wonder such as Dunbar described:

> The grit victour agane is rissin on hicht
> That for our querrell to the deth wes woundit;
> The sone that wox all paill now shynis bricht,
> And, dirknes clerit, our fayth is now refoundit.

Lallans released in MacDiarmid a strongly authentic and tender voice. For him it was almost a magic language with "datchie [secret] sesames and names for nameless things," a language that linked past and present and, working with the poet's imagination, effected a synthesis of the disparate elements. No other language used by MacDiarmid has supported his paradoxical vision as Lallans has done. As he admits, only Lallans brings him "fully alive." The language itself becomes part of the paradox.

The extravagance of his comic fantasy, meanwhile, is also traditionally Scottish. The wildly exuberant spirit, irrepressible, delighting in its lack of either tact or taste, belongs to the world of Henryson and Dunbar and the fifteenth-century Scottish poets. This extravagance appears later in Burns, but much more sporadically than in the older tradition: e.g., "The Holy Fair," "The Jolly Beggars." A Dionysian spirit surfaces periodically in Scottish literature; and Burns, Dunbar, and MacDiarmid share the dubious but distinctively Scottish distinction of incorporating into their masterpieces ("Tam o' Shanter," "The Tua Mariit Wemen," and *A Drunk Man*) the revealing and distorting elements of strong drink and a fascination for womankind. MacDiarmid's Dionysus, however, is as Ouspenskian as he is Scottish, providing a "direct contact with *eternity*," as sexual energy transforms itself "into a higher order of intuition, into a higher consciousness which will reveal to us a marvelous and mysterious world"[28]

For MacDiarmid, as for D. H. Lawrence, the release of sexual energies leads to the creation of a "new heaven and a new earth." MacDiarmid links this vision through Lallans to a release into folk language, and the combination of these two elements appears both startlingly modern and ancient—a wonderful development of Lawrence's experiments of combining sexual vision with colloquial tone and language. To the traditional elements of Scottish literature MacDiarmid has added a Lawrentian vision, and in doing so has bypassed the sentimentality of Burns and his successors. An ancient primal world meets the twentieth century under the aegis of paradox, sexual vision, Dionysus, and Lallans. There is no place here for nineteenth-century prudishness and sentimentality.

While Burns's sentimentality is the least attractive feature of his poetry, sentimentality is not germane to Scottish literature. It has no place in the work of the fifteenth-century poets, nor in the work of MacDiarmid. His voice is tougher than Burns's, and, paradoxically, more authentically tender because of its firmness. "Earth, thou bonnie broukit bairn" (beautiful deserted child) breaks the heart; and in comparison, "O, my Luve's like a red, red rose," is blurry and unfocused.

Sentimentality, however, had been Burns's legacy to the nineteenth-century contingent of Scottish poets, "minors in power," who "harped on the old strings, the more complacently because he had played so well."[29] The sentimental vein in Scottish verse grew, like Herrick's "vegetable love," "vaster than empires," into the full monstrosity of the "kailyard." As Duncan Glen has noted in relation to the Burns tradition,

> . . . the tradition he established was a rustic, parochial one. Soon after his death, the Industrial Revolution destroyed the old rural way of life of which his poetry had been a late product, but the versifiers of the nineteenth century continued to write sentimentally and nostalgically of a rural Scotland as seen in the poetry of Burns.[30]

It was in an attempt to shatter this decadent, drivelling tradition, that MacDiarmid adopted as the slogan of the Scottish Renaissance, "Not

Burns—Dunbar," and "Not traditions—precedents." He was searching for a more ancient, more authentic, and more vital Scottish voice, less Anglified and more European. In the figure of Dunbar he found an appropriate symbol. By going further back into the past, by examining the roots of Scottish genius, he hoped to go forward into the future and into line with Europe: "No revival of Scots can be of consequence to a literary aspirant worthy of his salt unless it is so aligned with contemporary tendencies in European thought and expression that it has with it the possibility of eventually carrying Scots work once more into the mainstream of European literature."[31] Once again MacDiarmid demonstrates his belief in the Blakean paradox that "Without contraries is no progression": by entering the past, one reaches the future; by becoming more national, one becomes more international.

MacDiarmid's view of his place in Scottish literature, his relationship to the Scottish Chaucerians and the essential genius of the Scottish race, owes much to G. Gregory Smith's 1919 *Scottish Literature*. (Even the title of MacDiarmid's first published volume, *Annals of the Five Senses,* is a direct quotation from this book[32]). Gregory Smith's analysis of Scottish literature and its essential characteristics is taken over *in toto* by MacDiarmid, and the source of its appeal must have lain in the paradoxical elements of Smith's theory of the "Scottish Antisyzygy." Smith viewed the chief characteristic of Scottish literature as being "the antithesis of the real and fantastic," which cannot be fully explained "by the familiar rules of rhetoric."[33] Extremes meet, unexpectedly and dramatically: "The sudden jostling of contraries seems to preclude any relationship by literary suggestion. . . . They are the 'polar twins' of the Scottish Muse."[34] It is difficult to remember that this was written in 1919 before MacDiarmid had, as far as we know, written any lyrics in Lallans, so accurately does Smith's description fit the early lyrics. The sudden, unexpected movement from one tone to a totally different one is the hallmark of MacDiarmid's most suggestive poetry, the movement itself providing a synthesis. He develops this characteristic for the first time in his Lallans lyrics, and it remains with him in the later poetry. Smith's theory of Scottish literature (a paradoxical synthesis of "contraries") had given to MacDiarmid a cultural mission—the giving back to Scotland of its ancient and vital heritage. In addition, it provided him with an intellectual point of reference to which he could link his poetry, and it encouraged him in experimentation with the "sudden jostling of contraries" that achieved its most perfect manifestation in *A*

Drunk Man. Both Lallans and the Smith interpretation of the Scottish tradition help MacDiarmid to achieve the paradoxical vision in his poetry.

Perhaps the "antisyzygy" that Smith describes derives ultimately from the Scottish ballads with their suddenly dramatic switches of tone as past touches future, and man touches the supernatural:

> O our Scots nobles wer richt laith
> To weet their cork-heild shoone;
> Bot lang owre a' the play wer playd
> Thair hats they swam aboone.

Even the stanza in "Sir Patrick Spens" that describes the omen of the new moon "wi' the auld moone in hir arme" seems to bring together the tone of warm protection with that of sinister threat, while linking birth and death, the inhuman and the human (moon and mother). MacDiarmid's best poems have a similar effect (e.g., "O Wha's the Bride," "Harry Semen").

The leap of imagination that makes the paradox possible and that typifies both MacDiarmid's poetry and the Scottish ballads, is ultimately a romantic one: "the seal's wide spindrift gaze towards Paradise." The trembling link between this world and the world beyond it, "where Alph, the sacred river, ran / Through caverns measureless to man / Down to a sunless sea," is the axis upon which MacDiarmid's poetry turns. Opium or Scotch whisky may provide a symbolic entry, and as Fruman has pointed out with regard to Coleridge,[35] plagiarism may accompany the vision, but the major impulse is a Romantic one.

Scotland and Romanticism seem to go hand in hand. Scotland has given the world its ballads, its *Ossian,* its Sir Walter Scott, and even its Byron. Queen Victoria herself seems to mellow in the Balmoral air. And if we gather together the Romantics of this century (Lawrence, Thomas, Crane, Edwin Muir, Yeats, Pound), MacDiarmid belongs in their company. He is braver than most, with the exception of Yeats and Pound, in his synthesis of the crude, the disgusting, and the barbarically appalling, with the unchanging, immortal elements of the vision. Like Yeats and Blake, he stands Janus-like between the worlds of innocence and experience, men and gods, time and eternity, violence and tenderness. The most unique and moving ingredient in his vision is this ability to hold a balance between the two and to effect a synthesis within the poetry.

Attempting to place MacDiarmid within a tradition becomes a confusing business. With Crane and D. H. Lawrence he shares a belief in the revelation into the mystery of life made possible by intense sexual experience, a belief that comes to all three from Ouspensky. MacDiarmid's Dionysus belongs, like Lawrence's, to an ancient, vital, and elemental world, a world that is brought close through the moment of sexual vision and, in MacDiarmid's poetry, through the elemental qualities of Lallans. Both MacDiarmid and Lawrence look to this ancient world as the source of the future "new heaven and earth." By re-establishing contact with the life-force, one moves forward into the world of future paradise, and the paradoxical movement is complete.

The link with Lawrence and Crane is also a link with Pound and his sexual vision, his counterbalancing of the insanity and disorder of war with a world of "Grecian orgies." In addition, MacDiarmid shares with Pound a tough, aggressive quality, a "hard voice," and he often demonstrates a Poundian tendency towards being a "village teacher." Both became avid supporters of the economic theories of C. H. Douglas, and MacDiarmid's nationalistic zeal almost led him, as Pound's economic theories did, into support of Hitler.[36] Both began with the lyric and "opened out all along the line."

Meanwhile MacDiarmid's experiments with language probably owe much to Joyce—he delighted in thinking of them as Joycean—and *A Drunk Man* can be viewed as a Scottish response to *The Waste Land*—once again MacDiarmid invites the comparison:

> T. S. Eliot—it's a Scottish name—
> Afore he wrote "The Waste Land" su'd ha'e come
> To Scotland here. He wad ha'e written
> A better poem syne—like this, by gum!   (p 74)

His omnivorous reading and his habit of incorporating into his poetry quotations from his reading link him not only with Pound and Eliot (a similarity of technique), but through the quotations with almost all modern literature, with the Gaelic tradition in Scotland and Ireland, with Russia (Dostoevski, Blok, Pasternak), with India and China, and with twentieth-century scientific theories and discoveries.

His debt to English literature is greater than he would like to acknowledge. The 1924 one-act play "The Purple Patch" suggests a link with Donne, and the conceits of *A Drunk Man* confirm the link. Blake's vision of the marriage of heaven and hell, where "all wholesome food is caught without a net or a trap,'' is never far distant. Sometimes the language he uses sounds as ancient as the language of *Beowulf,* while the intellectual frame of reference belongs to the twentieth century.

What are we to make of this chaotic *pot pourri* that resists categorization? The critic can do little more than draw attention to it and attempt to discover how the poetry effects a synthesis. In his attempt to establish a relationship between past and present, between order and disorder, between the individual and the tradition, between the part and the whole, MacDiarmid is very much a man of his time. Pound, Eliot, and Yeats were, in their individual ways, seeking to establish a similar kind of relationship. MacDiarmid, however, is unique in the balance of tension he creates in his best poetry—a trembling moment of unity that concentrates within itself these ''contraries.''

Like Hart Crane, he is very much aware of the abyss that threatens at any moment to shatter the precarious vision. Possibly they both gained this awareness from Ouspensky's descriptions of the intermediary stage between consciousness: ''He will sense a precipice, an abyss everywhere, no matter where he looks; and experience indeed an incredible horror, fear and sadness, until this fear and sadness shall transform themselves into the joy of the sensing of a new reality.''[37] Both MacDiarmid and Crane are specially daring in their undermining of the vision, in their continued awareness of the abyss *after* the presentation of the vision and the heady joy that accompanies it. Both poets frequently follow up their presentation of the vision with a wish or a prayer that the vision might be true. Each makes the leap, only to become aware of vertigo—a recognition that the vision may only be ''für Schwindelfreie'' (for those without vertigo), as Shestov had warned. The peculiar courage required to see and then to be aware that what was seen may only be a delusion, to create a myth and then to question the validity of that myth, demanded more than Crane was capable of giving. While MacDiarmid's courage and integrity led him to attempt what Crane also attempted, his unshakeable faith in man's ultimate fulfilment has enabled him to preserve his sense of vertigo while ascending to heights ''nur für Schwindelfreie.''

Paradoxically his Marxism helped him in the maintaining of this precarious balance. By identifying the enemy of man's progress as capitalism, as ''breid-and-butter'' problems that stand in the way of man's development and that, given the right conditions, could be removed, he makes the vision of the New Jerusalem a human possibility.

Marxism is for MacDiarmid a means, a method of enabling the flower to bloom. His interest is not so much in relieving human misery, as in seeing what happens *after* that misery is relieved:

> Man does not cease to interest me
> When he ceases to be miserable.
> Quite the contrary!
> That it is important to aid him
> In the beginning goes without saying,
> Like a plant it is essential
> To water at first,
> But this is in order to get it to flower
> And I *am concerned with the blossom*.   (p 432)

However Romantic MacDiarmid's Marxism may be, it has proved a lasting and valuable ingredient in his paradoxical vision. The hope of reaching a New Jerusalem, a "city of friends and lovers," has never failed him. It has served as an anchor between MacDiarmid and the rest of the human race, a symbol of the frailty and vulnerability of the flesh, while at the same time a promise for new kingdoms of the spirit.

Anything or anyone that comes in the way of this vision earns his relentless hatred. His list of enemies has grown. In the early thirties he was quoting Dostoevski's "All human organizations become conspiracies to short-circuit the development of human consciousness,"[38] and he has attacked most of these human organizations:

> The enumeration of these in itself manifests awareness of all that makes for the robotization of humanity; the perpetuation of needless drudgery which keeps most people cut off from any opportunity for a full life; the interposition of an arbitrary and artificial and war-causing financial system in which we are pot-bound between the vast majority of people and Nature's inexhaustible resources on the one hand and mankind's illimitable producing power on the other; and all the attendant phenomena of a corrupt and brain-destroying Press, a degraded and degradir.g cinema, Government propaganda radio, those elements of organized "religion" rightly stigmatized as the "opium of the people", the deliberate cultivation of false sport interest to "keep people from thinking", the subversion of the educational system, and so forth. It is necessary to mobilize the spirit of man against these anti-human agencies and to manifest means whereby any attempt to short-circuit human consciousness may be defeated.[39]

In this cultural-social-religious campaign MacDiarmid's attacks on individuals have been savage and relentless: Harry Lauder, Lauchlan Maclean Watt, and, the most savage of all, Edwin Muir. Anyone whom he views as a traitor to the human cause is one who deserves no quarter and must, if possible, be annihilated. A Swiftian anger descends, implacable, out of all proportion, and often revoltingly petty in its vindictiveness. The grandness of his vision is counterbalanced by the pettiness of his feuds. Within the context of the poetry, however, this pettiness is usually transmuted into daring and brilliant satire. Like MacDiarmid's Marxism, his satire establishes a firm connection between men as they are and men as they will be in the new city of "friends and lovers." In combination with the Romantic leap of imagination, the satire provides a link between the two sides of the paradox.

One of the most frustrating problems in approaching MacDiarmid's work is the issue of plagiarism, an issue connected both with the paradoxical nature of the man himself and with his vision of synthesis. It has become a problem because of MacDiarmid's lack of frankness and his deviousness. The notorious *Times Literary Supplement* controversy in the early months of 1965 made it very clear that MacDiarmid was doing everything in his power, including evasion and deceit, to wriggle out of the issue. Since then more evidence of plagiarism has poured in.[40] And I have no doubt that more evidence is still to come.

The lack of frankness, both in the original use of the material and in his responses to accusations of this sort, is the core of the problem—and it is probably as much a psychological problem as a moral one. If he had only acknowledged his sources, he would have been honourably incorporating into his own work the work of others—and this is a central part of his whole aesthetic. *Everything* in human experience up to the given moment of creation is the material with which the artist has to work and of which the "ideal observer of art at work" should be familiar. This must obviously include all written material. In his first published volume, *Annals of the Five Senses* (1923), MacDiarmid informs the reader that his work is to be seen through a "strong solution of books,"[41] and he apologizes, for one of the few times in his life, for an occasional failure to track down his sources. The devious element, however, is not long in following. In the 1924 playlet "Purple Patch," the minister of a Scottish Church accidentally includes in his sermon a section from Donne, and upon discovery of his error decides to leave it in: "It may be an accident, or it may be the hand o' God. It'll no' dae ony ill in either case. Them that comes to the kirk i' the richt frame o' mind'll never notice that onything's amiss, an' them that dae notice'll be puzzled to death to ken what to mak' on't. . . ."[42] Presumably MacDiarmid is equally as guilty as his fictitious minister. A few well-placed footnotes or a willingness to acknowledge his sources when challenged would have removed this problem altogether. As it stands, there is a meanness and a lack of integrity about the whole business that rests uneasily beside the greatness of his vision.

And so the paradoxical elements in the man and in his vision remain as paradoxical elements in the poetry, and find suitably paradoxical forms. His insecurity and his fear of losing control push him into long, rambling, plagiarized passages. His delight in extremes and in shocking the bourgeois lead him into exuberant bawdiness, brutal blasphemy, and wickedly comic satire. In his best poems—and these are often his poems in Lallans—vulnerability and confidence achieve a balance and come together, bringing with them an awareness of present horror, a memory of lost glory, and a hope of future paradise.

These elements and the trembling, precarious link between them combine then to create a poetry that is stamped with MacDiarmid's courage, disgust, integrity, wonder, strength, vulnerability, and tenderness. In these poems, paradox, vision, emotion, and language climax in a moment of epiphany:

> A watergaw wi' its chitterin' licht
> Ayont the on-ding,

(an indistinct rainbow with its shivering light beyond the heavily falling rain).

And at such moments, the "terrible crystal" unites all that is separate.

CHAPTER THREE

'Chitterin' Licht'

Annals of the Five Senses, Sangschaw and Penny Wheep

Sangschaw (1925) and *Penny Wheep* (1926) brought together the vision of paradoxical synthesis and the language of Lallans, thereby making possible epiphanies such as "the watergaw wi' its chitterin' licht." But MacDiarmid did not begin with *Sangschaw*, and the paradoxical vision formed slowly, drawing various elements to itself.

Between the young Christopher Grieve of Langholm and the Hugh MacDiarmid of *Sangschaw* and *Penny Wheep* lie the years of the First World War and the poet's first stumbling steps in the direction of the "terrible crystal." Grieve owes much to George Ogilvie, his English teacher at the Broughton Student Centre, who encouraged and guided his early attempts at writing. Their relationship reveals both Grieve's insecurity and the desire to succeed that pushed him into the writing of poetry *sui generis*. In many ways he looked to Ogilvie to take over the role of his father who had died while Grieve was attending the Broughton Student Centre. Ogilvie becomes the sympathetic and encouraging parent, the father-figure whom Grieve had sought. In a recently published letter, probably written in 1911 just after his father's death, Grieve reveals the depth of the relationship with Ogilvie: "I look back to you as I look back to my dead father, to my mother and one or two others."[1]

Ogilvie's influence upon Grieve continues long after Grieve left the Broughton Student Centre, and his dependence upon Ogilvie may well have been a major factor in his determination to become a great poet. After spending some years as a newspaper reporter in various parts of Scotland and Wales, Grieve left with the Royal Army Medical Corps for Salonika in 1916. A letter from this period reveals the intensity of the relationship with Ogilvie and the desperate need to please his former teacher: "Never a day has passed, however, but what I have thought of you. Never a day has passed but what I have said, 'Tomorrow I will write the Fine Thing—then I will write to him again.' But the tomorrow has never come."[2] In 1918 he was invalided home to a hospital in North Wales because of malaria, married Margaret Skinner in June of that year before leaving for a nine-month spell of duty in the Lahore Indian General Hospital near Marseilles: "We had always several hundred insane there and the death rate was very high, culminating in the great Influenza epidemic in 1918 when our patients . . . died in great numbers."[3] Such experiences left their mark. Army life must have been terribly difficult for a man of Grieve's shyness, intelligence, and sensitivity; and his feelings are revealed slightly in this description of the other soldiers:

> They certainly had no intellectual interests of any kind and except on the merest trivia it was impossible to have any sort of conversation with them. I think I would have felt the same with any other mob of army associates, and indeed that is just how I feel if inadvertently I get mixed up with a group of other men anywhere. I have no use for their horse-play and resent any familiarity, even if it falls far short of back-slapping jocosity. No wonder I have always been an outsider except to a chosen few; I do not share any of the interests of the mass. Their unexamined lives do not seem to me worth having.[4]

Although this description was written at some distance from the events it describes, it doubtless gives a true picture of Grieve's isolation from the other men, whether or not he felt, at the time, so confidently superior. The Langholm lad who was never "to be found where there was a pack of boys"[5] could not easily have adapted to the enforced intimacy of army life. And Ogilvie must have seemed like a distant god through whose worship the young soldier maintained his faith both in his poetry and in himself.

Shortly after being demobilized in 1919, Grieve and his new bride moved to the Scottish east-coast town of Montrose where he had obtained a job as editor-reporter of the *Montrose Review* and where he was to remain, constantly busy on literary projects of one kind or another, until the late twenties. During the war he had attempted, via Ogilvie, to arrange the publication of a volume of poems entitled "A Voice From Macedonia," but although this venture had not materialized, Grieve had taken the first step. The summer of 1919 saw the publication in *The Broughton Magazine* of "Beyond Exile—Salonika 1917," a rather sentimental Rupert-Brooke-type lyric, whose concluding stanza provides the first example of MacDiarmid's use of paradox. By dying, the speaker will have come home:

> And if I pass the utmost bourne
> Why, then, I shall be home again—
> The quick step at the quiet door,
> The gay eyes at the pane. (p 289)

By 1923 when *Annals of the Five Senses,* Grieve's first published volume, appeared, he had moved far beyond the simplicities of "Beyond Exile," with its quaint diction, its awkwardly forced alliteration ("quick," "quiet"), and its sentimental resolution. The paradoxical movement, however, remains, and while many of the poems in this volume are as derivative as "Beyond Exile," a stronger and more authentic voice is beginning to make itself heard. MacDiarmid is moving, step by step, with the encouragement of Ogilvie, towards the clear formation of his own vision, his own voice, and his own poetry.

The volume as a whole provides valuable information about where Grieve is beginning. The introduction, the prose pieces, and the lyrics, all reveal interests, themes, ideas, images, and styles, that he will develop and modify in his later work. The various elements that come together to form the paradoxical vision of synthesis are present in *Annals,* although in a somewhat chaotic form.

The introduction is tentative and apologetic: "these poems and these . . . psychological studies, essays, mosaics (call them what you will) which I have (perhaps the best word in the meantime is) 'designed'."[6] Grieve's hesitant use of the words "mosaic" and "designed" betrays a certain degree of indecision and insecurity about the precise nature of his role as a poet and about the relationship between his work and his sources. This introduction foreshadows the difficulty MacDiarmid will experience in establishing a line of demarcation between sources and original work; the border between the two will always be a shadowy one. And it also points towards the "mosaic" technique of his early poetic sequences.

Both the pitfalls and the strengths of this mosaic technique appear in two similes that Grieve uses to depict the thought-processes of an idealized Grieve-figure. In these similes lies the clue to one of MacDiarmid's basic techniques—the exploration of possibilities inherent in an idea or an image, and the chaos or the pattern that ensues. One of the similes gives the impression of confusion: "He was like an ant-heap stirred: thoughts and memories ran about in all directions at the same moment.''[7] The second gives the impression of creative freedom and excitement: "His memory was like the shooting of frost crystals on a window-pane; never was there a crystal which was not attached by traceable lines to the main body, yet no one could prophesy whether each fine filament might strike out on its own undivided adventure."[8] MacDiarmid's poems bear witness that his mind resembles both similes. In his best poems the frost crystals form magically on the window panes of our imagination. In his worst poems the ants crawl frantically and to no avail. In both the best and the worst, "each fine filament might strike out on its own undivided adventure," and it is this willingness to explore possibilities and to move towards the extreme, often in several directions at once, that makes the paradoxical vision possible. The technique can seem surprisingly and convincingly effective, or the result of wilful self-indulgence, depending upon the intrinsic interest of the filament and of the pattern which the development of that filament reveals or fails to reveal. On the whole, its advantages outweigh its dangers.

The central character in several of the short stories in *Annals* resembles Grieve in other ways than in his mental habits: he is a journalist; he has experienced the war; in "Four Years Harvest" he has served at Salonika and has a wife named Peggy. Meanwhile the major themes of the future MacDiarmid emerge undisguised: the Ouspenskian illumination into the mystery of life through sexual experience, often highly reminiscent of D. H. Lawrence; synthesis, the desired result of the various thought-explorations ("humanity's bewilderment of thought is a mighty net which somehow holds the whole truth," "his tendency was always to the whole, to the totality, to the general balance of things,"[9]); social concern as a step towards a universal synthesis, the first indication of MacDiarmid's paradoxical link between politics and religion ("the fullest participation in the treasure of the one life"[10]). Even the image of light, MacDiarmid's guiding image, plays a prominent part in establishing the essentially paradoxical nature of the desired synthesis, the movement from sexual experience into illumination. For example, the Lawrentian and Ouspenskian "Consummation" holds at its centre this image of light, the visible symbol of the paradox:

> Ablaze yet unconsumed I lay in thee
> And instantly flame blended into flame,
> As in a rising wind the light fires came.
> Curve after curve climbed shining into me

> I felt light flowing from your hands and feet,
> I lay in incandescence 'twixt your thighs,
> And saw the radiance mounting in your eyes
> And heard your soaring heart's delirious beat.
>
> Ablaze yet unconsumed I lie in thee.
> Once lit such fires blaze to the end of time
> To keener, clearer flaming still set free.
> The spirit like a wind moves to and fro
> Until in crystal heat, O Love Sublime,
> One with eternity our bodies glow![11]

The image of the burning bush, "ablaze yet unconsumed," is the central paradox, the manifestation of the vision and the synthesis of body and spirit. Parallels to this central paradox emerge throughout the poem as the miraculous light flows from the body: "from your hands and feet," "incandescence 'twixt your thighs," "radiance mounting in your eyes," "one with eternity our bodies glow." Significantly the light flows from the body of the woman—she is the source, not the speaker. Her flame sets him aflame, so that in the final lines both flames merge in climactic unity: "One with eternity *our* bodies glow" (my italics).

The theme that is presented here in its crudest form is a theme that MacDiarmid will use over and over again, a theme that he will develop and ramify in much of his later poetry: the vision made possible by woman, the light that flows from her sex and that unites both partners with eternity. We have it here in its simplest form, exuberant, rather adolescent, and overwhelmingly optimistic. Although paradoxical in origin, the vision itself reveals nothing but good. Later it will become more complex, drawing to itself the contraries of grief and joy, pain and pleasure, disgust and wonder. The vision will also become more transitory and more elusive as MacDiarmid moves beyond the easy confidence of "Once lit such fires blaze to the end of time / To keener, clearer flaming still set free." And paradoxically as the vision becomes more complex and elusive, it becomes more convincing. In "Consummation" Grieve is writing as he thinks he ought to write, attempting to imitate Lawrence, and putting forward a secondhand vision. Everything is a little too easy, a little too simple, and much too sentimental.

The secondhand experience of this poem stands implicitly behind the most important poem in *Annals*. The closing line, "One with eternity our bodies glow,'' leads directly into the opening lines of ''A Moment in Eternity,'' even although they are separated in the text:

> The great song ceased
> —Aye, like a wind was gone,
> And our hearts came to rest,
> Singly as leaves do,
> And every leaf a flame. (p 1)

The sexual experience of ''Consummation'' has made possible the ''moment in eternity,'' and now the speaker is free to focus on the vision itself and on its effects upon him. The woman's role is over, and the "our hearts" of the first stanza give way immediately to "*My* shining passions stilled" (my italics).

The debt to Ouspensky and to his descriptions of Jacob Boehme's visions is great. When MacDiarmid writes in *Lucky Poet*, ''. . . there are few of the great mystical experiences I have not had, and I can certainly claim that in Scotland, like Jacob Boehme on a green before Neys Gate at Goerlitz in 1600, I have on occasion been able to sit down, and, viewing the herbs and grass in my inward light, see 'into their essences, use, and properties', discovered to me 'by their lineaments, figures, and signatures','' he is doubtless quoting Ouspensky's description of Boehme's vision.[12] He neglects, however, to quote the passage from *Tertium Organum* that probably forms the basis of ''A Moment in Eternity,'' another vision of Boehme's: ''He now recognized the divine order of nature, and how from the trunk of the tree of life spring different branches, bearing manifold leaves and flowers and fruit, and he became impressed with the necessity of writing down what he saw and preserved the record.''[13] Grieve also ''preserved the record,'' but it is a record of secondhand experience, and it fails to convince:

> I was a multitude of leaves
> Receiving and reflecting light,
> A burning bush
> Blazing forever unconsumed,
> Nay, ceaselessly,
> Multiplying in leaves and light
> And instantly
> Burgeoning in buds of brightness. (p 1)

The incantatory effect, however, with its heavy alliteration, aureate diction, singing present participles, and free verse form, convinces on another level. Often the effect is terribly crude and amateurish ("Pealing pellucidly / And quivering in faery flights of chimes"), but occasionally a direct and powerful statement breaks through the surface decoration: "I shone within my thoughts / As God within us shines."

It is only at odd moments such as these that Grieve shows he has the makings of a great lyric poet. The poem suffers from an overabundance of exotic and Latinate adjectives, Milton gone wild:

> I was a crystal trunk,
> Columnar in the glades of Paradise,
> Bearing the luminous boughs
> And foliaged with the flame
> Of infinite and gracious growth.   (p 3)

This exotic plant is a strange precursor of the "gurly thistle" in *A Drunk Man*.

Sporadically and dramatically, however, the strong voice of conviction makes itself heard, and when it sounds, it is the voice of paradox:

> —Meteors for roots,
> And my topmost spires
> Notes of enchanted light
> Blind in the Godhead!
> —White stars at noon!   (p 3)

If we remove the flowery "And my topmost spires / Notes of enchanted light," we are left with three powerfully paradoxical images, simple, uncluttered, daringly evocative in their presentation of the union between God and man.

And so, despite its many failings, "A Moment in Eternity" gives an indication of the path that MacDiarmid will follow. Pruning and discipline will remove some of the less desirable tendencies, at least in his best poems, while the delight in extravagance and in exotic diction will find a more suitable medium. While his own voice will grow more confident and compelling, its origins are there, just as the paradoxical vision is there, in the "white stars at noon." In "A Moment in Eternity," Grieve has taken his place in the tradition of the poet-seer, the link between heaven and earth, the visionary who prophesies in lyrical language. And like Blake, he had found the means to this vision in the paradox.

Grieve also shared with Blake the ability to "run about in all directions at the same time," as evidenced by another poem in *Annals*—"The Fool," a welcome and healthy counterpart to the exuberances of "A Moment in Eternity":

> He said that he was God.
> "We are well met," I cried,
> "I've always hoped I should
> Meet God before I died."
>
> I slew him then and cast
>   His corpse into a pool,
> —But how I wish he had
>   Indeed been God, the fool!　　　　　　　　(p 6)

Surprisingly this too may find its origin in *Tertium Organum,* where the holders of "cosmic consciousness" are "exalted to the ranks of gods or are adjudged insane."[14] But if this is the case, Grieve has ironically complicated the concept by introducing the possibility that the speaker is more "insane" than the god-like fool. Also, although the tone of the first stanza is at the opposite pole from the tone of "A Moment in Eternity," even this does nothing to prepare the reader for the emotional shock of the violence that follows. Traditional Scottish irony, going beyond irony into the blackest of black humour, increases the shock value of the final two lines.

Viewed in conjunction, "A Moment in Eternity" and "The Fool" seem an odd couple. Each seeks union with God, but in a very different manner. One is violent, blasphemous, physical in its approach; the other is reverent, worshipful, awed, quickly moving from the physical to the purely spiritual. At this stage in his writing Grieve has to keep the two approaches separate. When he is able to combine them or to bring them into contact with each other, the paradoxical moment of synthesis emerges from the tension and the interaction of the two paradoxical approaches. Revulsion and wonder are both attendant at the meeting of flesh and spirit. Tenderness and disgust hover around the mystery of the paradox.

In these two poems are to be found the major elements of MacDiarmid's poetry: the Lawrentian theme of illumination through sexual experience, the moment of paradoxical vision, the desire to meet God, the instant of union, the soaring sweep of lyricism, the dynamic juxtaposition of tone, the sudden burst of violence. It is an exciting combination, both shocking and evocative, and it is a combination that has produced some of the greatest lyric poetry of the twentieth century.

The one missing ingredient, the ingredient that was to make the achievement possible, was already in Grieve's possession when he published *Annals,* although the public was unaware of its link with C. M. Grieve. "Hugh M'Diarmid" had already seen in print, first anonymously and then under the MacDiarmid *nom de plume,* his Lallans lyric "The Watergaw," the first and perhaps one of the most impressive results of his addition of Lallans to the ingredients already present in "A Moment in Eternity" and "The Fool." Lallans, whatever the theory behind its adoption, had released in MacDiarmid a strength, a conviction, and a tenderness that had not been present in the English lyrics and sonnets. He had found his voice. The ancient language of Scotland, a tangible link between past and present, was to provide the paradoxical aegis under which the paradoxical vision could finds its fulfilment.

Grieve had come to Lallans gradually. He had moved step by step from his 1921 position of opposition to the Vernacular Circle of the London Burns Club, an organization devoted to the revival of the Doric as a literary language, into support of their campaign, and, through his editorship of *The Scottish Chapbook,* into leadership of the newly born Scottish Renaissance. The aims of the *Chapbook,* set forth in the first number on 26 August 1922, were formulated thus:

To report, support, and stimulate, in particular, the activities of the Franco-Scottish, Scottish-Italian, and kindred Associations; the campaign of the Vernacular Circle of the London Burns Club for the revival of the Doric; the movement towards a Scots National Theatre; and the "Northern Numbers" movement in contemporary Scottish poetry.

To encourage and publish the work of contemporary Scottish poets and dramatists, whether in English, Gaelic, or Braid Scots.

To insist upon truer evaluations of the work of Scottish writers than are usually given in the present over-Anglicised condition of British literary journalism, and, in criticism, elucidate, apply, and develop the distinctively Scottish range of values.

To bring Scottish Literature into closer touch with current European tendencies in technique and ideation.

To cultivate "the lovely virtue."
And, generally, to "meddle wi' the Thistle" and pick the figs.[15]

The emphasis on internationalism through nationalism, on anti-Anglicism, and on the cultivation of distinctively Scottish values (a movement back into the past before the English influence was so strong) is an emphasis that MacDiarmid has retained throughout all the twists and turns of his beliefs. Of much greater importance however are the *results* of this creed, results which were soon evident in the anonymous publication of "The Watergaw" on 30 September 1922, and in its reappearance under the MacDiarmid pseudonym in the 22 October issue of *The Scottish Chapbook*. Lallans with its "names for nameless things" was to provide MacDiarmid with a magic language, a path back to the lost Eden, and a method of making the paradoxical vision a reality. "The Watergaw," possibly his first attempt at a lyric in Lallans, reveals its power:

> Ae weet forenicht i' the yow-trummle
> I saw yon antrin thing,
> A watergaw wi' its chitterin' licht
> Ayond the on-ding;
> An' I thocht o' the last wild look ye gied
> Afore ye deed!
>
> There was nae reek i' the laverock's hoose
> That nicht—an' nane i' mine;
> But I hae thocht o' that foolish licht
> Ever sin syne;
> An' I think that mebbe at last I ken
> What your look meant then.

(p 7)

The "chitterin' licht" (shivering light) of the rainbow and of the illumination felt by the dying man and by the speaker is in its own way as strange and exotic as the light in "A Moment in Eternity," "burgeoning in buds of brightness," but it carries with it the ring of truth and the stamp of authenticity and immediacy, while retaining the supernatural suggestiveness of the earlier vision. Indeed the sense of supernatural strangeness is *increased* through the language. Lallans has made possible a stronger emotional tone and a whole host of effects that are barred to standard English.

The theory behind the adoption of Lallans emphasized its strange

50

vitality and the complex thought-processes that lie behind the words, the words themselves providing a tangible link with an earlier and more mysterious world:

> There are words and phrases in the Vernacular which thrill me with a sense of having been produced as a result of mental processes entirely different from my own and much more powerful. They embody observations of a kind which the modern mind makes with increasing difficulty and weakened effect. [16]

When "The Watergaw" appeared in *The Scottish Chapbook,* it came equipped with a translation that served to emphasize the comparative inadequacy of standard English. It is a pathetically weak counterpart: "One wet afternoon (or early evening) in the cold weather in July after the sheep-shearing I saw that rare thing—an indistinct rainbow with its shivering light above the heavily falling rain." Much has been lost: the strength and the strangeness of the Lallans words; the image of "forenicht" with its component of "nicht" that suggests both night and nothing—this is the moment that precedes death; the trembling motif of "yow-trummle" (literally "ewe-tremble") and "chitterin' licht"; the finality of death, a finality that thuds in the short, bitter lines, "Afore ye deed," and "Ayont the on-ding." The second stanza is just as resistant to translation. "There was nae reek i' the laverock's hoose / That nicht—an' nane i' mine" translates into the obscure "There was no smoke in the lark's house that night and none in mine." The metaphor is no longer viable and must become the mundane "It was a wild stormy night outside, and in my heart." The central image and the beauty of the language have both been lost—the desolate monosyllables, the link between man and the non-human (rainbow, lark, eternity), and the powerful echoes ("reek"-"laverock," "nicht"-"nane"-"mine," and the aural link with the introductory "Ae weet forenicht"). In the original, the vulnerable, trembling moment of illumination felt by the speaker perfectly parallels the "last wild look" of the dying man, with *its* "foolish licht": a moment of "chitterin' " contact between man and the inhuman. And the strangeness of the language makes the experience of the poem even more strangely mysterious.

The discovery that this is probably one of the poems to which MacDiarmid was referring when he claimed that poetry is not "an idea gradually shaping itself in words, but deriving entirely from words" does not detract from the intrinsic power of the poem. When "The

Watergaw" was published anonymously, Grieve introduced it as the work of a "friend" who had busied himself with Sir James Wilson's *Lowland Scotch as Spoken in the Lower Strathearn District of Perthshire.*[17] The section in Wilson's text that deals with weather provides, on one page, "weet," "yow-trummul," and "waatur-gaw" (Wilson's phonetic representation of the words), together with their meanings. The "proverbs and sayings" section contributes "Dhur'z nay reek ee laivruck's hoose dhe-nikht" (there's no smoke in the lark's house tonight).[18] But these ingredients by no means make the poem. The shaping power of the "makar" brings these ingredients together and sets them in a relationship to each other and to the emotional reverberations of the link between the two men faced with death, the dying man himself and the grieving speaker.

Most likely these emotional reverberations stem from the impact of Grieve's father's death. In *Lucky Poet* he describes it more explicitly:

> Afore he dee'd he turned and gied a lang
> Last look at pictures o' my brither and me
> Hung on the wa' aside the bed, I've heard
> My mither say . . .

and,

> He looked in vain, and I again.[19]

The intensity of the emotion, however, emerges much more clearly in the dense Lallans of "The Watergaw," and this is partly due to the movement from the literal to the symbolic level, partly to the vividness of the Lallans itself. The poem seems to hover, like the "chitterin' licht" of the watergaw, above the mystery of life and death, above the foolishly brave and beautiful movements of man.

In *Lucky Poet* MacDiarmid recognizes that the "sounds" of the Scots language "bring me fully alive": "so it is only in the Scots language I can achieve or maintain if not, in certain senses, integrity of expression, at least 'the terrible crystal'."[20] Style and content interweave through the media of Lallans and of the intensity of emotion that, for MacDiarmid, accompanies Lallans. Vision and language come together in the trembling moments of synthesis between man and the unknown as the "terrible crystal" of paradox takes form. And Lallans itself is a kind of "terrible crystal," full of paradoxes: the words themselves form a paradoxical link between past and present; the *sounds* are both more gentle and more fierce than the sounds of standard English. This gentleness (the soft "ch," like "licht") and this fierceness (the exploded consonants, the guttural "ch" like "och," the rolling "r"s) seem to have released in MacDiarmid a corresponding tenderness and violence, brought together by the language itself. Thanks to Lallans, the two opposing approaches of "A Moment in Eternity" and "The Fool" can meet.

"The Watergaw" comes with an additional bonus, unsuspected so far by those who have written on the poem. In it, MacDiarmid has provided a solution to the problem that Burns avoided in "Tam o' Shanter": a lyrical Scots version of the unfortunate "rainbow's lovely form / Evanishing amid the storm." MacDiarmid's rage in 1936 when Edwin Muir praised these lines by Burns at the expense of the Scots lines in "Tam o' Shanter" is understandable. Muir was correct, however, in his insistence upon the emotional power of Lallans, and a poem such as "The Watergaw" demonstrates its ability to conjure up deep emotion while preserving a sense of mystery:

> . . . for here's a language rings
> Wi' datchie sesames, and names for nameless things. (p 58)

The language itself is a kind of illumination, a movement into a strange, unknown, but somehow familiar world.

MacDiarmid was obviously comfortable with his new poetic language and his new name. As Norman MacCaig delights in recalling, he took to it "like a duck to glue."[21] What may have begun as a casual experiment turned out to be an effective way of extending human consciousness. In practice, the language serves as a vehicle for lyrical effects set cheek by jowl with philosophical speculations or implications, the whole often enlivened by dry Scottish irony. Flickering transitions of tone are traditional in Scottish poetry, the language itself helping to bridge any otherwise obstrusive gap. This unique quality of Lallans stems partly from Scottish history and the Scottish class system. The language of the ruling classes in Scotland, unlike that of the ruling classes in England after the Norman Conquest, did not differ substantially from that of the lowliest man in the kingdom. Hence, *without a change in language* bawdy folk humour could be placed side by side with the courtly love tradition or with philosophical concerns (e.g., Dunbar). The effect would be somewhat akin to *Piers Plowman* with the Latin phrases removed.

Grieve was quick to recognize the unique qualities of Lallans and the importance of MacDiarmid's "Watergaw." Thanks to the pseudonym, he was able to comment in the same number of the *Chapbook:* "Mr. M'Diarmid has disclosed—shall I say?—a hope of resuscitation. He has done more. Stripping the unconscious form of Vernacular of the grotesque clothes of the Canny-Sandy cum Kirriemuir Elder cum Harry Lauder cult, he has shown a well-knit muscular figure that has not been seen in Scottish literature for many a long day."[22] This "well-knit muscular figure" of MacDiarmid's Lallans lyrics was soon a familiar part of *The Scottish Chapbook*; and by 1923 Grieve was beginning to formulate a battleplan for the Scottish Renaissance—based largely on Gregory Smith's Scottish-Antisyzygy-theory:

> We base our belief in the possibility of a great Scottish Literary Renaissance, deriving its strength from the resources that lie latent and almost unsuspected in the Vernacular, upon the fact that the genius of our Vernacular enables us to secure with comparative ease the very effects and swift transitions which other literatures are for the most part unsuccessfully endeavouring to cultivate in languages that have a very different and inferior bias.[23]

The fruits of this theory are evident in the 1925 collection of lyrics by "Hugh M'Diarmid," *Sangschaw.* The "genius" of the vernacular, when brought together with the vision and imagination of Christopher Grieve, has produced a singularly moving manifestation of the "polar twins" of the Scottish muse. Swift, flickering transitions of tone, brought about as man faces and touches the unknown, are the most distinctive features of this volume; and these transitions of tone usually indicate a dramatic movement from one side of the paradox to the other. Under the aegis of Lallans and with the full cooperation of the speaker's emotions, the paradox takes shape. "The Bonnie Broukit Bairn," with its dramatic switch of focus and tone as the speaker moves from one of the elements in the paradox to the other, is a fine example of this kind of effect. The "bonnie broukit bairn" (the beautiful deserted child) is the central, paradoxical image: she is revealed first as "broukit," then as "bonnie" and "broukit," and finally as "bonnie" in her triumph:

> Mars is braw in crammasy,   *fine in scarlet*
> Venus in a green silk goun,
> The auld mune shak's her gowden feathers,   *golden*
> Their starry talk's a wheen o' blethers,   *lot of nonsense*

> Nane for thee a thochtie sparin',   *little thought*
> Earth, thou bonnie broukit bairn!
> *—But greet, an' in your tears ye'll droun*   *weep*
> *The haill clanjamfrie!*   *whole bunch*

(p 7)

The theme here—the potential place of man within creation—has been presented in a short lyric, not a philosophical treatise; and the leap of imagination involved is convincing because of this treatment. The reader is swept along with the speaker from one tone to another, as his emotions undergo a series of transformations. It opens sardonically as the speaker, tongue very much in cheek, praises the planets' costumes. "Braw" in the first line indicates careful dressing on the part of Mars, rather than innate worth. Venus's colour comes from her "green silk goun," and "goun" smacks of pretension; while the moon appears like a fat, golden hen: "The auld mune shak's her gowden feathers." Their talk is as pretentious as their dress—"starry," appropriate in a description of the planets' conversation, while it simultaneously prepares the way for the speaker's disparagement of their talk: "a wheen o' blethers." The images and the language have reduced the planets to a collection of pretentious, empty gossips. A sudden, skilfully smooth movement draws the reader's attention away from the planets to the earth, correspondingly reduced to child size; and the tone becomes infinitely gentle and tender: "Nane for thee a thochtie sparin', / Earth, thou bonnie broukit bairn." Suddenly and without warning, but in a movement prepared for by the rising emotion of "bonnie broukit bairn," the poem soars upward and embraces the planets and the universe beyond: *"But greet, an' in your tears ye'll droun / The haill clanjamfrie!"* Earth's tears are magnified into a deluge greater than any known to man and capable of swallowing the planets themselves and all their foolish talk. The tone moves correspondingly into one of triumphant vindication and excitement.

The lyrical impact of the poem depends partly on the unusual rhyme scheme (a b c c d d b a, almost a magical formula), which creates a subtle echoing effect in the final lines: the climax seems appropriate because of the half-remembered and half-forgotten rhyme, and mysteriously appropriate too. The singing quality comes from the skilful and rich use of internal rhyme, half rhyme, and assonance, made possible by Lallans ("Mars"-"crammasy"-"starry," "goun"-"mune"-"nane"-"bonnie"-

55

"droun," "goun"-"gowden"-"wheen"-"greet"). Alliteration abounds, with special emphasis on "b" and "r," the concentration of "r"'s in the final lines contributing to the richly triumphant quality of the assertion: *"But greet, an' in your tears ye'll droun / The haill clanjamfrie!"* The metre is just as skilful. A pair of lines beginning with an unstressed syllable alternates with a pair beginning with a stressed syllable, and this contributes to the creation of a mysteriously appropriate ambience. The metre, in conjunction with the reduced number of feet in the final line and the enjambment leading into it, the only enjambment in the lyric, adds to the emphasis and the power of the final lines which confidently envision the victory of earth, and by implication the victory of mankind: this flood is irresistible. The combination of the image of the "bonnie broukit bairn" and Lallans, the language of childhood, and the lyrical and emotional powers that Lallans released in MacDiarmid, makes this victory a true "ferlie" (wonder, marvel, magic), a peculiarly moving marriage of Wordsworth and Blake with the Scottish language.

There is a great deal of this kind of experimentation in *Sangschaw:* the addition of Lallans and an unexpected viewpoint to familiar ingredients. Thus the Cophetua legend becomes: *"OH!* The King's gane gyte [mad], / Puir auld man, puir auld man, / An' an ashypet lassie / Is Queen o' the lan' " (p 19). This "ashypet lassie" (scullery maid) reminds us of the bonnie broukit bairn who achieves a similar kind of elevation. The paradoxical rise to power by one who is helpless gains focus in the concluding stanza where the beggarmaid, dressed in a silken apron, carries a silver bucket:

> Wi' a scoogie o' silk
> An' a bucket o' siller
> She's showin' the haill Coort
> The smeddum intil her!　　　　　(pp 19-20)

The "scoogie o' silk" and the "bucket o' siller" are extensions of the central paradox, the lassie herself, both scullery maid and queen. The down-to-earth "smeddum" (spirit) of this beggarmaid is irresistible. She is indomitable and wonderful, truly fit to be a queen, in a way that the pale heroines of the nineteenth century could never have contemplated.

The technique here is typical of the technique in *Sangschaw* as a whole. Familiar myths—the Day of Judgement, the birth of Christ, the Crucifixion, the Creation—become subject to a strange unexpected approach, reinforced by the eery and earthy associations of Lallans (e.g., "Crowdieknowe," "O Jesu Parvule," "The Innumerable Christ," "Whip-the-World"). In general, MacDiarmid is using familiar and traditional materials—the great mythic moments—but when he approaches them from a surprising angle and when he dresses them in the guise of Lallans, these materials become transformed into something very new, strange, and mysterious. The essentially paradoxical elements of the familiar myths are brought to new light through an unexpected focus on one side of the paradox. For example, in "Crowdieknowe," at the Day of Judgement the "muckle men wi' tousled beards" rise up, terrifying in their physical presence, scrambling "frae the croodit clay [crowded clay] / Wi' feck [plenty] o' swearin' " (p 16). The paradox of the resurrection becomes startlingly mysterious through MacDiarmid's focusing upon the *physical* aspects. Similarly in "The Eemis Stane" (the precariously balanced stone), the movement of the world through space appears unearthly and terribly vulnerable, and the reader is shocked into new vision:

<table>
<tr><td>I' the how-dumb-deid o' the cauld hairst nicht</td><td>midnight, autumn</td></tr>
<tr><td>The warl' like an eemis stane</td><td></td></tr>
<tr><td>Wags i' the lift;</td><td>sky</td></tr>
<tr><td>An' my eerie memories fa'</td><td></td></tr>
<tr><td> Like a yowdendrift.</td><td>counterswirl of snow</td></tr>
<tr><td></td><td></td></tr>
<tr><td>Like a yowdendrift so's I couldna read</td><td></td></tr>
<tr><td>The words cut oot i' the stane</td><td></td></tr>
<tr><td>Had the fug o' fame</td><td>moss</td></tr>
<tr><td>An' history's hazelraw</td><td>lichen</td></tr>
<tr><td>No' yirdit thaim.</td><td>buried</td></tr>
</table>

(p 17)

The speaker, of course, is as unidentifiable as the speaker in "The Bonnie Broukit Bairn." Is it God who sees in this way? Or man's imagination? The mystery that surrounds the speaker extends and deepens in the "eemis stane" itself: a wobbly stone that moves precariously through space and through the "cauld hairst nicht," a transitional period leading into winter, just as the "forenicht" in "The Watergaw" led into night; a stone that appears in the "how-dumb-deid" of the night, and then is recognized as a tombstone ("deid"), wrapped in the protective and impenetrable moss and lichen of the past. The

57

atmosphere is reminiscent of Scottish ballads or of Middle English lyrics. What is given in the poem appears as the remnant of some greater whole, a tantalizing clue to the mystery which somehow resists all attempts to simplify it or supply the missing parts. The movement of the poem, partly through the uneven length of line and rhythm and through the counterswirl that moves at its centre, "wags i' the lift," just like the "eemis stane," making the mystery of life seem very familiar and then very strange, hovering at the gateway of perception and recognition. The echo of "eemis stane" in "eerie memories," and of "warl' " in "wags," the repetition of "yowdendrift" at the centre of the lyric, the strong link of alliteration in "fug o' fame" and "history's hazelraw," all these echoes reassure and suggest a unity, a clear relationship, while the empty vowels of "how-dumb-deid" and "cauld hairst nicht" and "yowden" suggest that the central mystery will defy man's reason. Paradoxically they counterbalance the movement towards understanding and simplification.

While this ballad atmosphere of superhuman mystery is present in many of the lyrics in *Sangschaw,* the ballad *form* also makes an appearance, both in "I Heard Christ Sing" and "The Ballad of the Five Senses." Why should MacDiarmid in his attempt to bring Scottish poetry into line with twentieth-century Europe have chosen such an apparently retrogressive form?

His use of the ballad parallels his use of Lallans. Both the ballad form and Lallans suggest a more ancient world, a strange world where men and gods meet one another, a world where paradox predominates. By entering this world of elemental forces and by maintaining a twentieth-century frame of reference, MacDiarmid attempts to transcend time. He recreates the past in order to reach the future. While both Lallans and the ballad appear as odd choices for a Scottish poet who is trying to bring Scottish poetry into line with modern European poetry, they are consistent with MacDiarmid's insistence upon a paradoxical union of opposites, and they are symbolic of his desire to recreate the lost Eden in order to reach the future paradise. Although he has presented no theoretical justification for his use of the ballad form, as he has done for his adoption of Lallans, the two are obviously related. An examination of what he achieves with the ballad form strengthens this suggestion.

MacDiarmid is not writing other "Sir Patrick Spens"es; rather he is using the ballad, as Coleridge did in "The Ancient Mariner," to create an ambience of terror, mystery, and fate, within which the speaker contemplates the place and meaning of man. The traditional link between Lallans and the ballad helps to reinforce this kind of ambience. Desolation and isolation (as in "The Eemis Stane"), moving into triumphant assertion of man's potential (as in "The Bonnie Broukit Bairn") form the major axes of the poetry in this volume. ("The Watergaw" marks the junction of these two axes). Meanwhile, unusual and unexpected viewpoints continually jolt the reader into awareness of the world created anew by the imagination of the poet. The size of objects is frequently deceptive. The speaker uses his mind in telescopic fashion, and shows no hesitation in looking through each end of the mind-telescope in quick succession—and sometimes simultaneously (e.g., in "The Eemis Stane," the shrinking of the world into a stone, and then the expansion of this stone into a gravestone with all the mists of history swirling around it). Alice-in-Wonderland transformations, facilitated by the ballad ambience, abound. This particular technique is a variation upon the more general technique of expectation-reversal that MacDiarmid uses throughout the volume, the paradox taking form as he leaps in the opposite direction from what the reader expects. The fateful and tragic ending (to which one is accustomed in the ballad) is appropriately transformed into a vision of man-created, rather than fate-created splendour. And this vision gains enormous emotional conviction from the ballad context and from the language. We had been prepared for a miracle of sorts, but not this kind of miracle.

Look, for example, at the ballad "I Heard Christ Sing." To the basic ingredients (the lyrical and emotional suggestions of Lallans, the ballad form and atmosphere), MacDiarmid has added the implied framework of the medieval dream vision. Thus he is able to manipulate the tensions, expectations, and suggestive qualities of these three factors. He creates a world where mystery and fate are acknowledged forces and where philosophical questions are posed in terms of mythic figures and images. While the expected ballad ending is both tragic and fate-created, the expected dream vision ending is God-oriented and God-created. MacDiarmid makes use of both these expectations in order to create dramatic and emotionally compelling reversals. Neither expectation is fulfilled; instead mankind and the eventual achievement of his potential become the focus. This modern re-working of traditional mythic materials, in combination with Lallans and the ballad form, provides an effective link between past, present, and future. Both the language and the form of these Lallans ballads reinforce the paradoxical core of MacDiarmid's vision.

The central metaphor of "I Heard Christ Sing" is the Christian myth:
the man-God who will free mankind, the paradoxical link between man
and God, lost Eden and future paradise. Both this figure and the ballad
aura that surrounds him appear in the opening line, as direct and to the
point as "The king sits in Dumferling toune." The speaker plunges into a
description of the vision, without any preliminary details about lying
down to sleep or anything of that sort. Quite simply,

> I heard Christ sing quhile roond him danced
> The twal' disciples in a ring,
> And here's the dance I saw them dance,
> And the sang I heard them sing. (p 8)

While the atmosphere is reminiscent of "The Ancient Mariner" ("My
hert stude still, and the sun stude still, / But still the dancers plied"), it is
both very ancient and very modern. Christ becomes the centre of ancient
fertility rites (the maypole), the central point in time (the hands of the
clock standing still while the figures "gaed bizzin roon' "), and the
central point in space ("The twal' points o' the compass / Made jubilee
roon' and roon' "). Christ, the point where extremes meet, is the
paradoxical man-God. As a man, however, he begs God to consent to his
plan to release humanity from all that binds it. This reversal of the
traditional version of the myth is a typical MacDiarmid technique. The
reader is shocked into new vision: Christ, nailed down, is like man caged:

> *Sweet is the song*
> *That is lost in its throat,*
> *And fain 'ud I hear*
> *Its openin' note,*
> *As I hang on the rood.* (p 10)

Christ's song dies when he dies—his harp, composed of *"tremblin'
sunbeams,"* has broken—but *man's* song will continue: "As a white
sword loupin' at the hert / O' a' eternity." The movement of this section
of "I Heard Christ Sing" parallels the climax of "The Bonnie Broukit
Bairn": the soaring triumphant surge, through the enjambment, into
eternity. Man, rather than God, is the focus—man who has himself
become a kind of God through the full development of his powers.

The combination of light and song that appears in the harp of
"tremblin' sunbeams" and in the "white sword" is a characteristic
combination in *Sangschaw*. When all that fetters man is removed and

when his potential is released in a moment of pure vision, light and music fill the universe—just as the tears of the "bonnie broukit bairn" were able to "droun / The haill clanjamfrie." The light of "Consummation" flickers in these tears, in the "chitterin' licht" of "The Watergaw," and in the "tremblin' sunbeams." All the miraculous transformations have obvious sexual overtones, and D. H. Lawrence is never far absent—even in a poem such as "Ex Vermibus." The tone is very different, of course: much coarser than that of either "I Heard Christ Sing" or "Consummation." But the connection between light and music reappears, and once again in relation to the Christian myth and to the transforming power of sex. Neither receives explicit allusion, but both are suggested in the image of the miraculous worm that will save mankind:

Gape, gape, gorlin',   *fledgling*
For I ha'e a worm
That'll gi'e ye a slee and sliggy sang   *sly and cunning*
Wi' mony a whuram.   *grace note*

Syne i' the lift   *sky*
Byous spatrils you'll mak',   *wonderful notes*
For a gorlin' wi' worms like this in its wame *belly*
Nae airels sall lack.   *notes*

But owre the tree-taps
Maun flee like a sperk,   *fly, spark*
Till it hes the haill o' the Heavens alunt   *alight*
Frae dawin' to derk.   *dawn, dark*

(p 13)

The ambiguity surrounding the speaker (on the first level, a mother bird feeding her fledgling; on other levels, a lover addressing a coy mistress, or Gabriel explaining the Incarnation to Mary, or Grieve feeding the worm of Lallans to MacDiarmid, or Christ dying on the cross that man might live) makes for a wonderful mélange of suggestion and tone—earthy, sacrilegious, epiphanic, as spirit and flesh unite. The long third line in each stanza plays an important role: emphasizing the conniving intimacy of the first stanza; bringing the tone back to comic, elemental awareness in the second; and finally ringing forth triumphantly in "Till it hes the haill o' the Heavens alunt / Frae dawin'

61

to derk.'' The movement of this third stanza is once again similar to the climax of ''The Bonnie Broukit Bairn,'' as it soars into the transcendent vision, all the more powerful because of the elemental and earthy atmosphere of the first stanza. The extremes make possible the paradox. The expectations of the first stanza act upon the reader in a similar fashion to his expectations aroused by the ballad form and atmosphere. They establish a tone which moves suddenly in an unexpected direction under the aegis of Lallans, imagery, and surging rhythm, into an unexpected and unknown country, a country that appears as very beautiful, precarious, yet somehow familiar. At the climactic moment, we reach a kind of epiphany.

In *Sangschaw* MacDiarmid has clearly continued to develop the role established in ''A Moment in Eternity,'' that of the poet-seer, the visionary who, like Blake, sees man-as-God, rather than God on his own, as the focus of his vision. His concept of the *nature* of the vision has changed: the ''white sword'' is ''loupin' '' at eternity; the song ''maun flee like a sperk''; the light is ''chitterin' ''; the sunbeams are ''tremblin' ''; and the flood which will ''droun / The haill clanjamfrie'' is composed of tears. The vision has become more transitory, more precarious, and more painful, but, simultaneously and paradoxically, more convincing and more powerful. Just as Lallans confidently and convincingly bridges the gap between the supernatural and the elemental, between the past and the present, so MacDiarmid in these poems makes the vision more qualified and more real, more ''chitterin' '' and more ''alunt.''

Not only does this volume hark back to *Annals*—it also looks forward to *A Drunk Man*. MacDiarmid seems to be rejoicing in his new voice, testing it out, and attempting to find its limits in ballads, translations, lyrics, and some tentative poetic sequences. He is assembling all the ingredients that will come together to form his masterpiece, *A Drunk Man Looks at the Thistle*. These small sequences or constellations are created by the juxtaposition of two or three related lyrics, each of which gains by being placed in proximity to the others, and each of which contributes one element to the paradoxical vision of synthesis formed by the *interaction* of individual lyrics. For example, ''O Jesu Parvule,'' of the Christ-lullaby genre, is followed by ''The Innumerable Christ.'' This poem bears the epigraph, ''Other stars may have their Bethlehem, and their Calvary too,'' which picks up the reference to stars (''An' a' the starnies an' he are sib'') and develops the already established theme of the nativity. The endless process of Christ's birth and crucifixion gains poignancy through juxtaposition with the innocent loving tone of "O Jesu Parvule," and simultaneously this innocent indomitable love seems hopelessly but courageously vital in contrast to the bleakness of "The Endless Christ." Similarly "Farmer's Death" and "The Diseased Salmon" balance each other, as each explores in a different way the relationship between the animal and the human worlds in the context of death. While the animal world persists triumphantly and unfeelingly in "Farmer's Death," "The Diseased Salmon" reverses the situation as the speaker contemplates the body of the dead fish and ironically wishes that neither he nor his friends may meet a similar fate—a fate already guaranteed by "Farmer's Death." The speaker's hopeless wish is parallel to the innocent love of "O Jesu Parvule," in that the reader is forced to look upon it in the light of tragic experience. The Christ child must hang on the cross, and the farmer must die. In these small constellations the paradoxical mystery emerges from two related, but very different approaches to the one theme. It is the combination that makes the paradox possible.

MacDiarmid is also experimenting with an explicit poetic sequence in *Sangschaw*. "Au Clair de la Lune" was published in *The Scottish Chapbook* in July 1923, an indication of the speed with which MacDiarmid went about the testing of effects in Lallans. In many ways, it is a primitive and simple try-out for *A Drunk Man*. The four lyrics that form the sequence treat, each in its different way, the image of the moon; and the treatment is as varied as that given to the thistle in *A Drunk Man*. It almost looks as if MacDiarmid had set himself the task of inventing four conceits, each making use of the moon as a major ingredient. In the first lyric, the moon plays on the chanter of death, as earth crumbles into dust. In the second, the sinister white crow-figure (reversal of expectation—usually crows are black) leaps on the speaker and leaves him moon-struck: "An' the roarin' o' oceans noo / Is peerieweerie [the faintest sound] to me: / Thunner's a tinklin' bell: an' Time / Whuds [flits] like a flee"—a dramatic telescopic movement. The third lyric presents the figure of the man-in-the-moon as a "dumfoun'ered Thocht," peering out over the mystery of man's place in the universe: "Earth, the bare auld stane . . . White as a mammoth's bane"—more playing around with the *size* of the focal object. And in the final lyric the figure of Artemis, as gigantically erotic as Hart Crane's sea in "Voyages," dominates:

> Oot owre the thunner-wa'
> She haiks her shinin' breists,   *heaves up*
> While th'oceans to her heels
> Slink in like bidden beasts.

(p 15)

The "mad leap into the metaphor" and the transformations that result are magnificent.

Quite apart from the ingenuity of the conceits, the sequence is remarkable. It is unified through various motifs. The images of the moon and of whiteness interweave throughout the sequence, and a host of secondary motifs back them up: music ("whatna music is this," "a tinklin' bell," "the sang / That frae the chaos o' Thocht / In triumph braks or lang"); the oceans ("the roarin' o' oceans," "the seas o' Space," "th'oceans to her heels"); thunder ("Thunner's a tinklin' bell," "Oot owre the thunner-wa' "); and gold ("the quhither o' cauld gowd," "the gowden wave," "yellow hair . . . The colour o' Cairngorm"). The effect is to make the various conceits seem extraordinarily clever and fitting.

The only other sequence effect in *Sangschaw* is "The Ballad of the Five Senses," a weird mélange indeed. It combines Ouspensky's theory that the senses have to be left behind in the gaining of a higher consciousness, a very human reluctance to part with the five senses, the vision of "A Moment in Eternity" transposed into this context, and the Lallans ballad format. The whole is not very successful, although it has moments of intensity and power:

> I felt I could haud a' earth's trees   *hold*
> Dancin' upon my bluid,
> As they were ba's that at a Fair   *balls*
> Stot in a loupin' flood. . . .   *bounced, leaping*

(p 26)

The unexpected, yet appropriate image of balls at a fair-ground bouncing joyfully and easily on the top of a jet of water has a conviction and a power far beyond the "crystal trunk / Columnar in the glades of Paradise" in "A Moment in Eternity."

The visionary experience is also less simple. *Both* the world that is revealed by the senses and the world that is revealed by the higher consciousness seem inadequate; and the speaker is left, in the fifth section of the ballad, poised between these two worlds, dissatisfied with

64

both, wanting a synthesis that neither can offer. In its recapitulation of themes, phrases, and emotions, and in its painful yearning for something beyond what has been experienced, this section parallels the ending of *A Drunk Man:*

> O I wist it is a bonny warl'
> That lies forenenst a' men,   *in front of*
> And that ony man wi' his senses five,
> As weel's the neist may ken.
>
> And I wist that that is a shaddaw show
> To the warl's that can be seen
> By men wha seek as I ha' socht
> And keep their senses keen.
>
> But O I'm fain for a gowden sun,
> And fain for a flourishing tree,
> That neither men nor the Gods they'll ken
> In earth or Heaven sall see!   (p 29)

Nostalgically the speaker looks back to the joy of discovery through the senses, and with resignation to the mystery of the "shaddow show." The final stanza, in a lyrical outpouring and an upward surging movement, envisions the possibilities that would satisfy. Paradoxically and ironically this vision resolves the tension of the preceding stanzas by ignoring the evidence of the poem, and is tempered by this evidence—a new tension is set up. The effect is similar to Crane's technique of ending with a prayer that the vision may be true.

The "gowden sun" and the "flourishing tree" represent all that could unite flesh and spirit, man and god, the full development of the "chitterin' licht." But the "chitterin' licht" of this world is vulnerable, the golden sun only hoped for, and the repetition of "fain" in the final stanza emphasizes the disparity between what is known ("O I wist") and what could be known. MacDiarmid has moved beyond the simplicity of *Annals.* The five senses no longer lead to eternity; but they do provide a *moment* of vision, transient but very real. The sunbeams may be "tremblin'," and man may be a "bonnie broukit bairn," but MacDiarmid has found both his vision and his language.

Almost half of the lyrics in *Sangschaw* (1925) had been published in *The Scottish Chapbook* before its demise in December 1923, and a good third of those in *Penny Wheep* (1926) had similarly made their début in its pages. The principle of selection (which lyrics should belong to which volume) seems to consist of placing in *Sangschaw* the most impressive and powerful of the published lyrics ("The Bonnie Broukit Bairn," "The Watergaw," "The Eemis Stane," "Crowdieknowe"), and of holding in reserve for *Penny Wheep* those lyrics and poems that took greater risks and made more daring experiments. MacDiarmid's vision, which Edwin Muir had hailed as "profoundly alien to the spirit of English poetry" and as comparable to the "materialistic" vision of Villon,[24] appears in *Penny Wheep* as even more materialistic, strange, and daring. For example, in "Blind Man's Luck," which appeared in *The Scottish Chapbook* in June of 1923, the eyes of the blind man appear grossly and disgustingly as "twa oon eggs" (two eggs without shells), which in turn become the eggs of heaven's nest:

> "I've riped the bike o' Heaven," quo' he   *plundered the nest*
> "And whar ma sicht s'ud be I've stuck
> The toom doups o' the sun   *empty shells*
> And mune, for luck!   (p 31)

The rough violence of this lyric has no equivalent in *Sangschaw*. It is a development and exaggeration of the coarse earthiness to be found in such lines as the "muckle men wi' tousled beards."

"Penny Wheep" means "small beer," a beer to be bought for a penny, and suggests both a kind of ironic self-deprecation and the distorting qualities of drink that make the "materialistic vision" possible. The most renowned appearance of "penny wheep" in literature before this date is in Burns's "Holy Fair," and its context merits consideration:

> Leeze me on Drink! it gies us mair   *my blessing on*
> Than either School or College:
> It kindles Wit, it waukens Lair,   *learning*
> It pangs us fou o' Knowledge.   *stuffs*
> Be't whisky gill or penny wheep,
> Or ony stronger potion,
> It never fails, on drinkin deep
> To kittle up our notion,   *tickle*
> By night or day.

Thus, even the title of this volume suggests some sort of preparation for

A Drunk Man, where "whisky gill," rather than "penny wheep," will "kittle up our notion" and make possible the extreme, which in turn makes possible the paradox. Just as in "Tam o' Shanter," drink will enable the poet-speaker to see the world in a different light and to give free rein to his imagination. At the same time, by its very nature, drink is a less reliable catalyst than either the classical muse or the medieval dream vision. The validity of the revelation remains suspect, although the reality of the vision remains unquestioned. Its character is Dionysian rather than Apollonian; and it delights in extravagance and in extremes.

At first glance *Penny Wheep* seems remarkably similar to *Sangschaw.* The short, intensely concentrated, sparkling lyrics predominate once again—lyrics which MacDiarmid has added, in general, to *The Scottish Chapbook* contribution. Most frequently these present the Lawrentian life-death-sexuality theme through various powerful images. "Servant Girl's Bed" provides a fine example:

<table>
<tr><td>The talla spales</td><td>tallow runs down</td></tr>
<tr><td>And the licht loups oot,</td><td>leaps</td></tr>
<tr><td>Fegs, it's your ain creesh</td><td>fat</td></tr>
<tr><td>Lassie, I doot</td><td></td></tr>
<tr><td>And the licht that reeled</td><td></td></tr>
<tr><td>Loose on't a wee</td><td>for a moment</td></tr>
<tr><td>Was the bonnie lowe</td><td>flame</td></tr>
<tr><td>O'Eternity.</td><td align="right">(p 49)</td></tr>
</table>

The brightly flaming and guttering candle is the focus of the paradox as it draws to itself suggestions of life at its most intense and meaningful moments (a Lawrentian view of sexuality) and connotations of death. The impact rests partly on the suggestiveness of the image, and to an even greater extent on the choice of language. The lovely long vowels, the weaving pattern of the "l"s, the ominous intrusion of "r," the down-to-earth rough effect of "Fegs," and the magnificent echo of "loups" in "lassie," "loose," and the climactic "lowe," all combine in a crystallizing movement that is centred on the burst of light from the dying candle. The fires of "Consummation" seem ridiculous and excessive in comparison to the poignant beauty of this flame.

A favourite technique of MacDiarmid's has contributed to the success of "Servant Girl's Bed." It consists of the presentation—early in the poem—of a compelling image, which is followed by an explanation of sorts, whether explicit, qualified (as in "Servant Girl's Bed"—"I

doot''), or mysterious. MacDiarmid had already used this technique in
Sangschaw, for example in "The Watergaw" where the explanation is
both qualified and mysterious: "An' I think that mebbe at last I ken /
What your look meant then." "Ex Ephemeride Mare" is one of the best
examples of explicit explanation in *Penny Wheep:*

> I ha'e seen the Egypt herrings
> Eelyin' in an emeraud sea,   *vanishing*
> And it's fain I could ha'e gane
> In their skinklan' company.   *shining*
>
> Sae in deeps Thocht canna faddom
> Dern the dreams that glint a wee   *hide*
> Through Time's shawls, and syne are tint   *then are lost*
> In dowf immensity.   *unfeeling*

(pp 30-1)

While the image of "Egypt herrings / Eelyin' in an emeraud sea" is
richly suggestive (partly through the connotations of Egypt, a beautiful
lost civilization), the skilful manipulation of language and sound adds to
the mysterious and incantatory effect ("seen"-"sea," "Egypt"-
"eelyin' "-"emeraud," "fain"-"gane"-"skinklan' "-"company"). With
a similar deftness the interweaving effect of "d"s and "t"s in the
second stanza develops the suggestion of "eelyin' " (vanishing),
reinforced by the insistent "a wee." This vision, like that of "Servant
Girl's Bed," is only to be glimpsed. And simultaneously this sound
pattern prepares the way for the climactic and emptily inhuman "dowf
immensity."

The lyrics that remain tenaciously in the reader's imagination,
however, are those in which the explanation remains suggestive and
mysterious, as mysterious as the central paradox itself. In these poems,
the second stanza gains enormous strength. It absorbs into itself the
image of the first stanza and suggests a great deal more—rather than
serving as a kind of Wordsworthian appendix to the image ("For oft,
when on my couch I lie / In vacant or in pensive mood"). A lyric such as
"Empty Vessel" exemplifies the power of this technique:

> I met ayont the cairney   *behind the cairn*
> A lass wi' tousie hair   *tousled*
> Singin' till a bairnie
> That was nae langer there.

68

Wunds wi' warlds to swing   *winds*
Dinna sing sae sweet,
The licht that bends owre a' thing   *everything*
Is less ta'en up wi't.   (p 50)

As in "Ex Ephemeride Mare," the original image is suggestive: the girl with "tousie hair" singing to a baby that is "nae langer there" (dead? . . . carried away by the fairies?) in a strangely ambiguous setting—does "beyond the little cairn" indicate a hilltop, or a grave? There is a strong indication of desolation and inhumanity, at any rate, in the "ayont the cairney" setting. The suggestive qualities of the original image are reinforced by the music of the words, in this case the repetition of nasal sounds ("ayont," "cairney," "singin'," "bairnie," "nae langer"). Meanwhile, the simple syntax, vocabulary, and metre seem to indicate a unity and a simplicity which yet elude us—as in Blake's lyrics. The second stanza increases this sense of unity and simplicity, while paradoxically deepening the mystery, through the presentation of two powerful and related images: the "wunds wi' warlds to swing," and the "licht that bends owre a' thing." In part the suggestiveness of these images comes from their unusual viewpoint. We do not normally think of winds playfully swinging worlds about, nor of light bending maternally over all creation. With the title as an aid, the zealous reader can clear up some of the mystery. The mother singing to the dead child is like an empty vessel. There is no separation between her and her grief, as there is between the winds and the worlds, between the light and everything that it illuminates, between God and his creation. But does this suffice? On the whole such an explanation betrays the original in the attempt to clarify it. The mystery of the relationship between the woman, the winds, and the light, remains, or should remain, as it does in the poem itself. And this mystery is enhanced by the euphonic quality of the second stanza: the combination of "w"s and "s"s in the first two lines, the gently pervasive "licht" of the final couplet. The speaker claims that the song of the "lass wi' tousie hair" is even more beautiful than this song. Imagination takes flight in attempting to hear it—the song which, like the light of the vision, unites all that is separate.

While MacDiarmid is experimenting with increasing the sense of mystery that surrounds his paradoxical vision of synthesis (and the ballad connotations of Lallans help him in this), he is also experimenting with a more wild and unexpected humour, a humour that is often brutally comic in its forced juxtaposition of incongruous elements. MacDiarmid seems to be stretching the wings of Lallans, seeing how far it will fly. For example, consider "Morning," a four-line lyric that shatters the romantic connotations of dawn ("Bliss was it in that dawn to be alive"):

> The Day loups up (for she kens richt weel — *leaps*
> Owre lang wi' the Nicht she mauna lig) — *must not lie*
> And plunks the sun i' the lift aince mair — *sky*
> Like a paddle-doo i' the raim-pig. — *frog in the cream jug*
>
> (p 43)

The humour results from the expectations aroused by the title "Morning" and based on dignified allegorical treatments of Day and Night and on the aubade tradition, juxtaposed now with earthy language and homely image. The figure of the sun "plunked" squatly and comfortably in the middle of the sky like a frog in a jug of cream is wickedly daring and successful; and the words "paddle-doo" and "raim-pig" emphasize the gross physicality of the image.

A similar grossly physical image climaxes "Jimsy: An Idiot," where Jimsy's laugh swallows heaven, earth, and God himself:

> And afore God kens whaur He is
> He's under the pap o' his hass — *uvula*
> And his teeth are closin' ahint Him
> And His pass is Jonah's pass. (p 50)

Eliot's "Hysteria" or "Sweeney among the Nightingales" may have provided models for Jimsy, but the unadulterated and totally unsophisticated physicality of MacDiarmid's language goes far beyond any of Eliot's effects. There is nothing gentlemanly about this kind of humour that delights in the unredeemed, unregenerate, unpretentious earth of which man is made. In such lyrics the emphasis lies on the physical elements of the central paradox: God becomes body.

The continued experimentation evident in *Penny Wheep* seems to declare MacDiarmid's readiness to branch out. A lyric which was saved for this volume, but which had been published in *The Scottish Chapbook* in December 1922, indicates how early MacDiarmid realized the limitations of Lallans—a realization that all the experimentation within the confines of the lyric did nothing to dispel. While the quality of the lyrics is justification enough for the short poem medium, MacDiarmid gives explicit justification in "To One Who Urges More Ambitious Flights":

> Dinna come tae bauld my glead,   *stir up my fire*
> It'll be a bear-meal-raik.   *fruitless task*
> Wee bit sangs are a' I need,
> Wee bit sangs for auld times' sake!
> Here are ferlies nae yin sees   *wonders*
> In a bensil o' a bleeze.   *big fire*

(p 41)

The image of light, here contained in the image of fire, serves MacDiarmid well and helps to set up a strange and ironic tension. While the speaker is stating on the surface that he would rather create "ferlies" in a "glead" than a "bensil o' a bleeze," the *movement* of the poem suggests that "ferlies" are also possible in a big fire. In the first two lines MacDiarmid establishes the "b" and "l" consonance. The second couplet threatens to plunge the poem into Burnsian sentimentality ("auld times' sake"), while maintaining the "b" and "l" echoes. The "wee bit sangs" in themselves constitute a tension. Is the poet-speaker ironically disparaging his work (as in "penny wheep")? Is he trying to be modest? Or is he really content to work in a medium that he recognizes as limited? In the final two lines the poem soars climactically as the "b"'s and "l"'s emerge in triumph: "Here are ferlies nae yin sees / In a bensil o' a bleeze." Through a sort of aural osmosis the "ferlies" have been transferred into a "bensil o' a bleeze." The movement of the lyric is like the glowing ember, first showing a spark, then threatening to die, and finally fanned into vigorous life; and this movement works against the speaker's stated theme. Everything about the poem is paradoxical.

The theme of "To One Who Urges" is, within the context of *Penny Wheep,* both valid and ironic. The "ferlies" in the "wee bit sangs" are there without a doubt. MacDiarmid, however, is already engaged on "more ambitious flights" and needs no urging—as the four long philosophical poems in *Penny Wheep* bear witness: "Sea Serpent," "Bombinations of a Chimaera," "Gairmscoile," and "Your Immortal Memory, Burns!" Each is very different from the others. It looks as if MacDiarmid is taking "more ambitious flights" in several different directions and exploring the newly discovered territory to determine its suitability for future use. While tone and form may vary immensely, three of them—"Your Immortal Memory, Burns!" is the

71

exception—have a great deal in common. The basic method is really an extension of that used in the lyrics, namely the presentation of a compelling image accompanied by an explanation of sorts. In these long poems, MacDiarmid has room to develop the image at length and to explore leisurely the various possibilities, even to balance several possibilities against each other. In this way a large amount of philosophical speculation is possible. The speaker ventures down different paths which may well lead in opposing directions, but which radiate out from the image which remains as the focal point, the symbol of the central paradox. Typically the image supports the proffered explanations, while at the same time suggesting a great deal more. An unexplored and perhaps unexplorable mystery remains at the centre of these poems.

In "Sea Serpent," for example, MacDiarmid uses the image of the sea serpent to recreate the myth of paradise lost and to speculate upon the chances of regaining paradise. The first four stanzas present the serpent, the first life made by God, incandescent with energy, beauty, and power—a fitting symbol of the Lawrentian life force. This Leviathan is no Satan chained to a burning lake, but primal life itself:

> His joy in his wark gied it lint-white lines
> Brichter than lichtnin's there.
> Like starry keethins its fer-aff coils   *circles in water*
> Quhile the nearer rings   *indicating fish*
> Ran like a raw o' siller girds   *hoops*
> On the wan-shoggin' tap o' the waters   *shaking*
> And soupled awa' like wings.   (p 34)

The excitement and joy of the creator match the whirlings of the sea serpent: "God like a Jonah whirled in its kite [belly] / But blithe as a loon [boy] in the swings." This homely and surprising image has the same kind of punch as the "ba's that at a Fair / Stot in a loupin' flood" in "Ballad of the Five Senses." The vision of the serpent reaches a climax when it "gethered in on itsel' again / And lowed [flamed] like the plans o' Heaven, / A michty puzzle o' flames that mirrored / The ends o' the thocht." While the Lallans is considerably less dense than in the lyrics, it adds immeasurably to the vision, a vision of primeval life that is presented in language that *sounds* more ancient than English.

The relevance of this vision gradually emerges as past is contrasted to present: "And the serpent's turned like a wud sin' syne / That canna be seen for the trees.'' As a result, the speaker is only occasionally able to glimpse the synthesizing movement of the serpent. Having established through the image of the serpent the relationship between past paradise and present paradise lost, MacDiarmid can proceed to speculate on future possibilities: man can raise a cry to ''fetch God back / To the hert o' His wark again''; the serpent movements that man feels are only the death-throes of the creature, not a sign of life, and man will be left to ''skinkle [shine] ahint like pools in the san'.'' These two contrasting possibilities sound like the voices of innocence and experience, focusing on the central paradoxical meeting place of past and future, hope and despair: the image of the serpent, the deity to whom the prayer that paradise be regained is addressed:

> Loup again in His brain, O Nerve, *leap*
> Like a trumpet-stang, *sting, prick*
> Lichtnin-clear as when first owre Chaos
> Your shape you flang
> —And swee his mind till the mapamound, *sway, map of the world*
> And meanin' o' ilka man,
> Brenn as then wi' the instant pooer *burn*
> O' an only plan!
>
> (pp 35-6)

The resonantly strong rhymes, the short lines, the alliterative pattern, and the brightly flaming image make this a triumphant climax. The language moves us, ''swees'' our minds as it demonstrates how primal paradise can be regained. Dunbar is resurrected (''Dungin is the deidly dragon Lucifer, / The crewall serpent with the mortall stang''), while the serpent of Eden becomes the saviour of mankind, rather than his betrayer. The combination of these elements results in an ancient, yet peculiarly modern vision; and the host of connotations that surround the serpent (Old Testament, Celtic, Lawrentian) remain connotations. The serpent himself is magnificent and unique, almost as mysterious and powerful as Blake's tyger.

''Bombinations of a Chimaera,'' as the title would indicate, is a much stranger fish. It is an inferior poem, on account of its loose construction, its unconvincing ending (which almost gives the impression that MacDiarmid got tired of the experiment and quickly threw in a conclusion), and the vagueness that surrounds the central images (foxes, eagles, light, and Christ descending into hell) and the relationship between them and the various possibilities suggested by the speaker. It is a jumpy work that suffers from an uncomfortable lack of focus as the speaker rejects each possibility that appears, leaping from extreme to extreme:

> *Christ descendit into Hell*
> And for a' that we can tell
> A' that's guid on Earth may be
> Gaen' like Him through devilry.
> .   .   .
>
> O the Earth may be in Hell,
> I may be a Deil mysel',
> Mebbe Christ gaed through it but
> Ithers in't foraye are shut.   (p 46)

The agility with which the speaker leaps from one possibility to another, from one side of the paradox to the other, begins to establish itself as one of MacDiarmid's trademarks. The study of possibilities, strictly limited in "Sea Serpent" and the early lyrics, expands as the speaker attempts to cover all possible possibilities. While "Bombinations" is a sloppy and largely unsuccessful work, it marks an important stage in MacDiarmid's development. The method of leaping easily from one extreme to another will be one of the most important and exciting elements in *A Drunk Man;* and it is this movement that makes the various paradoxes of the *Drunk Man* possible.

The two other long poems in *Penny Wheep* also mark a new development for MacDiarmid, a different kind of half-way stage between the early lyrics and *A Drunk Man*. In "Gairmscoile" and "Your Immortal Memory, Burns!" he turns for the first time towards explicitly Scottish concerns as subject matter. In the lyrics and other long poems, the speakers had contemplated a cosmic no-man's land, or the animal world, or the mysterious world of the ballad. While the language was undoubtedly Scottish, the setting was not necessarily Scotland, the subject not necessarily Scottish. With "Gairmscoile" and "Your Immortal Memory," MacDiarmid first focuses on explicitly Scottish themes.

"Your Immortal Memory," like "Bombinations," is not a work of the first intensity. It presents a Rabelaisian view of the Scottish Philistine who is willing to honour Burns if he can fill his stomach at the same time:

> Thought may demit
> Its functions fit

> While still to thee, O Burns,
> The punctual stomach of thy people turns.   (p 60)

The rhymes are sometimes almost Byronic in their cleverness, but the central conceit soon becomes boring, and the relatively standard English seems "thin" in relation to the gutsy Lallans of the rest of *Penny Wheep*. The importance of "Your Immortal Memory" lies in the attitude of the speaker towards the Philistine—disgust, hatred, contempt. These emotions will be as strong, but much more effective, in *A Drunk Man* where they will find an intensity and purpose lacking here.

"Gairmscoile" is much more exciting. Like "Sea Serpent," it succeeds as a poem, and not merely as an experiment. Dunbar and the old Scots Makars are in evidence throughout. The naked power of MacDiarmid's vision here goes beyond the primeval elements of "Sea Serpent" into an even more ancient and terrifying world; and this naked power is as dependent upon the primitive elements in Lallans as it is upon the images that MacDiarmid presents:

> Aulder than mammoth or than mastodon
> Deep i' the herts o' a' men lurk scaut-heid   *scrofulous*
> Skrymmorie monsters few daur look upon.   *dreadful*
> Brides sometimes catch their wild een, scansin' reid,   *eyes, glinting*
> Beekin' abune the herts they thocht to lo'e   *warming*
> And horror-stricken ken that i' themselves
> A like beast stan's, and lookin' love thro' and thro'
> Meets the reid een wi' een like seevun hells.
> . . . Nearer the twa beasts draw, and, couplin' brak
> The bubbles o' twa sauls and the haill warld gangs black.
>
> (p 56)

While the vision of these primeval monsters coming together in the mating ritual is more violently suggestive than anything MacDiarmid has written up until now, the Lallans is appropriately ferocious and terrifying ("scaut-heid," "skrymmorie"), and the strong Scottish accent makes possible a line such as "Meets the reid een wi' een like seevun hells," where the long "ee" vowels are like hammer blows, building towards the coupling in the following line: "Nearer the twa beasts draw. . . ." The *sound* of the Lallans here is a major ingredient in the ferocity of the orgasmic experience, and it makes possible something that is outside the range of poetry written in standard English. The violence that sputtered in "The Fool" emerges now in all its raw power. MacDiarmid's vision is correspondingly unique, comparable perhaps to the sexual vision of Lawrence or Pound, but less Mediterranean in quality. The ancient north is untouched by any mellowing sun; the life force is more nakedly terrifying.

The speaker-hero takes upon himself the role of venturing into this ancient realm: "My bluid sall thraw a dark hood owre my een / And I sall venture deep into the hills." This movement, together with the suggestion that it is "deep i' the herts o' a' men" that these monsters lurk, links together past and present. And when the purpose of the speaker's exploration emerges—to hear the "beasts in wha's wild cries a' Scotland's destiny thrills"—past and future are also linked, through the speaker and through Lallans (the "wild cries" themselves). The implications of this vision are rich, combining a Freudian investigation of the "skrymmorie monsters few daur look upon," a Lawrentian attempt to resurrect the life force, and an exploration of the role that language plays in linking past, present, and future. The first two implications add enormously to the strength and suggestiveness of the vision, while the third is the implication (or possibility) that MacDiarmid chooses to develop in the rest of the poem. The basic technique is similar to that in "Sea Serpent," but the link between this vision of primal paradise and the present is stronger, thanks to the close connection between Lallans and the vision. Without Lallans, this paradoxical vision would not have been possible.

The remaining sections of "Gairmscoile" develop these possibilities. The speaker sees a kindred spirit in Wergeland, the champion of the Norwegian *Landsmaal* experiments. Both men share the heritage of the beasts: a language that is a "dour dark burn [stream] that has its ain wild say / Thro' a' the thrang [busy] bricht babble o' Earth's flood." An Ouspenskian view of time helps to link past and future as the speaker imagines the invasion of civilization by the animal world: "A foray frae the past—and future tae / Sin Time's a blindness will thraw [cast] aff some day!" The result of this invasion is illumination, an illumination akin to the vision in "Ex Vermibus," "Consummation," or "Bonnie Broukit Bairn":

. . . Lo! what bricht flames o' beauty are lit at
The unco' een o' lives that Life thocht deid   *strange eyes*
Till winnock efter winnock kindles wi' a sense   *window*

O' gain and glee—as gin a mair intense
Starn nor the sun had risen in wha's licht
Mankind and beasts anew, wi' gusto, see their plicht.   (p 57)

The importance which the speaker attaches to language had been suggested implicitly in the link between the language of the poem and the vision, and explicitly in the reference to Wergeland. He now makes the insight clear: "And there's forgotten shibboleths o' the Scots / Ha'e keys to senses lockit to us yet / —Coorse words that shamble thro' oor minds like stots [oxen], / Syne turn on's muckle een wi' doonsin [dazzling] emerauds lit." The animal world and the human world, linked—as in the introductory section of "Gairmscoile"—through language, vision, and the motif of shining eyes, are now linked even more closely through references to Chesterton's donkey, to "Jammes' Prayer to Gang to Heaven wi' the Asses," and to Gabriel's "cock-a-doodle-doo" on the Day of Judgement; and each of these references also contributes a suggestion of Christian salvation.

MacDiarmid is obviously up to something. In this poem he is recognizing the debt that his vision owes to the Scottish language. The "datchie [secret] sesames" had supported his vision from "The Watergaw" on: Lallans, the language of the poet-seer and of the Scottish people, the language of vision that unites both senses and spirit. The revitalizing of man and the revitalizing of Scottish language and literature are now seen as *one* quest, a foray into the past in order to regain paradise, a movement back before the fall of man. In "Gairmscoile" the speaker's personal vision and his personal language are brought together as representatives of the future salvation of man, a salvation to be based on forgotten experiences. The lost Eden will be recovered and will provide the key to the future paradise.

The second section of "Gairmscoile" concentrates on all that stands in the way of this future paradise: the Philistines, and the Scottish artists who have betrayed their art and their vision. The flyting dealt to "Rae, Martin, Sutherland—the dowless [feeble] crew" is worthy of Dunbar himself. The *tour de force* of "d"'s ("Wee drochlin' craturs drutling their bit thochts / The dorty bodies) which stretches for fourteen lines and for which MacDiarmid must have pillaged the "d" section of *Jamieson's Dictionary,* ends in a vision of these "deltit craturs" in hell, a fate that will contribute to the achievement of the future paradise: "For we ha'e faith in Scotland's hidden poo'ers / The present's theirs, but a' the past and future's oors."

What do we make of such a poem? It is like nothing else in English or in Scottish literature: a peculiar mixture of tones, of quality, and of themes (Scotland, Christ, poetry, sexuality, hell, Eden, paradise, and language), all squeezed into one mould. The opening is magnificent, while the ending is disappointing and sudden, as in "Bombinations." It is an uneven but important experiment, a modern sensibility that presents in ancient language a vision that hovers paradoxically between past, present, and future.

The reason for its sudden ending becomes obvious when we look at the earliest form of "Gairmscoile." It appeared in the last issue of *The Scottish Chapbook* at the end of 1923 under the title "Braid Scots: An Inventory and Appraisement." MacDiarmid dedicated it to Edwin Muir and explained that it had been written "extempore on receipt of a letter from Mr Muir suggesting that 'a long poem in the language you are evolving would go tremendously'."[25] Muir's suggestion that MacDiarmid explore the possibilities of Lallans had rich consequences. The original version in *The Scottish Chapbook* includes a *third* section that ends with an identification between the speaker and his nation, and with the metaphor of a tree running its roots down into the depths of the nation, taking upon itself the misery, and bearing strange fruit:

> Strang an' deep-suckin' are the roots I rin
> Into my race; an' a' its misery
> I'll raise into mysel'—an' towards the sun!
> Let whasae may lament the poverty
> O' mind an' saul they say aboonds to-day,
> An', coorin' frae reality, fin' bield   *shelter*
> For craven wits whar cynicism hauds sway.   *small crabbed people*
> *—Oor tree's nae daised wud yet but's routh*   *discoloured, abundance*
>   *o' fruit to yield.*[26]

Here, without a doubt, springs the tree that will become the thistle of *A Drunk Man,* a much more complicated growth than the tree in "A Moment of Eternity," as it draws to itself the contraries of grief and joy, past and future, sterility and fruitfulness, disgust and wonder, man and god. It is a fitting symbol for the central paradox of MacDiarmid's vision.

Muir's suggestion not only led to the finding of the central suggestive image; it also led to the form that the *Drunk Man* would take. While Muir had hoped for a "long poem," MacDiarmid in "Braid Scots: An

Inventory and Appraisement" was working on a poetic sequence. The poem, as it appears in the *Chapbook,* consists of a prologue and three sections. MacDiarmid carefully, or optimistically perhaps, added a note about what was to follow. The plan is a grand one:

> The other sections of this poem, which it is hoped to publish later, are as follows:—IV., The Voice of Scotland; V., Invocation to the Old Makars; VI., Scotland as Mystical Bride; VII., Braid Scots and the Sense of Smell; VIII., Braid Scots, Colour, and Sound; IX., Address to the World-Poets of To-day; X., Edinburgh; XI., Glasgow; XII., Sunrise Over Scotland and an Epilogue. Each section consists of four or five eight or ten-line verses. [27]

By the time *A Drunk Man* appeared in 1926, this plan had undergone vast amendment and transformation. Nevertheless, several elements remain: the "Mystical Bride"; the "Old Makars"; the "World-Poets of To-day"; the structuring of the poem in sections composed of individual lyrics. "Gairmscoile," as it appears in the *Chapbook,* is the missing link between the Lallans lyrics, the experimental poems of *Penny Wheep,* and that strange and magnificent work—*A Drunk Man Looks at the Thistle.*

Gradually MacDiarmid has been finding his way, with an occasional stumble, towards the medium he will use in *A Drunk Man.* Not only had he found his language and his form; he had been experimenting with the themes that stand at the centre of *A Drunk Man:* the relationship between the senses and the spirit, life and death, vision and eternity. The paradox is taking shape. Scotland is becoming a symbol for mankind, with Lallans the link between Eden and paradise. Man may be a "bonnie broukit bairn," but the "datchie sesames" of the poet's vision remain. And the "chitterin' licht" illuminates earth and reveals what it means to be a man faced with glimpses of eternity.

CHAPTER FOUR

'A Routh o' Contraries'

A Drunk Man Looks at the Thistle

The "chitterin' licht" of the paradoxical vision achieves its finest manifestation in *A Drunk Man Looks at the Thistle,* published five months after *Penny Wheep* on 22 November 1926. The paradoxes quickly form as the drunken speaker, the thistle, and the moon are brought together in a series of startling and often violent confrontations.

Without a doubt *A Drunk Man* is MacDiarmid's masterpiece. The paradoxical vision of synthesis which he had gradually been developing achieves here its most dramatic, most convincing, most unique, and most sustained manifestation. He gives us one of Scotland's chefs d'oeuvre, one of the most interesting pieces of modern poetry. The limits of Lallans and of its "synthetic" power are tested as they have never been tested before. The book aroused a storm of controversy at the time of its publication and has subsequently influenced almost every Scottish writer. Edwin Muir, Maurice Lindsay, and Douglas Young are only a small sample of writers who have openly expressed their enthusiastic admiration of the work and who have drawn attention to the impact it made upon them. The kailyaird tradition quailed before MacDiarmid's singlehanded establishment of a new tradition in Scottish literature.

On 17 December 1925 MacDiarmid had advertised *A Drunk Man* as "expressly designed to show that braid Scots can be effectively applied to all manner of subjects and measures," and on 13 February 1926 he announced in another *Glasgow Herald* advertisement its demonstration of the "hitherto unrealized potentialities of Braid Scots."[1] The relationship between this intention and the early version of "Gairmscoile," "Braid Scots: An Inventory and Appraisement," is obvious.

MacDiarmid's choice of Lallans as the poetic language is crucial. Douglas Young has described its dramatic impact:

> . . . I coft a copy,   *bought*
> and was kind o dumbfoundert a wee as gin I'd been drinkan
> to see in prent a chiel thinkan as I'd been thinkan,   *man*
> to hear at last the authentic voice of Scotland,
> *la voix du sang, de mon sang,*
> and nae the muffin-mouit mummle o Saxonie and Jutland   *muffin-mouthed mumble*
> that had threepit at me sae lang.[2]   *nagged*

Although MacDiarmid's first lyrics in Lallans were so much superior to those of his contemporaries and predecessors, they had not marked a dramatic departure from the convention of his day. The lyric had become the accepted medium for Lallans, and his lyrics are unique because of their scope, their subject matter, their unusual treatment of familiar materials, and their eerie beauty, and not merely because they are lyrics written in Lallans. The longer poems in *Penny Wheep* with their explicitly philosophical content are more of a departure from the comfortable kailyaird tradition. *A Drunk Man* deals, or attempts to deal, the *coup de grace:* a sustained, structured sequence, *written in Lallans,* an iconoclastic break with the familiar and limited kailyaird. The influence of *The Waste Land* is obvious. Translations, references to other writers, foreign quotations and allusions are sprinkled throughout the poem. The concept itself—a Lallans "masterpiece," a Scottish poem to rival *The Waste Land,* an attempt to "re-establish the distinctively Scottish contribution in the literature of Europe"[3]—is nothing less than staggering.

What did Lallans offer? First of all, the impact of its novelty as a poetic language in a serious consideration of the fallen state of man, his past glories, and his future triumph, is considerable. As Daiches has written, the shock value of *A Drunk Man* was similar to that of a "childbirth in church,"[4] and much of the credit for this must go to the Lallans ingredient. Secondly, the flexibility of Lallans aids in the sudden transitions and in the violent juxtapositions that make up one of the basic structuring elements. The language itself is one of the major unifying forces in the sequence. And thirdly, the tangibly elemental qualities of Lallans and its primal toughness help in the establishment of the basic axis of the poem: the relationship between "contraries," the coming together of extremes to form the paradoxical synthesis. The flesh, the earth, and the physical world are revealed in the guts of the language ("lap up the ugsome aidle wi' the lave"—lap up the disgusting slop with the others), in contrast to the shining vision and the world of the spirit ("a maze o' licht, a siller-frame"). The common language helps to unite these contraries, and at the same time to create a greater distance between them than is possible in standard English. Blake's "Then old Nobodaddy aloft / Farted and belched and coughed" comes as close as any other lines in English literature after Chaucer to the purely physical and revolting effects that MacDiarmid achieves here. "Lap up the ugsome aidle wi' the lave," when read correctly, makes one physically nauseous.

While he was making a dramatic break with the convention of his day as regards the form of the poem, he was returning to the Scottish tradition in his use of Lallans and in his personal version of the Scottish Antisyzygy, one of the major elements in the poem. Gregory Smith had claimed that Scottish literature "is remarkably varied, and that it becomes, under the stress of foreign influence and native division and reaction, almost a zigzag of contradictions."[5] He concluded that the "sudden *jostling of contraries* [my italics] seems to preclude any relationship by literary suggestion. The one invades the other without warning. They are the 'polar twins' of the Scottish Muse."[6] *A Drunk Man* owes much to Smith's theory: "in the routh [abundance] / O' contraries that jostle in this dumbfoondrin' growth" (p 102).

MacDiarmid's version of the Scottish Antisyzygy, however, owes as much to Blake as to Gregory Smith. In *A Drunk Man* the speaker is searching for a "marriage of Heaven and Hell": "To pit in a concrete abstraction / My country's contrair qualities, / And mak' a unity o' these" (p 129). Man's nature is revealed through contraries, and any possible unity must take place at the point where extremes meet, where flesh and spirit join in paradoxical synthesis:

> I'll ha'e nae hauf-way hoose, but aye be whaur
> Extremes meet—it's the only way I ken
> To dodge the curst conceit o' bein' richt
> That damns the vast majority o' men.   (p 67)

The whole approach is close to Blake's "If the fool would persist in his folly he would become wise," and "Without contraries there is no progression." Blake and MacDiarmid share a common vision: the ultimate triumph and liberation of mankind from all that binds him, a liberation that is made possible by reaching the depths and the heights of all that is human. Paradoxically, the extreme of the contrary makes possible a unity.

While more critical effort has been expended on *A Drunk Man* than on any of the rest of MacDiarmid's poetry, more nonsense has been written about it as well. This is partly due to the paradoxical nature of the work itself and to the ironic and misleading "Author's Note" which attempts to increase the mystery surrounding the central paradox and the structure by moving the whole issue into the world of drunkenness:

> Drunkenness has a logic of its own with which, even in these decadent days, I believe a sufficient minority of my countrymen remain *au fait*. I would, however, take the liberty of counselling the others, who have no personal experience or sympathetic imagination to guide them, to be chary of attaching any exaggerated importance, in relation to my book as a whole, to such inadvertent reflections of their own sober minds as they may from time to time—as in a distorting mirror—detect in these pages, and of attempting, in, no doubt, a spirit of real helpfulness, to confer, on the basis of these, a species of intelligibility foreign to its nature, upon my poem. It would have been only further misleading these good folks, therefore, if I had (as, arbitrarily enough at best, I might have done) divided my poem into sections or in other ways supplied any of those "handrails" which raise false hopes in the ingenuous minds of readers whose rational intelligences are all too insusceptible of realising the enormities of which "highbrows" of my type are capable—even in Scotland.
>
> I would suggest, on the other hand, if I may, that they should avoid subtleties and simply persist in the pretence that my "synthetic Scots" presents insuperable difficulties to understanding, while continuing to espouse with all the impressiveness at their command the counter-claims of "sensible poetry."
>
> The whole thing must, of course, be pronounced *more Boreali*. [7]

As a result of these two factors (the nature of the work itself and the author's note), a host of related problems has arisen. The structure of the work has never emerged clearly, and its genesis remains wrapped in mystery. Before I can examine the sequence in detail, I must attempt to deal with these problems, problems caused ultimately by the paradoxical nature of the man who wrote it. I hope that as I attempt to shed light on these problems, I will also be shedding light upon the sequence as a whole and upon its relationship to the central vision of synthesis. At least in this introductory section I can eliminate certain approaches and suggest a more valid framework.

The preface, of course, is as ironic and as deliberately misleading as Twain's introductory warning at the beginning of *Huckleberry Finn* or Pound's footnote to "Mauberley." When the book was first published, one reviewer took it seriously enough to claim that, as the author himself thought the poem unintelligible, there was no point in trying to understand it.[8] His sense of frustration is common to most critics of *A Drunk Man*. When faced with such provocation, the critic has four choices. He can accept the introduction at face value as a sincere expression of MacDiarmid's point of view. In this case, if he is a teetotaller, he will push aside the book as firmly as he would push away a proffered glass; or, if he has a reputation as a bacchanalian, he can make drunken pronouncements on the work with all of MacDiarmid's backing. Neither of the alternatives offered by this reading of the introduction is very appealing. He can, however, accept the introduction with qualifications, seizing upon a phrase or an idea as a guiding light in his approach to the poem—a dangerous path to follow. Or, the third and most acceptable possibility, he can put aside as ironic and misleading the entire "Author's Note," interpreting it as a riproaring attack on the Philistines, delivered by the war-like MacDiarmid, cheered on by the insecure Grieve.

A recently published letter from Grieve to Ogilvie confirms the validity of this judgement. It throws light on the care with which MacDiarmid conceived and worked on *A Drunk Man* and on the paradoxical relationship between Christopher Grieve and Hugh MacDiarmid. The serious tone of the letter is enough to give the lie to the cocksure bravado of the official introduction:

> We both [F. G. Scott and Grieve] felt that the section I've been re-writing—which comes about midway in the book and should represent the high water mark, the peaks of highest intensity, could be improved by being recast and projected onto a different altitude of poetry altogether—made, instead of a succession of merely verbal and pictorial verses, into a series of metaphysical pictures with a definite progression, a cumulative effect—and that is what I've been so busy with. . . . I'm out to make or break in this matter. There are poems in the book (which is really one whole although many parts are detachable) of extraordinary power, I know . . . but that's not what I'm after. It's the thing as a whole that I'm mainly concerned with, and if, as such, it does not take its place as a masterpeice—sui

generis—one of the biggest things in the range of Scottish literature, I shall have failed.[9]

I am going to take these private remarks of MacDiarmid seriously. I shall consider the work as a poetic sequence, a structured whole, and shall resist the easiest and most attractive of the possibilities open to the critic—the avoidance of the basic issue through consideration of individual poems taken out of context. This is what most critics have done. While much of what they write is of interest and importance, they cannot come to grips with the sequence as a whole if they employ this method. Those critics who have discussed the work most extensively—David Daiches, Kenneth Buthlay, and John C. Weston (I am excluding Duncan Glen here as he provides a historical approach to MacDiarmid's work rather than a critical one)—have diverged in their treatment of the poem, although they all do treat the work as a whole. Each has had difficulty in establishing a valid perspective.

Daiches has chosen the second possibility open to the critic. He half-accepts MacDiarmid's introduction by picking up the hint of the "logic of drunkenness" and twisting it to suit his theory: "Drunkenness serves for MacDiarmid the same purpose that the mediaeval poet found in the dream. The logic of dreams and the logic of drunkenness are similar; both give poetic probability to those violent transitions of mood and *tempo*. . . ."[10] This argument provides a convenient handle for the poem. But despite its attractiveness, the argument is demonstrably specious. Consider first the sleight of hand in the switch from "same" to "similar." The logic of the dream, from the Freudian point of view, may indeed be similar (but not identical) to the logic of drunkenness. In both the dream and the drunken state, inhibitions are removed as the subconscious plays a more powerful role than in everyday waking life. However this is a very different kettle of fish from the medieval dream vision. Try to imagine *A Drunk Man Looks at the Pearl,* or *A Drunk Man Looks at the Rude.* In the medieval dream vision everyday reality quails before the reality and the permanence of the vision. Drunkenness presents a different kind of vision, more suspect and more qualified, more closely linked to everyday life. And in *A Drunk Man,* even if we view the work as an amalgam of conflicting and counterbalancing visions—no single vision is presented—the lack of a unified, harmonious vision makes possible only a contrast with the medieval dream vision, and hardly a comparison or identification between the two.

Why then the drunken speaker? There are more precedents in Scottish literature for a drunken speaker or observer than in other literatures. One need only think of the key role that drink plays in "The Tua Mariit Wemen and the Wedo" and in "Tam o' Shanter." *A Drunk Man* is closer in nature to "The Tua Mariit Wemen." Both poems operate on several different levels. In "The Tua Mariit Wemen," the worlds of courtly love and grossly bawdy reality are juxtaposed through the medium of the drunken speaker. If the women had not been drinking and if they did not continue to drink throughout the poem, there would be little incongruity between their appearance and their speech. *A Drunk Man* operates on a much more complex scale while using the same basic technique. The convention of the drunken speaker facilitates the movement from level to level and makes credible the rapid switches in tone, which in turn make the paradox possible. The distortion of drink creates the extreme that leads to synthesis. Sometimes the speaker is a drunk man on a hillside, sometimes a poet in contemporary Scotland with a plan for a poem, sometimes a heroic Ulysses-Christ figure. More frequently he is various combinations of these. Likewise, Jean is a stock nagging wife (like the wife in "Tam o' Shanter"), awaiting with wrath the return of a drunken husband; then a mysterious female figure who can bring revelation through intense sexual experience; and finally the female principle. Cruivie and Gilsanquhar are the drunk man's cronies, contemporary Philistines, and unredeemed mankind that makes every effort to thwart the efforts of the hero on its behalf. Similarly Scotland is both a country in the 1920's and humanity in general, fallen man capable of reaching a new salvation. The drunken framework results in a blurring of the speaker's relationships with these forces. His attitude to them is often ambiguous, careening from hatred to disgust to love. Moreover, one relationship often blends into another. His relationship with Jean is the matrix for the other relationships. Male and female come together in the sexual act and make a unity of flesh and spirit. This Lawrentian movement towards release and fulfilment is an integral part of all the other relationships: the fulfilment of Scotland and humanity.

Moving onward in his argument, Daiches claims that basically the poem is "a kind of dream allegory where the poet visits Hell and finds that every feature of its landscape reminds him of home."[11] This theory allows for the hellish elements in the poem, but completely discounts the counterbalancing paradisiacal elements which play an equally important part: the lost Eden, the future triumph of man, the trembling moments of illumination, the "breists like stars" of the bride who "cairries the bunch / O' thistles blinterin' white." The speaker himself states quite clearly one of the major axes of the sequence: "Whisky mak's Heaven or Hell and whiles mells [mixes] baith" (p 98). The drunken viewpoint enables the speaker to see infernal and paradisiacal elements in his world and results in a paradoxical mingling of the two. However, while Heaven and Hell swirl around each other, the major focus rests elsewhere:

> Whisky mak's Heaven or Hell and whiles mells baith,
> Disease is but the privy torch o' Daith,
> —But sex reveals life, faith! (p 98)

Heaven and hell, revealed and united through whisky, and death, revealed through disease, are far less important than the revelation into life (which paradoxically contains heaven, hell, spirit, flesh, and even death). All are revealed in the "licht" that shines forth in the love of woman, not in the "logic of drunkenness."

Daiches's concentration on the hellish elements in the sequence neglects the major premiss of the work, the meeting place of extremes, the moment of paradoxical unity: "I'll ha'e nae hauf-way hoose, but aye be whaur / Extremes meet." Throughout the sequence these "extremes meet": heaven and hell, man and woman, spirit and flesh. They converge on man, the ultimate paradox and the ultimate subject of the poem, in agony locked between heaven and hell: "the tug-o'-war is in me still / The dog-hank o' the flesh and soul" (where "dog-hank" signifies a male dog's inability to withdraw during mating). The speaker presents a contemporary "Essay on Man," the struggle between flesh and soul epitomized in the thistle as moonlight accentuates the beauty and the ugliness of its prickles and roses. A never-ending crucifixion takes place before our eyes. The thistle stretches from earth to heaven, its roots running deep, its highest roses touched by the moon. All the ugliness of man and all his beauty focus here. Symbolically and paradoxically it yokes extremes, links earth and heaven.

MacDiarmid found this symbol, of course, in Scotland's traditional plant. Despite its history, the symbol was fresh, unused in literature before *A Drunk Man*. And while MacDiarmid takes it over from Scottish history and uses historical associations, he recreates the thistle in order to make it the grand symbol of his paradoxical vision. As he presents it here, the thistle is richly suggestive, its prickles linked with Christ's crown of thorns, with the phallus, and with all that constricts and binds man. Its topmost branches burst forth in flowers, and by calling these "roses" MacDiarmid is able to add to the thistle and to the connotations suggested by its prickles all the traditional associations of the rose: perfection, beauty, love, woman, England, fulfilment, Christ. These traditional associations, however, are seen in a new light because of their connection here with the ugliness and the agony of the thistle. The symbol he creates is the ultimate symbol for his paradoxical vision of synthesis. Its unifying effect, its suggestive power, and its versatility are major elements in the poem. "Extremes meet" in the symbol of the thistle, and these extremes and their meeting-place seem convincing through the power of the symbol and the technique of the drunken speaker.

The various styles and tones of the individual lyrics do everything in their power to illustrate "whaur extremes meet." Relentlessly MacDiarmid juxtaposes gentle evocative lyricism with gross and violent effects, parallel to the juxtaposition of thistle and rose. Sometimes these are separated into counterbalancing poems. For example, the brutally coarse "Millions o' wimmen bring forth in pain / Millions o' bairns that are no' worth ha'en" shatters the gentle rising lyricism of "O Wha's the Bride" (p 85). Sometimes, like heaven and hell, contrasting tones interweave or "mell" within one poem, as in the "tug o' war" section. The anguished opening is followed by a blasphemous and violent accusation of God:

> The tug-o'-war is in me still,
> The dog-hank o' the flesh and soul,
> Father in Heaven, what gar'd ye tak'   *made*
> A village slut to mither me,
> Your mongrel o' the fire and clay?   (p 110)

The language becomes even more brutal and shocking as the speaker imagines the mating of whore and deity:

> The trollop and the Deity share
> My writhen form as tho' I were
> A picture o' the time they had . . .

Suddenly and without warning two powerfully evocative lines thrust the poem upward:

> When Licht rejoiced to file itsel'
> And Earth upshuddered like a star.

The strength of "upshuddered" is almost Miltonic. For a brief moment the speaker breathes clear crystal-like air, only to plunge downward again into the most brutal and bawdy blasphemy:

> A drucken hizzie gane to bed
> Wi' three-in-ane and ane-in-three.

Phallus and testicles, Father, Son, and Holy Ghost, all merge in this violent and drunken trinity.

This flowing together of styles under the aegis of the drunken speaker and Lallans illustrates within itself the paradoxical theme of "whaur extremes meet." When the poet adds to this *pot au feu* the unifying power of rich imagery, a certain harmony does indeed manifest itself. Buthlay speaks sense when he describes this unifying imagery: "The key-symbols of Thistle and Rose, Moon and Woman, Whisky and Sea-Serpent, are fecund themes on which imagination and fancy alike play variations with a flow of figurative invention unequalled by any other modern poet."[12] He comes to grief however in his attempt to grasp the poem as a whole. Buthlay claims, without convincing evidence, that the "ultimate subject of the work is the creative process itself, as though the author were showing us what came before and after and between his separate poems, as well as these poems themselves."[13] *Any* poetic sequence could be interpreted in this manner. Such a claim merely avoids the basic issue of *this* poetic sequence. It is extremely difficult to find the correct perspective for this particular work. Buthlay, in attempting to stand back far enough, has placed himself at such a distance that he fails to see much of the intrinsic nature of this very unusual work.

Weston, a more recent critic of *A Drunk Man,*[14] repeats much of the material provided by Buthlay (e.g., MacDiarmid's debt to Dostoevsky, Solovyov, and Shestov), and in general his treatment is spotty. In a rough attempt at understanding the structure he has identified two central sections (11. 121-810; 11. 1104-2243), an ideological climax (11. 2230-35), and a dramatic climax (after 1. 2646).[15] All this does not take us very far. His major contribution is the gathering together of various quotations relating to the genesis of the work. From these quotations he draws the conclusion that MacDiarmid originally conceived the work as a demonstration piece of "Scottish literary expansionism," but that as he progressed, he realized that he had "a great poem in itself."[16] Weston's conclusion seems justified. In December 1925 MacDiarmid was advertizing the poem as "expressly designed to show that braid Scots can be effectively applied to all manner of subjects and measures,'' and in February 1926 he advertized his intention to show that ''Braid Scots is adaptable to all kinds of poetry, and to a much greater variety of measures than might be supposed from the restricted practice of the last hundred years.''[17] (The original concept doubtless derives from Muir's suggestion and from the experimentation in the early version of ''Gairmscoile''). But by August 1926 (admittedly in the letter to Ogilvie, in the private rather than in the public voice) he was concerned that his work be a ''masterpiece.'' While MacDiarmid's public pronouncements are not always a reliable indication of his private feelings, Weston's conclusion is probably as close as we shall ever come in this particular area.

Weston fails, however, to draw attention to a much more vital piece of information contained within the two *Glasgow Herald* advertisements—namely, that *A Drunk Man* is ''a long poem . . . split up into *several sections,* but the forms within the sections range from ballad measure to vers libre,'' and that ''it is divided into *various sections,* affording scope for a great variety of forms''[18] (my italics). The obvious conclusion is that the poem was conceived as a series of sections. Later, MacDiarmid—either in an attempt to make the poem appear as one single indivisible entity, or, more probably in an attempt to disguise his insecurity about its structure—removed the ''handrails'' against which he fulminates in the unfortunate introduction. The coy confession that ''arbitrarily enough at best'' he could divide the poem into sections is a deliberate manoeuvre in the opposite direction from where the truth lies.

Weston also provides another vital piece of information, although once again he seems unaware of its significance. Tucked away in a footnote is a reference to yet another letter from MacDiarmid to Ogilvie: ''I have *incorporated* in my 'Drunk Man' a long 'Ballad of the General Strike' ''[19] (my italics). The use of the word ''incorporated'' suggests that ''The Ballad of the Crucified Rose'' (obviously the poem to which MacDiarmid refers) was placed in positon after the major portion of this section of the poem had been written. It did not develop organically as part of the poem.

Other details support this interpretation. The poem ''Love,'' originally published in *Penny Wheep* earlier in 1926, presumably before MacDiarmid realized its appropriateness to *A Drunk Man,* is ''incorporated'' into the section dealing with illumination through sexual experience. ''All the Ins and Outs,'' a poem in *A Drunk Man* ''suggested by the German of Else Lasker-Schuler,'' is an adaptation from Babette Deutsch and Avrahm Yarmolinsky's translation in *Contemporary German Poetry* (1923). MacDiarmid had already used this book as source material in "The Dead Liebknecht" (*Penny Wheep*) and in "You Know Not Who I Am" (*Sangschaw*). It is highly likely, therefore, that the translation of "All the Ins and Outs" took place *before* MacDiarmid conceived *A Drunk Man,* and that subsequently he moulded the poem into suitable shape for the appropriate section.

All these jigsaw pieces fit together to form a rather hazy picture of the genesis of *A Drunk Man:* a poem conceived as a demonstration of the as yet unrealized potential of Lallans; a poem structured into several sections but later *presented* as a "gallimaufry" (hodge podge), with the logic of drunkenness as the basic structuring element; a *chef d'oeuvre* into which MacDiarmid incorporated earlier poems and translations, moulding them to fit into what he hoped would be a seamless garment. Whatever their differences, Daiches, Buthlay, and Weston, all do the poem the credit of tackling it as a carefully planned and progressive whole despite MacDiarmid's injunctions to the contrary. The original 1926 misunderstandings have mushroomed out of all proportion thanks to Maurice Lindsay's account of one bacchanalian evening in which Grieve and F. G. Scott sat down with a bottle of whisky and "got the thing into order," the "thing" being lots of little scraps of paper with "no arrangement."[20] The "logic of drunkenness" theory gained enormous support from this account. According to Lindsay, it was F. G. Scott who provided both title and ending, Jean's final comment, " 'And weel ye micht,' / Sae Jean'll say, 'efter sic a nicht!' "

I do not intend to dispute that Scott helped in the making of *A Drunk Man.* MacDiarmid openly admits that Scott "was not long in seizing on the essentials and urging the ruthless discarding of the unessentials."[21] Even the private letter to Ogilvie acknowledges that "we both" had certain ideas about one of the major sections of the poem. MacDiarmid both welcomed and acknowledged Scott's collaboration, and fittingly the work is dedicated to this friend and former teacher. (Scott seems to have taken over Ogilvie's role—the former teacher to whom one looks for support and advice). Whatever the extent of the collaboration, the fog of one evening's or several evenings' drinking should not act as a smokescreen to MacDiarmid's concept of the work as a whole, nor should it disguise the structure which consists of much more than the logic of drunkenness, but which falls short of being a seamless garment.

William Soutar, a fellow Scotsman and poet, was willing to grant to the whole work a "consistency of emotional tone."[22] Buthlay grants to the poem a unity deriving from the "key-symbols." Weston makes note of the "dramatic unity." But there is much more than that. The sequence consists of separate sections, unified by thought, linked to the others by imagery and by the movement of the sequence as a whole. Transitional poems link the different sections. Frequently an image will serve as a connection between poems, the major unifying images being the thistle and the moon. Thus the last two lines of "All the Ins and Outs" ("O' this great thistle, green wi' jealousy, / That breenges 'twixt the munelicht and my hert") seem to lead naturally into the opening lines of the following poem ("Plant, what are you then? Your leafs / Mind me o' the pipes' lood drone"). At other times a concept will serve as the link. For example, the concept of a lost Eden presented in "The Mortal Flaw" and focused in the final "nocht but a chowed core's left whaur Jerusalem lay / Like aipples in a heap" carries over into the following poem, "The Tragic Tryst": "It's a queer thing to tryst wi' a wumman / When the boss o' her body's gane." The rattling of her "banes in the wund" takes over the role of the "chowed core" image. These connections are the most obvious structuring devices in the sequence, apart from the dramatic unity that centres on the drunken speaker as he switches from role to role.

Ultimately, however, the structure is much more complex than the above discussion has indicated. "Yank Oot Your Orra Boughs," a poem which comes about half way through *A Drunk Man,* marks a turning point in the sequence. The sections before this point are characterized by a structure based on the juxtaposition of clashing tones, and the paradox emerges from the forced and violent juxtaposition. The individual poems in these early sections are, in general, intensely focused lyrics, using a dense Lallans, counter-balancing in tone the lyrics immediately surrounding them. As Daiches has pointed out, one of the major weapons in MacDiarmid's arsenal is the shock tactic.[23] In these early sections of the sequence, the individual lyrics appear in a suspended state of unrelieved tension. The necessary narrative and ratiocinative parts are kept at a minimum, the major exception consisting of the introductory section ("Sic Transit Gloria Scotia"—"A Vision of Myself"). Very rarely does the tone of one lyric carry through into the succeeding lyric. For example, the brutal final stanza of "The Looking Glass" ("But what aboot it—hic—aboot it . . .") leads directly, without other transition than the cooperation of the reader and the flexibility of Lallans, into the lovely reverence of "I ha'e forekent ye! O I ha'e forekent. / The years forecast your face afore they went. / A licht I canna thole is in the lift."

It seems highly likely that these sections were the most receptive to "incorporations." (Significantly there are no translated or adapted poems after the midway mark). The major themes are presented mainly through what I shall call "poetic kernels," the moments of highest intensity, in this case individual lyrics that illustrate the theme, the theme itself presented explicitly in a brief expository manner, or not at all. For example, the poem "Love," which appeared originally in *Penny Wheep,* must have appeared as a likely candidate for the illustration of the theme, "Man's spreit is wi' his ingangs twined / In ways that he can ne'er unwind." It is perfectly possible that other earlier poems fitted as easily into the structural scheme of this half of the sequence.

In the letter to Ogilvie, from which I quoted earlier, MacDiarmid indicates that "about midway in the book" he plans to "recast" several sections, making them "instead of a succession of merely verbal and pictorial verses, into a series of metaphysical pictures with a definite progression, a cumulative effect." The results of this decision are obvious. From "Yank Oot Your Orra Boughs" to the end of the sequence, the structure within the individual sections is markedly different from the structure of the sections preceding this midway point. The short intense lyrics fade largely from view, and are replaced by longer poems. Lallans gives way to English with a Scottish accent and an odd word of dialect. The poetic kernels are no longer individual lyrics, but now appear as moments of intensity *within* longer poems. They are embedded in explicitly thematic material. Tortuous thought will suddenly be broken by a few lines that soar upward, combining a suggestive image or a cluster of suggestive images with evocative language, rhythm, and movement:

> The thistle like a snawstorm drives . . .
> Or like a swarm o' midges hings,
> A plague o' moths, a starry sky.   (p 109)

The lines following these poetic kernels usually pull slowly and inexorably away from the heights that have been reached, rather than clashing in violent combat—the technique in the early sections of the sequence. This has the effect of suggesting an evolutionary kind of synthesis, unity gradually emerging from diversity. The paradox seems to grow out of the various components, to emerge slowly and painfully, and then to fall apart after the climactic moment of unity.

The major exception to this new structure consists of the final coda with its return to the intense illustrative lyric. Appropriately the sequence is framed by exceptions, the introductory section providing the major exception in the first half of the sequence, and the concluding section providing the major exception to the second half. This device rounds the sequence out. We feel that we are beginning where we ended, ending where we began, and the structure itself illustrates the paradox.

The original format of the sequence, with no division between the individual poems and with no separate titles, is both helpful and obstructive. While it aids in the viewing of the sequence as a whole, it adds fuel to the "logic of drunkenness" theory by camouflaging the inherent pattern. While MacDiarmid, according to Weston,[24] later regretted these divisions, the titles are his own. The fact that MacDiarmid supplied the titles for the first edition of the *Collected Poems* and consented to the breaking up of the sequence into individual poems indicates to some extent that he viewed the sequence as a collection of "fragments . . . shored against my ruins," rather than as one indivisible whole. His correspondence with M. L. Rosenthal, the editor of the first *Collected Poems,* reveals that he readily accepted the suggestion to divide the sequence and that he quickly provided the titles. These facts, together with his later repudiation of the divison, suggest nothing less than an indecisive insecurity about the structure of *A Drunk Man*. When we add to this his unfortunate introduction (his defence of the poem before the date of the trial has been set), the bolstering up of his decision to recast several sections in the letter to Ogilvie ("we both"), the strange collaboration that stands behind the poem, then we are drawn to the inevitable conclusion that MacDiarmid himself was unsure about the structure and desperately in need of reassurance, whether that of Scott, Ogilvie, Rosenthal, or, more recently, Weston. (All these men, incidentally, were or are teachers). MacDiarmid's insecurity about the structure, however, does not necessarily imply that there is no structure. We know that he wanted it to be a "whole": "It's the thing as a whole I'm mainly concerned with." And it is a whole, although probably less of an organic whole than MacDiarmid indicated in his "logic of drunkenness" resolution to all structural problems.

Iain Crichton Smith has recently put forward the most interesting theory of all about *A Drunk Man*. He claims that it is basically a confessional poem, with "more to do with Sylvia Plath and Robert Lowell than many care to think."[25] He argues convincingly that at this stage in his career MacDiarmid was confronting an impossible problem and that the experience of this agonizing choice is what stands behind the poem and shapes it:

> For all practical purposes when we are confronted by a logical or mathematical paradox we can forget about it: in life we have to live perpetual paradoxes. We cannot dismiss them; we have to endure them.
>
> To select from experience and set up categories is to limit one's experience. Not to select is to die from a plethora of images. What one sees in this poem is a man creating a clearing in order momentarily to exist. There are manic sets of images crowding in on him and these represent the multifariousness of life perpetually raging around him. The creation of the artistic image and artistic order is a strategy by which, for the moment, the poet survives.[26]

The crowding in of "manic sets of images" and the self-defeating attempt to impose order on what cannot be ordered suggest strongly a connection between personal psychological problems and the problems of being a poet. These are what give the poem its energy; these provide its informing spirit. The chaotic elements are reinforced by the explicitly Dionysian ambience. Sexual energy and whisky are constantly at work to blur the issue, to smash through superimposed order, to rise in defiance of man and god. The clashing juxtapositions and the orgasmic moments of intensity upon which the sequence is based are the formal correlatives of the instinctual drive released in the Dionysian world of the thistle and the drunk man.

Lallans and the Caledonian Antisyzygy add to the rapidity of the transitions. MacDiarmid had sought in Lallans "the very effects and swift transitions which other literatures are for the most part unsuccessfully endeavouring to cultivate in languages that have a very different and inferior bias."[27] Neither Lallans nor the Caledonian Antisyzygy, however, had produced any work that matches *A Drunk Man* in rapidity of transition or range of association. Lallans and Dionysus are a powerful combination, and the world that they help to create is filled with elemental and instinctual forces that, in the early sections of the sequence, not only "jostle," but crash against each other, and, in the later sections, emerge slowly and orgasmically from the formal thought that surrounds them.

Throughout the entire sequence the lines between formal thought and instinctual expression are blurred, and both Lallans and Dionysus with their emphasis upon instinctual expression contribute greatly to this blurring action. MacDiarmid will later use a similar technique in "Harry Semen," where formal thought, instinctual expression, and madness whirl around the image of semen—just as here formal thought, instinctual expression, and drunkenness whirl around the image of the thistle. Drunkenness seems to serve as a dramatic equivalent for the distortions of an agonized and maddened psyche. Meanwhile Dionysus and Lallans continually thrust the sequence towards the moment of release, out of the world of formal logic and into the world of paradox. Ouspensky and Lawrence meet as the drunk man faces the thistle.

The blurring action that Lallans and Dionysus help to create also has an effect upon the formal structure of the sequence. It is not the seamless garment that MacDiarmid desired, but the seams that are visible are only just visible—the remnants of the "sections" to which MacDiarmid referred in his letter and in his advertisements. And the sequence is no less a masterpiece because of these seams. Accordingly I shall make use of MacDiarmid's own "handrails," the titles he has given to the individual poems, in my effort to establish the larger structural units— the long-lost sections.

For the sake of clarity and perspective I shall present the sections in an overall view before plunging into a deeper consideration of each of them and an examination of how the paradoxical vision appears in the poems themselves. To a certain extent the divisions must be arbitrary. I have placed transitional poems in the section that follows rather than in the section that precedes. What I see as two sections could well be viewed as two halves of a larger section, and *vice versa*. When I first attempted to rediscover the lost sections, I was unaware of the existence of "Braid Scots: An Inventory and Appraisement" with its plan for twelve sections. Consequently I did not try to force *A Drunk Man* into twelve sections in order to form a parallel with "Braid Scots." This new evidence, however, would tend to confirm my division of the poem into twelve. Roughly the structure is as follows:

I "Sic Transit"—"A Vision of Myself": The speaker establishes his character, the roles he will play, and the setting. He introduces the major motifs. He considers the struggle between heroes and philistines and takes his place among the heroes, in particular Burns and Christ.

II "Poet's Pub"—"Unknown Goddess": Woman becomes the focus. MacDiarmid sets up a contrast between the serious mystical qualities of woman and the coarseness of the drunk man.

III "My Nation's Soul"—"The Ineducable": The speaker establishes the link between his own soul and that of Scotland. His role is to save that soul, or at least to wander like Ulysses in an attempt to save it.

IV "The Psycho-somatic Quandary"—"The Problem Child": The thistle becomes a phallus. Sexual experience is the clue to the mystery of life.

V "The Skeleton at the Feast"—"Tussle with the Philistines": The speaker examines Scotland's barren state.

VI "The Splore"—"Reductio ad absurdum": The speaker examines mankind's barren state and the discrepancy between lost Eden and present hell.

VII "The Spur of Love"—"Love Often Wins Free": The female principle, when linked to the masculine principle, leads to possible illumination.

VIII "Yank Oot Your Orra Boughs"—"The Form and Purpose of the Thistle": The speaker examines the rose-plus-prickles problem.

IX "Ballad of the Crucified Rose"—"The Fork in the Wall": The thistle becomes a Christ figure as heaven and hell are joined in one agony.

X "The Goal of Scottish History"—"Farewell to Dostoevski": The speaker takes his place in world literature in an attempt to make a unity out of the "contrair qualities."

XI "The Barren Tree"—"The Great Wheel": The speaker presents the vision of the great wheel. This vision *is* comparable to the medieval dream vision. Scotland is seen as part of the cosmos.

XII "The Stars Like Thistle's Roses Flower"—"Yet Ha'e I Silence Left": The speaker considers the result of the vision, its effects on himself. He is left with emptiness and silence, poised between despair and hope, the destructive and the healing.

Before I look at the individual sections, I should make some general comments on the major themes of *A Drunk Man*. While most of them have emerged through my approach to the structure, I shall now gather them together. The range of association makes possible a wide range of theme. The drunken speaker moves easily and rapidly from one theme to another, and the themes often interweave within the sequence as they do within the head of the drunk man. Just as the Dionysian thrust towards release controls, in a paradoxically wild manner, the movement within the sections and connects one section with another, so the theme of the liberation of sexual energy is in a sense the meaning of the poem. It links metaphorically and suggestively all the other themes: the need to liberate man from all that binds him; the need to free Scotland from England's domination; the need to free Scottish poetry from the atrocities of the Philistine and the kailyaird. At the centre of the poem, "the thistle rises and forever will," and this characteristic movement towards the release of sexual energy is a movement that manifests itself in all the other themes. Similarly the coming together of man and woman in the sexual act is a matrix for all the other meeting places of "contraries" (life and death, man and god, Scotland and the cosmos, past and future).

The burden that this places upon the speaker is a heavy one. It is in his mind, the mind of the drunk man as he looks at the thistle, that all these forces must meet. He and he alone is the link between the different worlds, and the connection that he must make between them is violent, tortured, and exquisite. In an almost schizophrenic manner his mind lurches from one end of the paradox to the other, the link between the unholy pairs of man and woman, earth and moon, thistle and rose, Jekyll and Hyde. The paradoxical nature of man is revealed through these contraries, MacDiarmid's Blakean and Lawrentian version of the Scottish Antisyzygy. The speaker's and the poet's role is that of the hero, the saviour, the contemporary Christ whose role it is to unite these contraries. He takes on himself the burden and the suffering of mankind. Meanwhile the vision of future paradise and the memories of lost Eden stand in powerful contrast to the hell of contemporary Scotland, to fallen mankind. These ultimate contraries are revealed through the uniting of their representatives, the male and female principles, which come together in trembling moments of illumination, in the most intense kind of sexual experience. In their unity each is revealed as it has never before been revealed, the flesh more fleshly, the spirit more spiritual, yet *one*. The vision is, by its very nature, transitory, just as the vision in "The Watergaw" is a "chitterin' licht." The emptiness that follows both the sexual climax and the vision can be either barren ("The Stars like

Thistle's Roses Flower") or fruitful ("Yet Ha'e I Silence Left"), just as the semen, in itself a symbol of the mystery, can be wasted ("The wasted seam that dries like stairch / And pooders aff, that micht ha'e been / A warld o' men and syne o' Gods") or fruitful ("The tree that fills the universe"). The thistle's world is a world filled with paradox.

This precarious moment of vision, this transitory but absolute moment of freedom through unity, of the release of potential, stands behind most of the poetry of *A Drunk Man*. The characteristic soaring movement, the all-embracing climax to many of the poems, unites the sexual climax and the "chitterin' licht" of the granted vision. In the first half of the sequence this vision emerges from the forcible clashing of the "contrair" forces; in the second half, as an inexorable and redeeming result:

> These are the moments when my sang
> Clears its white feet frae oot amang
> My broken thocht, and moves as free.
> As souls frae bodies when they dee.   (p 126)

Characteristically the vision is "white," the colour of the physical semen and of the spiritual light; and the moon is an appropriate presiding goddess.

These contraries (man and woman, the flesh and the spirit, the ugly and the beautiful, the fruitful and the barren) are concentrated on the thistle itself, the central symbol of the paradox. The "chitterin' licht" of the moon reveals to the eyes of the drunk man all the hopes and all the failures of the thistle. At the centre of the sequence, the drunk man, the thistle, and the moon appear locked in an eternal struggle, and in the moments of vision the beauty and the ugliness of the thistle merge with the unity of all creation. Man's contraries are *one*.

In order to arrive at some understanding of how these themes are presented, how they are related to the structural pattern, and how they are developed through language and imagery, I must now turn to the individual sections.

I "Sic Transit Gloria Scotia"—"A Vision of Myself"

This introductory section is the major exception to the structural pattern that establishes itself in the following sections. The reasons behind its structure are obvious. First of all, the apparently rambling dramatic monologue is a familiar form ("what's still deemed Scots and the folk expect''), a technique to grab the reader's attention, while at the same time leading him to expect something different from what MacDiarmid plans in the succeeding sections. He is preparing the ground for the reversal of expectation technique. Secondly, the direct statement of theme, as opposed to the illustrative lyric, offers the most economical method of establishing setting and characters, in particular that of the drunk man himself.

This economy is the most intriguing feature of the introductory section, an economy which is hardly apparent upon a first reading. It is made possible by the technique of the drunken speaker. The poems appear loosely knit, as though the speaker were haphazardly and drunkenly lurching from topic to topic, carried along by his loquacity and by a compulsion to make some sense out of the situation in which he has found himself, a drunk man wandering confusedly around on a Scottish hillside. But the apparently rambling monologue is as economical and as tightly packed as "My Last Duchess." Almost before we are aware, MacDiarmid has introduced the major figures, the roles which they will play, the setting, the major motifs, some of the main themes, the overall plan for the entire poem, and its most important axis (namely, the coming together of opposites and the relationship between extremes). While the speaker's virulent scorn of the Philistines and his choice of the Burns Supper as the epitome of Philistine stupidity may be reminiscent of "Your Immortal Memory, Burns!" in *Penny Wheep,* "Sic Transit" and "A Vision" are much more ambitious poems, more skilful technically and subject to a greater amount of artistic control.

MacDiarmid establishes the speaker's three roles with care. In the first stanza the speaker wryly describes his primary role: he is old, tired, and somewhat intoxicated, the major emphasis resting on his being "deid dune":

> I amna' fou' sae muckle as tired—deid dune
> It's gey and hard wark coupin' gless for gless   *very, drinking*
> Wi' Cruivie and Gilsanquhar and the like,
> And I'm no' juist as bauld as aince I wes.   *fit*

(p 63)

This offhand little hint about an earlier and grander state is picked up in the second stanza where the speaker concentrates on his loss of vigour and youthful strength—it is now hard work lifting up a glass of whisky and swallowing it:

> The elbuck fankles in the coorse o' time, *elbow tangles*
> The sheckle's no' sae souple, and the thrapple *wrist, gullet*
> Grows deef and dour: nae langer up and doun *stubborn*
> Gleg as a squirrel speils the Adam's apple. *eager, runs*
>
> (p 63)

Wilson, in his section dealing with parts of the body, had provided MacDiarmid with "thraapul," "elbuk," and "shaakul."[28] The comically moving treatment of the *ubi sunt* theme is, however, uniquely MacDiarmid's, with its lovely image of the Adam's apple bobbing up and down like a playful squirrel, suggestive of all the glory that has been lost. When we consider these two stanzas in relation to the title of the poem, "Sic Transit Gloria Scotia," it becomes obvious that beneath the surface of his primary role, the speaker has more significant roles to play. The substitution of "Scotia" for "mundi" suggests that the lost "gloria" of the squirrel-like Adam's apple applies not only to the speaker, but to Scotland, and to humanity in general. Adam has fallen; Eden has been lost. These hints, dropped so off-handedly and dryly, will be developed in succeeding sections.

MacDiarmid establishes the secondary role, that of the poet with a plan for his poem, quite explicitly:

> (To prove my saul is Scots I maun begin
> Wi' what's still deemed Scots and the folk expect,
> And spire up syne by visible degrees
> To heichts whereo' the fules ha'e never recked.
>
> But aince I get them there I'll whummle them *overturn*
> And souse the craturs in the nether deeps, *creatures*
> —For it's nae choice, and ony man s'ud wish
> To dree the goat's weird tae as weel's the sheep's!) (pp 63-4)

Economically he slips in another dig at the expense of the Philistines who insist upon an artist producing what they expect, while establishing the major axis of the poem, the coming together of opposites (in this instance, high and low, goat and sheep). He develops this point further in "A Vision of Myself":

> I'll ha'e nae hauf-way hoose, but aye be whaur
> Extremes meet—it's the only way I ken
> To dodge the curst conceit o' bein' richt
> That damns the vast majority o' men. (p 67)

With the Caledonian Antisyzygy, William Blake, and Ouspensky's "higher logic" as back-up troops, the poet-speaker is setting out to explore the relationship between extremes.

The third role of the speaker is more complex. In this introductory section he discovers and accepts the role of the hero. He makes a choice, and to a very large extent the following sections are dependent upon that choice. The heroic role is presented less explicitly than the other two roles, and largely through the speaker's position as an opponent of the Philistines. The Burns Supper, as in "Your Immortal Memory," becomes the focus of the speaker's scorn:

> You canna gang to a Burns supper even
> Wi'oot some wizened scrunt o' a knock-knee
> Chinee turns roon to say "Him Haggis—velly goot!"
> And ten to wan the piper is a Cockney.
>
> No' wan in fifty kens a wurd Burns wrote
> But misapplied is a'body's property,
> And gin there was his like alive the day
> They'd be the last a kennin' haund to gi'e—   (p 64)

The parallel between Burns and the speaker is limited here to a mutual opposition of the Philistine, but a parallel has been made. Skilfully the speaker moves from this position to a comparison between Christ and Burns, both as heroes whose followers have misapplied or ignored their gospels: "Mair nonsense has been uttered in his name / Than in ony's barrin' liberty and Christ" (p 65). An attack on these Philistine-followers moves even more skilfully into an identification of the speaker as a kindred spirit of Burns, and consequently of Christ:

> You left the like in Embro in a scunner   *Edinburgh, disgust*
> To booze wi' thieveless cronies sic as me.   *profligate friends*
> I'se warrant you'd shy clear o' a' the hunner
>
> Odd Burns Clubs tae, or ninety-nine o' them,
> And haud your birthday in a different kip   *whorehouse*
> Whaur your name isna ta'en in vain—as Christ
> Gied a' Jerusalem's Pharisees the slip . . .   (p 65)

This leaves the way clear for the suggestive and ambiguous ending of "Sic Transit":

> As Kirks wi' Christianity ha'e dune,   *churches*
> Burns' Clubs wi' Burns—wi' a' thing it's the same,
> The core o' ocht is only for the few,   *anything*
> Scorned by the mony, thrang wi'ts empty name.   *busy*

> A greater Christ, a greater Burns, may come.
> The maist they'll dae is to gi'e bigger pegs
> To folly and conceit to hank their rubbish on.   *fasten*
> They'll cheenge folks' talk but no' their nature, fegs!   (p 66)

Because of the speaker's self-alignment with Christ and with Burns, against organized Christianity and Burns Clubs and "the mony," the role which the speaker will accept *could* be that of "a greater Christ, a greater Burns." His hubris is not great enough for him to claim the role explicitly, and, even if he should, his scepticism regarding the results acts as a protective device. However the suggestion of this role as a possibility remains, despite the undercutting techniques.

Indeed the first stanza of "A Vision of Myself" indicates that the speaker *has* accepted the role of hero, a representative for his generation, a contemporary Christ in the Gethsemane of Scotland:

> I maun feed frae the common trough ana'   *after all*
> Whaur a' the lees o' hope are jumbled up;
> While centuries like pigs are slorpin' owre't   *slobhering*
> Sall my wee 'oor be cryin': "Let pass this cup?"   *hour*
>
> (p 67)

This is the first indication of the psychic agony that lies behind *A Drunk Man*. Not only must the speaker play the role of the crucified Christ, he must take on the role of the hero in an unheroic world. (The link with Grieve's childhood and the short story "Andy" is obvious: the understanding between mother and brother force him into the role of hero, while simultaneously making it impossible for him to fulfil that role). This is the first of the many impossible binds that the speaker of *A Drunk Man* will find himself in. He will wish to be more than human, yet will be unwilling to relinquish any of his humanness. He will wish for release, yet will dread the resultant emptiness. He will wish for unity, yet will cherish his separateness. All these impossible binds are a manifestation of the deeply painful conflicts that stand behind the poem. The role of the crucified Christ is the focus of the agony.

Having accepted the role, the speaker moves into a consideration of what he brings to the role, and he reviews his innate qualities with light derision, with humour, and with increasing confidence, bolstered by a contrast between himself and the Philistine:

> I lauch to see my crazy little brain
> —And ither folks'—tak'n itsel' seriously,
> And in a sudden lowe o' fun my saul   *flame*
> Blinks dozent as the owl I ken't to be.   *stupid*   (p 67)

The climax of this section occurs in the prayer that follows the self-appraisal, a prayer that the speaker be adequate to his task, in the most suggestive, most lyrical, and least ironic stanza of the entire introduction:

> Like staundin' water in a pocket o'
> Impervious clay I pray I'll never be,
> Cut aff and self-sufficient, but let reenge
> Heichts o' the lift and benmaist deeps o' sea.   *sky, furthest*
>
>   (p 68)

The vulnerability of his position at this point is quickly camouflaged through the technique of the drunken speaker. By a process of association (sea, water, whisky, angry wife), he wrenches the poem back from the heights it has reached and drops back into his primary role of a drunk man on a hillside:

> Water! Water! There was owre muckle o't   *too much*
> In yonder whisky, sae I'm in deep water
> (And gin I could wun hame I'd be in het,   *if, get home*
> For even Jean maun natter, natter, natter). . . .   (p 68)

But he *has* accepted the role, and because of this acceptance the tone of the final stanza is one of despair and enormous sympathy, rather than the rumbustious scorn which had preceded the acceptance of the role:

> And in the toon that I belang tae
> —What tho'ts Montrose or Nazareth?—
> Helplessly the folk continue
> To lead their livin' death! . . .   (p 68)

Meanwhile, the figure of woman, concentrated in the character of Jean, surfaces occasionally. Her primary role, that of the stock nagging wife, could have come from "Tam o' Shanter": "our sulky sullen dame, / Gathering her brows like gathering storm, / Nursing her wrath to keep it warm." Like Tam's Kate, Jean will have no patience with a drunken husband who has squandered their money: "Yin canna thow the cockles o' yin's hert / Wi'oot ha'en cauld feet noo, jalousin' [guessing] what / The wife'll say (I dinna blame her fur't)" (p 63).

But the speaker drops a few hints that there is something more to Jean than just a shrewish nagger. He is more sympathetic towards her than Tam is to his Kate, and a wry expression of his affectation and sympathy emerges, despite himself, in "I dinna blame her fur't." In his confusion as to whether he is dreaming or drunk, he calls out to her for help: "*Jean! Jean!* Gin she's no' here it's no' *oor* bed." This suggestive line establishes the possibility of a deeper relationship between the speaker and Jean than that between Tam and his "sulky sullen dame." Not only is Jean presented as a figure who could help the speaker to resolve his confusion, she is also presented in an explicitly sexual context, an area where Kate is conspicuously absent. In addition, the speaker presents with great subtlety some sort of connection between Jean and the image of the moon. The preceding stanza establishes the moon as a "doited jade" who is leading the speaker astray, and the appeal to Jean follows directly upon the confusion resulting from this image:

> That's it! It isna me that's fou' at a',
> But the fu' mune, the doited jade, that's led   *mad*
> Me fer agley, or 'mogrified the warld.   *astray*
> —For a' I ken I'm sae in my ain bed.
>
> *Jean! Jean!* Gin she's no' here it's no' *oor* bed.   (p 66)

Through the speaker's confusion, a parallel has been set up between Jean and the mysterious moon-woman. And the final reference to Jean in this section, as Daiches has pointed out,[29] confirms the earlier hints of Jean's importance:

> Water! Water! There was owre muckle o't
> In yonder whisky, sae I'm in deep water
> (And gin I could wun hame I'd be in het,
> For even Jean maun natter, natter, natter). . . .   (p 68)

While Jean has returned here to her role of stock nagging wife, the suggestion of greater qualities remains in the use of the word "even."

Also the parallel structure ("*Jean! Jean!*" and "Water! Water!") provides a serious link, in addition to the comic pun regarding hot water, between Jean and the "benmaist deeps o' sea." The speaker clearly indicates that while Jean may share some of the unpleasant characteristics of womankind, she possesses more important and valuable attributes than merely those of the average nagging wife.

MacDiarmid has also introduced his major motifs. While each of those has been dropped almost casually in the train of thought, the images themselves are strongly suggestive. The moon, of course, appears in her role of the "doited jade" with the power to "mogrify" the world. (Incidentally, *this* provides a link between the moon, Jean, and whisky, as whisky too has the power to "mogrify"). The thistle meanwhile is linked to an image of barren hopelessness: "A blin' bird's nest / Is aiblins [perhaps] biggin' [building] in the thistle tho'? . . . / And better blin' if'ts brood is like the rest!" (p 64). The bleakness of this image forms a powerful contrast to the mysterious qualities of the moon and to the beauty of the sea-serpent, the third major image. The splendour of the serpent is reinforced by the rising emotion and movement of the lines that follow its introduction:

> For I've nae faith in ocht I can explain,
> And stert whaur the philosophers leave aff,
> Content to glimpse its loops I dinna ettle   *try*
> To land the sea serpent's sel' wi' ony gaff.
>
> Like staundin' water in a pocket o'
> Impervious clay I pray I'll never be,
> Cut aff and self-sufficient, but let reenge
> Heichts o' the lift and benmaist deeps o' sea.   (p 68)

These two stanzas are really a concentrated version of the earlier experimental "Sea Serpent" in *Penny Wheep,* even to the use of the image of standing water ("tho' we skinkle ahint like pools in the san' ") and the prayer to be granted the power to explore high and low ("And lift and licht us eternally. / Frae the howe o' the sea to the heich o' the lift [sky]"). The concentration has been an improvement, with the magnificent enjambment leading into the climactic line and with the massed "ee"s that build up to "benmaist deeps o' sea" and link those "deeps" with "heichts," an aural link that is impossible in standard English.

Meanwhile the substitution of "Scotia" for "mundi" indicates that the background of the poem is not simply a particular Scottish hillside in the 1920's. The poem radiates out into other cultures, other centuries, and other traditions, through a host of allusions—a technique undoubtedly derived from *The Waste Land*. Burns, of course, is the major literary reference. The others form a mixed bag: Jean Elliot, an eighteenth-century Scottish poet ("a' the floo'ers / O' the Forest are wede awa' "); Wordsworth and Milton ("Rabbie, wadst thou wert here—the warld hath need, / And Scotland mair sae, o' the likes o' thee!"); Eliot himself ("A bauble in Babel, banged like a saxpence / 'Twixt Burbank's Baedeker and Bleistein's cigar"); G. K. Chesterton ("As G. K. Chesterton heaves up to gi'e / 'The Immortal Memory' in a huge eclipse"); and Thomas à Kempis ("Sic Transit Gloria Scotia"). Characteristically MacDiarmid meddles with each of the quotations, even the Scottish ones, forcibly twisting them to fit his poem. On the whole the tone is by no means one of wholehearted admiration. The poet-speaker is carefully placing his poem in reference to world literature, and the disparaging tone that he uses to all save Burns gives some indication of the value he attaches to the Scottish tradition and to his own work.

MacDiarmid however is careful not to limit the range of association to the world. In a brilliantly comic little stanza the speaker ventures out into the cosmos as he considers the declining quality of Scotch whisky:

> Forbye, the stuffie's no' the real Mackay,
> The sun's sel' aince, as sune as ye began it,
> Riz in your vera saul: but what keeks in   *peeks*
> Noo is in truth the vilest "saxpenny planet."   (p 63)

Once again the economy is magnificent. Not only has MacDiarmid suggested other worlds beyond this one, but through the link between present whisky and the grand spirit of the past, he has suggested a lost grandeur.

He has been sowing the seeds that will sprout later in the sequence. The scope of the thought and imagery will range out from a Scottish hillside, to Scotland in general, and from there out into the world, and finally into a superhuman world. Later in the sequence, just as in this introductory section, these various ranges will not always be clearly separate. One blends into another under the aegis of the drunken speaker, so that suggestions from one world (e.g., the sexual link between the speaker and Jean) carry over into another. The world of the drunk man is a world of metamorphosis, of changing shapes. In such a world paradoxical relationships quickly form to make a unity, and just as quickly disintegrate. The focus is continually changing.

Quite apart from the achievements discussed above, these two poems display vigour, muscle, and variety, despite the strict limitations of form. This is largely due to the strong alliterative pattern, often daring in nature ("deid dune," "sun's sel'," "deef and dour," "lap up the ugsome aidle wi' the lave"), to the startling images (the squirrel-like Adam's apple, the "blin' bird's nest"), to the Byronic skill with comic rhymes ("began it"—"planet," "knock-knee"—"cockney"), and most of all to the sudden lurches of movement and tone, helped along by the device of the drunken speaker. Almost before the reader is aware, the tone has moved from weariness to rising irritation, to bitterness, to confusion, to scorn, to heroic resolution, to hope, and finally back to sceptical weariness, now infused with a love and pity for mankind. MacDiarmid manipulates the reader's expectations in such a manner that he is continually taken aback by new and unexpected developments. The unexpected, ranging from "a bauble in Babel, banged like a saxpence / 'Twixt Burbank's Baedecker and Bleistein's cigar" to the sudden change of metre in the final stanza ("And in the toon that I belang tae / —What tho'ts Montrose or Nazareth?— / Helplessly the folk continue / To lead their livin' death! . . ."), infuses these poems with interest and vigour. Ironically this technique of the unexpected should alert the reader to the pattern of startling development and unexpected juxtapositions in the poems that follow. The speaker-poet states clearly the major principle guiding the movement: "spire up syne by visible degrees / To heichts whereo' the fules ha'e never recked. / But aince I get them there I'll whummle [topple] them / And souse the craturs in the nether deeps." Despite this explicit warning, the speaker-poet surprises us in this introductory section and in the sections that follow. Extremes will be forced into violent juxtaposition in order that the paradoxical vision might emerge.

II "Poet's Pub"—"The Unknown Goddess"

This section is the first to make use of a structure based on violently clashing tones. At no point in the section does the speaker state directly the theme. We are left to extract the theme from the lyrics themselves.

The three poems in this section, "Poet's Pub," "The Looking Glass," and "The Unknown Goddess," all bring together two contraries: mysterious woman, awesome in her power, and coarse masculine sexuality and drunkenness. "Poet's Pub" introduces the contraries, with the speaker acting as intermediary between them. He is linked to the drunken rabble through his drunken state, and also linked to the woman of supernatural connotations through this same state: "A'e freend's aye mirrored in my glass." Each of the poems that follow seizes on one of these contraries and develops it. Put in its simplest form, in "Poet's Pub" we have a drunk man and a mysterious supernatural woman; in "The Looking Glass" we have a *very* drunk man; and in "The Unknown Goddess" we have a *very* mysterious and supernatural woman. The highlighting of these contraries makes for a dramatic and dynamic contrast. The power and the mystery of woman, faintly suggested in the figure of Jean through her link with the "doited jade," now become transcendent. In "Poet's Pub," she is associated with the "horns o' Elfland," and in "The Unknown Goddess" her coming ensures that "the ends o' space are bricht," and that "generations that I thocht unborn / Hail the strange Goddess frae my hert's-hert torn." At the same time, the pleasantly drunken speaker of the introductory section and of "Poet's Pub" is transformed into the comically revolting and crude drunk of "The Looking Glass":

> Gurly thistle—hic—you canna   *savage*
> Daunton me wi' your shaggy mien,
> I'm sair—hic—needin' a shave,
> That's plainly to be seen.   (p 70)

It presents a brutal debunking of the tone of the preceding poem as the savage hiccoughs shatter the image of the "freend" mirrored in the glass. The mysterious woman is dethroned. In her place a reflection of the speaker's uglier qualities takes form: "And, fegs, I feel like Dr Jekyll / Tak'n guid tent [heed] o' Mr. Hyde."

The emphasis of this poem, however, is not the final one. "The Unknown Goddess" reverts back to the tone of wonder and awe which the speaker felt when confronting the serious and mystical qualities of woman in "Poet's Pub." While the tone of "The Unknown Goddess" is entirely unadulterated when considered in isolation, it is counterbalanced within the sequence by the drunken coarseness of "The Looking Glass." Each becomes *more* extreme through contrast with the other.

A major problem of approach to "Poet's Pub" and "The Unknown Goddess" results from Buthlay's research. [30] While MacDiarmid claims that "Poet's Pub" is "from the Russian of Alexander Blok," and that "The Unknown Goddess" is "freely adapted from the Russian of Alexander Blok," Buthlay suggests that these poems are "translated" from *English* versions by Babette Deutsch and Avrahm Yarmolinsky. And this is indeed the case. A comparison of the Deutsch-Yarmolinsky versions with the MacDiarmid poems leaves no room for doubt. [31]

THE LADY UNKNOWN

Of evenings hangs above the restaurant
A humid, wild and heavy air.
The Springtide spirit, brooding, pestilent,
Commands the drunken outcries there.

Far off, above the alley's mustiness,
Where bored gray summerhouses lie,
The baker's sign swings gold through dustiness,
And loud and shrill the children cry.

Beyond the city stroll the exquisites,
At every dusk and all the same:
Their derbies tilted back, the pretty wits
Are playing at their ancient game.

Upon the lake but feebly furious
Soft screams and creaking oar-locks sound.
And in the sky, blasé, incurious,
The moon beholds the earthly round. . . .

POET'S PUB

At darknin' hings abune the howff
A weet and wild and eisenin' air.
Spring's spirit wi' its waesome sough
Rules owre the drucken stramash there.

And heich abune the vennel's pokiness,
Whaur a' the white-weshed cottons lie;
The Inn's sign blinters in the mochiness,
And lood and shrill the bairnies cry.

The hauflins 'yont the burgh boonds
Gang ilka nicht, and a' the same,
Their bonnets cocked; their bluid that stounds
Is playin' at a fine auld game.

And on the lochan there, hauf-herted
Wee screams and creakin' oar-locks soon'
And in the lift, heich, hauf-averted,
The mune looks owre the yirdly roon'. . . .   (pp 68-9)

And so on. Similarly "The Unknown Woman" is undoubtedly the
source for "The Unknown Goddess":

THE UNKNOWN WOMAN

I have foreknown Thee! Oh, I have foreknown Thee. Going,
The years have shown me Thy premonitory face.
Intolerably clear, the farthest sky is glowing.
I wait in silence Thy withheld and worshiped grace.
The farthest sky is glowing: white for Thy appearing,
Yet terror clings to me. Thy image will be strange.

And insolent suspicion will rouse upon Thy nearing.
Thy features long foreknown, beheld at last, will change.
How shall I then be fallen! low, with no defender:
Dead dreams will conquer me; the glory, glimpsed, will change.
The farthest sky is glowing! Nearer looms the splendor!
Yet terror clings to me. Thy image will be strange.

THE UNKNOWN GODDESS

I ha'e forekent ye! O I ha'e forekent.
The years forecast your face afore they went.
A licht I canna thole is in the lift.
I bide in silence your slow-comin' pace.
The ends o' space are bricht: at last—oh swift!
While terror clings to me—an unkent face!

Ill-faith stirs in me as she comes at last,
The features lang forekent . . . are unforecast.
O it gangs hard wi' me, I am forspent.
Deid dreams ha'e beaten me and a face unkent
And generations that I thocht unborn
Hail the strange Goddess frae my hert's-hert torn! . . .

(p 71)

Quite apart from the literary ethics involved, MacDiarmid's achievement is substantial. A comparison of the Deutsch-Yarmolinsky versions with the MacDiarmid ones reveals not only MacDiarmid's skill with language, but also the deliberate departures he made from the originals. These in turn throw light on what he is attempting in this section.

Deutsch and Yarmolinsky had explicitly stated their aim: "What we continually sought was to produce, in the end, a poem."[32] MacDiarmid's versions reveal how far short they fell of that goal. Where they fail, he succeeds. The awkward and torturous lines of the English translation are transformed into flowing and suggestive phrases (e.g., "a humid, wild and heavy air"—"a weet and wild and eisenin' [lusting] air," "the Springtide spirit, brooding, pestilent'-—"spring's spirit wi' its waesome sough," "blasé, incurious"-"heich, hauf-averted," "strange, immutable"-"fey and fremt [lonely, with a suggestion of the German 'fremd'])," "A misty fainting perfume"-"a rooky dwamin' [misty dreaming] perfume," "the farthest sky is glowing"-"the ends o' space are bricht."

Meanwhile, in "Poet's Pub" MacDiarmid increases the coarseness of the world outside the speaker's vision ("exquisites" become "hauflins" [lads]), while simultaneously increasing the mystery of the woman: "I see enchanted shores' declivity / And an enchanted distance calls" becomes "See white clints [cliffs] slidin' to the sea / And hear the horns o' Elfland blaw." The contrast between these two "contrair" forces becomes much more pointed. Similarly MacDiarmid's entirely original poem "The Looking Glass" establishes a counterbalancing tone to "The Unknown Goddess," where, in comparison to the original, the present rather than the future tense adds a great deal of drama, and the woman is more intimately linked to the speaker ("frae my hert's-hert torn") and more powerful: she is a goddess whom "generations that I thocht unborn" will hail.

The two extremes, mysterious woman and coarse masculine sexuality,

112

meet under the auspices of intoxication with a clashing strength that is missing in the Deutsch-Yarmolinsky versions. Whatever path MacDiarmid followed in order to arrive at this meeting-place of converging forces appears almost irrelevant in the light of his achievement. His choice of these poems and the changes he brings to bear upon them are strong justification. But it is surely unfortunate that he did not truthfully acknowledge his source material. The ferreting out of his sources can often act as a red herring, drawing attention away from the poems themselves. The subterfuge involved necessitates this kind of exploration.

Much more important is the success of this section in the establishment of the theme of the revelation achieved through woman. At the moment it is not clear what is being revealed—something supernatural and powerful—and this theme will be developed more fully at a later date. The section has also exemplified the major axis of the sequence, the coming together of opposite but interdependent forces; and it has continued to put into effect the reversal of expectation technique as the speaker moves from one extreme to another. In "Poet's Pub" MacDiarmid gives enough suggestions of coarse masculine sexuality to justify "The Looking Glass." At the same time, the drunken lurch of tone and the savage hiccoughs make for a shocking juxtaposition. Similarly "The Unknown Goddess" reverts back to "Poet's Pub" for justification, but depends upon "The Looking Glass" for forceful contrast and effect. The juxtaposition of these extremes of tone, theme, and character has established the central paradoxical movement of the sequence as a whole. It has also created the explicitly Dionysian ambience, lightly suggested in the introductory section, within which contraries can meet.

III "My Nation's Soul"—"The Ineducable"

In "The Looking Glass" the speaker sees as his reflection in the glass the "shaggy mien" of the "gurly [savage] thistle." This identification prepares the way for the theme of the following section: the identification made between the speaker's soul and that of Scotland. Simultaneously, the structure of the preceding section, bringing together contrary forces and contrasting tones, leads into an easy metamorphosis—the thistle as the meeting-place of extremes, the central point of tension as the soul writhes in agony in a waste land. The transitional poem, "My Nation's Soul," effects the metamorphosis through the image of the thistle as a rising phallus, an unexpected and dramatically shocking reaction to the unearthliness of the "strange Goddess":

> Or dost thou mak' a thistle o' me, wumman? But for thee
> I were as happy as the munelicht, withoot care,
> But thocht o' thee—o' thy contempt and ire—
> Turns hauf the warld into the youky thistle there. *itchy*
>
> (p 71)

The sexual transformation (blending together the figure of Jean and the goddess) seems to lead naturally into the theme of man "torn in twa / And glorious in the lift [sky] and grisly on the sod," one of the many moments in *A Drunk Man* where different themes come together under the auspices of the Dionysian ambience.

In "The Gothic Thistle," the sexual connotations of the thistle ("its rigid virtue," "the bee / Mak's honey frae the roses on its thorns") have departed from the Scottish soul:

> And a' the country roon' aboot it noo
> Lies clapt and shrunken syne like somebody wha *shrunken*
> Has lang o' seven devils been possessed;
> Then when he turns a corner tines them a'. *loses*
>
> (p 74)

The desolation that results is even more total, in the speaker's view, than the desolation of *The Waste Land:*

> T. S. Eliot—it's a Scottish name—
> Afore he wrote "The Waste Land" s'ud ha'e come
> To Scotland here. He wad ha'e written
> A better poem syne—like this, by gum! (p 74)

The present horror is suggested even more evocatively in "The Octopus," with its climactic allusion to *Moby Dick,* the most radical departure MacDiarmid makes from the Deutsch-Yarmolinsky version:

> In mum obscurity it twines its obstinate rings
> And hings caressin'ly, its purpose whole;
> And this deid thing, whale-white obscenity,
> This horror that I writhe in—is my soul![33]

Seriously ("All the Ins and Outs"), and then playfully ("To the Music of the Pipes"), the speaker focuses on the thistle as the representative of these interlocking tensions and establishes the thistle as the central paradoxical symbol. It is almost a metaphysical conceit, reminiscent of George Herbert. Both poets represent opposing but related forces through a twisting or winding metaphor, a painful and inevitable agony of tension between the two sides of the paradox. Thus in "All the Ins and Outs," "Her pupils narraw to bricht threids that thrill / Aboot the sensuous windin's o' her thocht" (p 76). And in a lighter vein in "To the Music of the Pipes":

> Grinnin' gargoyle by a saint,
> Mephistopheles in Heaven,
> Skeleton at a tea-meetin',
> Missin' link—or creakin'
> Hinge atween the deid and livin'. . . .   (p 77)

Obviously the "creakin' / Hinge" with its painfully humorous enjambment is as representative of the agony of the thistle as the "bricht threids that thrill / Aboot the sensuous windin's o' her thocht." Both indicate a paradoxical and painful union of extremes.

The lyrical kernel of the section is to be found in "The Crying of the Fair" and "Man and the Infinite." These two central poems bring together the concepts of lost Eden and future paradise, contrasted by their position in the section to the present horror that surrounds them. The structure of the section reveals the paradox. Embedded in the present hell is a memory of lost Eden and a hope of future paradise—just as these two poems are embedded in the section. Quite apart from their key role in this section, they play an important role in their foreshadowing of future themes: the theme of the crucifixion, the ultimate paradoxical agony involved in the "dog-hank o' the flesh and soul," and the theme of the emptiness resulting from a vision, an emptiness both fruitful and barren at the same time, as paradoxical as the vision itself.

"The Crying of the Fair" presents the themes of past Eden, crucifixion, and future paradise, as they converge upon the image of the thistle, carried like a cross in the magical world of the "Muckle Toon," the large or great town, Grieve's childhood home of Langholm:

> Drums in the Walligate, pipes in the air,
> Come and hear the cryin' o' the Fair.

> A' as it used to be, when I was a loon   *boy*
> On Common-Ridin' Day in the Muckle Toon.   (p 78)

The speaker's role is that of the hero, bearing the cross-like thistle in a world where it is easier to carry the symbol of the fish or the rose, and easier still to search for monetary success:

> Beauty and Love that are bobbin' there;
> Syne the breengin' growth that alane I bear;   *hurtling*
>
> And Scotland followin' on ahint   *behind*
> For threepenny bits spleet-new frae the mint.   (p 79)

The speaker's earlier wry acceptance of the role of hero is now confirmed as a serious decision. The focus of the poem, however, does not lie in the agony of this contemporary crucifixion. The joyous magic of the world of childhood and the delight of the future paradise (closely linked to Christ's promise to the thief, "Tonight thou shalt dine with me in paradise") provide the major focus. And this focus is in turn undercut in the final stanza by an even greater joy—the joy that was once achieved in the arms of the virginal Jean and that can be achieved once more:

> But I'll dance the nicht wi' the stars o' Heaven
> In the Mairket Place as shair's I'm livin'.
>
> Easy to cairry roses or herrin',
> And the lave may weel their threepenny bits earn.
>
> Devil the star! It's Jean I'll ha'e
> Again as she was on her weddin' day. . . .   (p 79)

The link between this poem and the famous "O Wha's the Bride" is obvious. The "breists like stars" of the violated yet virginal bride are preferable to the stars themselves. Jean, magically still a virgin in the timeless world of paradox, links the speaker both to past Eden and to future paradise. Simultaneously the parallel between Jean and the stars harks back to the "strange Goddess" and confirms the link between Jean and the "doited jade" with the power to "mogrify" the world.

In contrast to "The Crying of the Fair," "Man and the Infinite" ignores past Eden and present crucifixion in order to focus on future paradise. The thistle becomes the sea-serpent of "A Vision of Myself" (a

116

good example of the constant metamorphosis in the sequence), twisting
and turning in all its beauty and power throughout the realms of space, a
Lawrentian link between man and the infinite:

> Frae laichest deeps o' the ocean   *lowest*
> It rises in flight upon flight,
> And 'yont its uttermaist motion
> Can still set roses alight,
> As else unreachable height
> Fa's under its triumphin' sight.   (p 80)

The final stanzas concentrate on the speaker's delight and power and
on the glorious liberation of the phoenix-thistle, yet another
metamorphosis:

> Lay haud o' my hert and feel   *hold*
> Fountains ootloupin' the starns   *out-leaping*
> Or see the Universe reel
> Set gaen' by my eident harns,   *busy brains*
> Or test the strength o' my spauld   *backbone*
> The wecht o' a'thing to hauld!
>
> The howes o' Man's hert are bare,   *hollows*
> The Dragon's left them for good,
> There's nocht but naethingness there,
> The hole whaur the Thistle stood,
> That rootless and radiant flies
> A Phoenix in Paradise! . . .   (p 80)

Typically MacDiarmid is not satisfied with this one point of view. The
following poem, "Man's Cruel Plight," reverses the focus from the
liberation of the phoenix-thistle to the resultant emptiness in the heart of
man. Instead of being liberated, man has been cheated:

> Thistleless fule,
> You'll ha'e nocht left
> But the hole frae which
> Life's struggle is reft! . . .   (p 81)

These two paradoxical reactions to the vision foreshadow the ending of
the entire sequence. Creative and worthwhile emptying, the liberation of
all that is at present hindered, is brought into sharp contrast with the

resulting emptiness, an emptiness that is even more devastating than the agony that had preceded it. This may be Ouspenskian in origin. In *Tertium Organum* Ouspensky describes the transitional state between the old logic and the higher logic as an awareness of a "bottomless pit," and he emphasizes that "in order to find the new world it must *lose* the old one . . . it must repudiate *everything* around it."[34] Obviously it is also linked, through the sexual connotations of the release of the phoenix, with post-coital sadness and emptiness. The tone is dramatically coarse and earthy, an effective counterbalance to the soaring vision of the thistle "rootless and radiant." The impossible bind that the speaker finds himself in is also linked to Grieve's psychic state. As Iain Crichton Smith has suggested,

> At a certain stage MacDiarmid was willing or was compelled to open himself out to life and being of an extremely sensitive nature he was nearly destroyed by it. To have sustained such insights would have been annihilating. Yet he wished to retain such insights for he knew that as a poet he was dependent on them. He was being more extreme than one has the power to be—and survive. But to survive—was that worth it when one could survive only as a bourgeois and lead a living death?[35]

From this dilemma comes the feeling of openness and of emptiness. The intensity of the gain has resulted in its immediate loss, and MacDiarmid has both found and lost his new world. Thus even the results of the paradoxical vision are paradoxical in nature. At this stage in the sequence the speaker qualifies future triumph by the necessity of future desolation. By the end of the sequence and because of the experience of the poem, future desolation will be qualified by the necessity of future triumph. The order of these two reactions to the vision will be reversed, and the focus will have shifted from one side of the paradox to the other.

IV "The Psycho-somatic Quandary"—"The Problem Child"

Just as "The Looking Glass" had prepared the way for the third section of the sequence, so "The Unknown Goddess" and "Poet's Pub" have prepared the way for this fourth section with its development of the theme of revelation made possible by the coming together of man and woman. Although this section is much shorter than most of the others, it is probably the most famous section in the sequence. It contains the much anthologized "Love," "O Wha's the Bride," and "The Problem Child." MacDiarmid's lyrical treatment of the revelation that comes from the most intense sexual experience has proved to be unforgettably moving. Yet, as interrelated poems, as part of a greater sequence, these poems have been totally neglected. They have never been studied in context, nor viewed in relation to each other.

The transitional and introductory poem, "The Psycho-somatic Quandary," establishes on a lower poetic level the frame of reference, the theme which stands behind the illustrative lyrics—namely the paradoxical relationship between body and spirit, each revealed more fully in the sexual act:

> Said my body to my mind,
> "I've been startled whiles to find,
> When Jean has been in bed wi' me,
> A kind o' Christianity!"
>
> To my body said my mind,
> "But your benmaist thocht you'll find   *inmost*
> Was 'Bother what I think I feel
> —Jean kens the set o' my bluid owre weel,
> And lauchs to see me in the creel
> O' my courage-bag confined.' " . . .   *scrotum*

(p 83)

And so the revelation felt by the mind is paradoxically qualified by the insistence of the body on *its* prior claim for attention. In a magnificently bawdy section, reminiscent of Burns's Merry Muses of Caledonia (e.g., the pun on "seemin' "), MacDiarmid graphically poses the problem as the speaker playfully moves from one side of the paradox to the other:

> I wish I kent the physical basis
> O' a' life's seemin' airs and graces.
>
> It's queer the thochts a kittled cull   *tickled testicle*
> Can lowse or splairgin' glit annul.   *free, splashing semen*
>
> Man's spreit is wi' his ingangs twined   *entrails*
> In ways that he can ne'er unwind.
>
> A wumman whiles a bawaw gi'es   *look of contempt*
> That clean abaws him gin he sees.   *abashes*

119

> Or wi' a movement o' a leg
> Shows'm his mind is juist a geg.   *deception*
>
> (p 83)

In the final two stanzas the thistle is transformed into a phallus, an echo
of the speaker's earlier reaction to the "Unknown Goddess," and
ironically it rises despite Jean's absence:

> I'se warrant Jean 'ud no' be lang
> In finding whence this thistle sprang.
>
> Mebbe it's juist because I'm no'
> Beddit wi' her that gars it grow! . . .   *makes*
>
> (p 83)

The following poems illustrate this paradoxical relationship between
body and mind, their interdependence and their conflict, as established
here. In keeping with the pattern established in the two preceding
sections, the high points in this section reside in the illustrative lyrics
where one tone counterbalances and merges into another. For example,
in "Love" the revelation made possible by the sexual experience is seen
as a flickering flame, moving between disgust and wonder, flesh and
spirit, life and death. The peculiarly Scottish "hovering" or trembling
quality of this lyric takes us back to the earlier "Watergaw." Rhythm
and movement illustrate within themselves the glimmering of the
revelation:

> A luvin' wumman is a licht
> That shows a man his waefu' plicht,
> Bleezin' steady on ilka bane,
> Wrigglin' sinnen an' twinin' vein,   *sinew*
> Or fleerin' quick an' gane again,   *flaring*
> And the mair scunnersome the sicht   *disgusting*
> The mair for love and licht he's fain
> Till clear and chitterin' and nesh   *shivering, nervous*
> Move a' the miseries o' his flesh. . . .   (p 84)

While the burning bush of "A Moment in Eternity" with all its attendant
present participles has been transformed here into the flickering and
revealing light of love, the concentration, intensity, and economy (when
contrasted with "A Moment in Eternity") represents the full
development of MacDiarmid's poetic powers.

The concept of the nature of the revelation has also developed. The eery "licht," shed by the woman in the act of love, reveals both flesh and spirit in their most extreme manifestations. The first line, through the evocative use of Lallans, presents the central paradox. The "luvin' wumman" is also a "licht," drawing to herself all the warmth of earth and all the mystery of the supernatural. Because of the choice of Lallans, "luvin' " and "wumman" seem much more intimately connected than "loving woman" would. The vowels of each word are similar, warm and tangibly earthy, possibly because of the present-day lower-class associations of "wumman." A "wumman" could never sit on a chair which "like a burnished throne, / Glowed on the marble." But although this woman is associated with the earth, she is also associated through metaphor and alliteration with the mysterious and supernatural "licht." Her earthiness is increased when it becomes apparent that the "luvin' wumman" is not merely an affectionate woman, but a woman in the act of love. And with this, the paradox is increased. While the "luvin' . . . licht" element reappears in "love and licht," the "wumman" part reappears in "waefu' " and, with greater resonance, in "scunnersome" (disgusting). "Love and licht" strip bare the body, laying open bone, sinew, and vein, as they focus a devastatingly revealing spotlight on all that is "scunnersome," all "the miseries o' the flesh." The flickering flame of revelation blazes mercilessly forth in the three climactic centres of focus: "scunnersome," "chitterin'," and "miseries." The metrical link between these three words highlights their agony. At the same time, the obvious parallel with the sexual climax, accentuated by the suspense-filled "clear and chitterin' and nesh," makes the final climactic line both more human and more mysterious.

Rarely has the typical MacDiarmid trick of ending a poem with ". . . ." been so effective. While this technique leaves the reader in a suspended position as the movement of the poem expands, it also serves as a guiding line into the next lyric. The reader pauses as his imagination ranges over possible implications, and then is firmly drawn back into MacDiarmid's line of thought. His most successful poems usually end this way, and significantly each of the poems in this section makes use of such an ending.

The following poem, "In the Last Analysis," switches focus. The "luvin' wumman" whose "licht" showed the speaker his "waefu' plicht" now becomes the centre of attention as the speaker considers the result upon *her* of the revelation. Her "bonny een" appear innocent of the terrible knowledge that has been gained: *"Gin you could pierce their blindin' licht / You'd see a fouler sicht! . . ."* (p 84). Miraculously the revelation which the woman has brought forth seems to have left her untouched. The "blindin' licht" forms an impenetrable barrier, and the full knowledge of the "miseries o' the flesh," that *she* has brought forth, have left her with "bonny een." She sees and does not see. Her innocence has been violated, yet left untouched. *This* is the context within which "O Wha's the Bride" should be viewed in order to do full justice to the poem. "In the Last Analysis" provides the link between "Love" and "O Wha's the Bride." Together they provide the background for the vision of the mysterious bride, violated yet virginal, a vision that had been suggested earlier in "The Crying of the Fair."

"O Wha's the Bride" creates a magic and a power of its own, as witnessed by its impact on readers and critics. The eerie world of the supernatural hovers around the figure of the woman, who appears almost as a composite of the "Unknown Goddess" and the "lass" with "bonny een":

O wha's the bride that cairries the bunch
O' thistles blinterin' white?　　　　*gleaming*
Her cuckold bridegroom little dreids
What he sall ken this nicht.

For closer than gudeman can come　　*husband*
And closer to'r than hersel',
Wha didna need her maidenheid
Has wrocht his purpose fell.

O wha's been here afore me, lass,
And hoo did he get in?
—A man that deed or I was born
This evil thing has din.

And left as it were on a corpse,
Your maidenheid to me?
—Nae lass, gudeman, sin' Time began
'S hed ony mair to gi'e.　　　　　(pp 84-5)

The ballad atmosphere and the parallel between this woman's plight and the legend of the virgin birth lead the reader to expect this as the vision.

122

However in the final stanzas MacDiarmid reverses expectation, and the first vision pales before the very real beauty and love that this archetypal woman offers to her husband. She moves from an apologetically humble tone to one of infinite compassion and love. The "gudeman" becomes the "lad" to whom the supreme vision is granted:

> *But I can gi'e ye kindness, lad,*
> *And a pair o' willin' hands,*
> *And you sall ha'e my breists like stars,*
> *My limbs like willow wands.*
>
> *And on my lips ye'll heed nae mair,*
> *And in my hair forget,*
> *The seed o' a' the men that in*
> *My virgin womb ha'e met. . . .*   (p 85)

The poem soars upward in an incantatory and compelling movement as the woman weaves her spell. "Willin' " and "willow," "breists" and "stars," "mair" and "hair," "heed" and "seed," and the gentle pattern of "m"s revolve around the miracle of this woman and her "virgin womb." Vision and language come together in a supremely moving climax as the mystery surrounding the paradox deepens. The figures of whore and virgin fuse, as the light of the "luvin' wumman" makes a unity of body and spirit, innocence and experience.

The lyric that follows, "Repetition Complex," brutally shatters the magical and awesome tone. The aspiration of the pregnant woman becomes the butt for cruel mockery, even if, like the Virgin Mary, she should produce a Christ. Yet at the same time the speaker retains a reluctant admiration for her stubborn faith, an ashamed backing away from the mystery that is woman, and a sympathy that goes half way to meet her intuition:

> Gin that's the best that you ha'e comin,'
> Fegs but I'm sorry for you, wumman!
> . . .
>
> Yet a'e thing's certain—Your faith is great.
> Whatever happens, you'll no' be blate! . . .   shy

(p 85)

"The Problem Child" ends this section and completes the cycle of thought. Man is contrasted to the Christ child. Indignity, misery, and

disease counterbalance redeeming beauty; and the speaker's sympathy
lies with the insistent bodily pain of man, the pain that is inescapable:

> Christ had never toothick,
> Christ was never seeck,
> But Man's a fiky bairn
> Wi' bellythraw, ripples, and worm-i'-the-cheek! . . .

troublesome child
colic, diarrhea,
toothache

(p 86)

As in "The Psychosomatic Quandary," the body's insistence deafens all
opposition (the horribly physical climax). But the jewel of light that
sparkled in "O Wha's the Bride," while framed by scepticism and
disgust, shines forth like Eliot's "garlic and sapphires in the mud." The
brilliance is both qualified and accentuated by the surroundings.

V "Skeleton at the Feast"—"Tussle with the Philistines"

The "miseries o' the flesh" that had been revealed in the light of love
are transformed in this section into the miseries of contemporary
Scotland and are subjected to the speaker's love for all that Scotland
could be—the bride who "cairries the bunch / O' thistles blinterin'
white." MacDiarmid focuses attention on Scotland's barren state as
symbolized in the ugliness of the thistle and in a host of images linked to
this ugliness and to the purely physical world. Senseless growth, disease,
deformity, and deadness form the centre around which the images
revolve: the "skeleton-at-the-feast," "an eaten and a spewed-like
thing," "a little-bodies' changeling," "my rawny bones," "*the* barren
fig," "a shot kail," "jags or stalk," "drumlie clood o' crudity and
cant," "my gnawin' canker."

In each lyric the poignancy of Scotland's present state emerges
primarily from the speaker's passionate concern, expressed in virulent
condemnation of what Scotland is. The violence of the attack and the
coarse humour that accompanies it provide a kind of healthful energy
which itself is not barren. Look, for example, at some lines from "The
Skeleton at the Feast":

> Dod! It's an eaten and a spewed-like thing,
> Fell like a little-bodies' changeling,
> And it's nae credit t'ye that you s'ud bring
> The like to life—yet, gi'en a mither's love,
> —Hee, hee!—wha kens hoo't micht improve? . . . (p 86)

124

Or the wonderfully comic, yet horrible vision in "To Be Yourselves and Make That Worth Being":

> Ploomen and ploomen's wives—shades o' the Manse
> May weel be at the heid o' sic a dance,
> As through the polish't ha's o' Europe leads
> The rout o' bagpipes, haggis, and sheep's heids!   (p 89)

At the same time, in each of these poems MacDiarmid provides either explicitly or implicitly an ideal counterpart to Scotland's present degradation, and this "contrary" contributes to the poignancy of Scotland's present plight. The poems that enclose the section ("The Skeleton at the Feast" and "Tussle with the Philistines") present the most suggestive counterbalancing images and the least closely defined counterbalancing concepts. The material they enclose is a detailed examination of the "skeleton at the feast" that is Scotland.

The introductory "Skeleton" picks up the image of the disease-ridden bastard child that had been presented in the concluding lyric of the previous section, "The Problem Child." The initial setting bears a strong resemblance to "Bonnie Broukit Bairn" as once again the "auld mune shak's her gowden feathers" on the occasion of some galactic festivity. The "bonnie broukit bairn," however, is now more "broukit" than "bonnie," and the tone is both more impudent and more devastating:

> Pure mune, ye needna thring your shouder there,   *shrug*
> And at your puir get like a snawstorm stare,   *bastard*
> It's yours—there's nae denyin't—and I'm shair
> You'd no' enjoy the evenin' much the less
> Gin you'd but openly confess!   (p 86)

The reversal of expectation technique, however, is once more at work as the inherent beauty of the bastard child is revealed. Just as in "Bonnie Broukit Bairn" earth's tears drown the "haill clanjamfrie," so now earth emerges as a dazzling light that overwhelms the combined powers of sun and moon. The hidden side of the paradox has been revealed:

> Nae doot that hidden sun
> 'Ud look fu' wae ana',   *very sad too*
> Gin I could see it in the licht
> That frae the Earth you draw! . . .   (p 87)

In "Tussle with the Philistines," the ideal alternative is appropriately more qualified, as the mass of intervening evidence makes the earlier confident vision no longer possible. The speaker's vision is now more dependent on himself, more easily shattered by consideration of the present horror:

> Eneuch! For noo I'm in the mood,
> Scotland, responsive to my thoughts,
> Lichts mile by mile, as my ain nerves,
> Frae Maidenkirk to John o' Groats! (p 90)

The poem acts almost as a résumé of the entire section. It opens in a tone of disgust ("O drumlie clood o' crudity and cant"), moves into the personal vision quoted above, qualifies this vision by the evidence that follows ("And Edinburgh and Glasgow / Are like ploomen in a pub"), and ends with a desperate quest for the ideal—while surrounded by a solid mass of cynicism about the value of the quest. In almost Brechtian fashion MacDiarmid uses italics to set off and to qualify the importance of this glimpse of truth:

> It sets you weel to slaver *slobber*
> To let sic gaadies fa' *howlers*
> *—The mune's the muckle white whale*
> *I seek in vain to kaa!* *trap*
>
> *The Earth's my mastless samyn,* *ship's deck*
> *The thistle my ruined sail,*
> *—Le'e go as you maun in the end,*
> And droon in your plumm o' ale! . . . *deep pool*

(p 91)

In contrast to "Bonnie Broukit Bairn," the engulfing action is one of disgust and failure, rather than of triumphant victory, as the revolting "ploomen in a pub" make the quest even more vain.

The intervening poems present Scotland's barren state in explicit terms. In "The Barren Fig" Scotland is contrasted with the "dry stick" which Moses transformed into a serpent. The Old and New Testaments merge with the speaker's vision as "Instantly it / Floo'ered in his hand." Moses' serpent, Christ's fig tree, and MacDiarmid's flowering thistle represent in conjunction all that Scotland is not. Obviously the focus rests on Scotland's spiritual state, now barren. "To Be Yourselves" opens with a reference to Burns, links the "shot kail" that has developed

126

from the Burnsian tradition to the neglect of Dunbar, and ends with praise of Dunbar: "I widna gi'e five meenits wi' Dunbar/For a' the millions o' ye as ye are." The emphasis rests on the barren state of Scotland's poetry. (Ironically and paradoxically the entire *Drunk Man* counterbalances this condemnation and confirms the speaker's position as hero—just as the virulence of the attack is in itself fruitful rather than barren). "My Quarrel with the Rose" considers the failure of Scotland's struggle for independence from England. The "rose" of England's power, prestige, and achievement shames Scotland's miserable thistle:

> Gin the threid haud'n us to the rose were snapt,
> There's no a'e petal o't that 'ud be clapt.   *shrunken*
> A' Scotland gi'es gangs but to jags or stalk,
> The bloom is English—and 'ud ken nae lack!   (p 90)

The link between Scotland's barren political state and the arts has been made explicit.

The solid basis of these three poems (their explicit and careful consideration of the problems that thwart Scotland's growth) provides a delineation of the barrenness which is counterbalanced by the visionary claims of the surrounding poems. They also help to delineate ways in which the vision can be achieved: a new Moses-Christ figure to lead in the establishment of a healthy religious state; a new Dunbar to resurrect Scottish poetry; a new political hero to lead in the establishment of a fruitfully independent state. The qualified ending to "Tussle with the Philistines" implies that the speaker will attempt to search for the achievement of the vision, while recognizing his limitations and the impossibility of success ("in vain," "ruined," "mastless").

VI "The Splore"—"Reductio ad absurdum"

This section takes us from a consideration of Scotland's barren state to a consideration of the barren state of mankind in general. The hint wryly dropped in "Sic Transit Gloria Scotia" is picked up and developed.

"The Splore" (the revel, frolic) provides the link between the two sections; and in its presentation of both the physical component of human sexuality and Robert Burns taken to the extreme, it is one of the most brilliant transitions in the whole *Drunk Man*. The coarse and drunken approach to sexuality harks back to the earlier atmosphere of

"The Looking Glass" and provides a strong contrast to the mysterious and delicately woven tone of "O Wha's the Bride." Just as in *Death in Venice* Aschenbach discovers Dionysus at the end of the aesthetic path, so here the speaker finds himself in a Scottish version of the Dionysian orgy. The poem is a logical extension of Burns's least sentimental poems—his bawdy poems, "The Jolly Beggars." Burns too is taken to the extreme to provide the contrary, another kind of "shot kail." We even have a little of the philosophical Burns: "Ilka pleesure I can ha'e / Ends like a dram ta'en yesterday." The speaker explicitly calls up the ghost of Burns in "Be't whisky gill or penny wheep" and in the reference to Cutty Sark and "Tam o' Shanter." Typically he attempts to out-do Burns. Unlike Tam, this speaker will not run away from the demoniac scene but will participate fully, seeking the extreme in order to make the synthesis of contraries possible:

> "Noo Cutty Sark's tint that ana',   *lost, too*
> And dances in her skin—Ha! Ha!
>
> I canna ride awa' like Tam,
> But e'en maun bide juist whaur I am.   *stay*
>
> I canna ride—and gin I could,
> I'd sune be sorry I hedna stude,
>
> For less than a' there is to see
> 'll never be owre muckle for me.
>
> Cutty, gin you've mair to strip,
> Aff wi't, lass—and let it rip!" . . .   (pp 92-3)

In contrast, both Burns and Tam had been remarkably reticent. Even Burns's muse had been put to flight:

> But here my Muse her wing maun cour,
> Sic flights are far beyond her pow'r:
> To sing how Nannie lap and flang. . . .

In "The Splore," neither the speaker nor his muse has any such reservations. In the final stanza drink and sexuality come together in a brilliantly comic version of the speaker's semen engulfing the world, the sexual equivalent of the tears which "droun / The haill clanjamfrie" in "Bonnie Broukit Bairn":

> I was an anxious barrel, lad,
> When first they tapped my bung.
> They whistled me up, yet thro' the lift *air*
> My freaths like rainbows swung. *foam*
>
> Waesucks, a pride for ony bar,
> The boast o' barleyhood,
> Like Noah's Ark abune the faem,
> Maun float, a gantin' cude. *yawning barrel*
>
> For I was thrawn fu' cock owre sune, *thrown full*
> And wi' a single jaw *spurt*
> I made the pub a blindin' swelth, *whirlpool*
> And how'd the warld awa'! . . . *scooped out*

While the expanding movement, linked with the motif of a released flood, parallels the ending of "Bonnie Broukit Bairn," the tone is obviously different, relentlessly coarse. Other elements belong very much to the frame of reference already established in *A Drunk Man*: the link between drink and sexuality; the shimmering quality of the vision ("freaths," "rainbows," "a blindin' swelth"); the emptiness that follows the release of potential ("a gantin' cude"); and the bawdy physicality. The rest of this section concentrates on the resultant emptiness—man's state after the Fall, barred from Eden. Significantly the speaker of "The Splore" was a virgin ("when first they tapped my bung"). The fall of Adam has never been presented in such brutally and comically physical terms.

In the remainder of the section, references to a past and lost paradise frame the images of death and emptiness: "echo and aiker," "flaw in a jewel," "nadryv" (tragical crack), "the worms'll breed in my corpse," "the slounge o' daith," "a fair forfochen [exhausted] man," "Sargossa Sea," "St. Vitus' Dance," "a chowed core," "banes," "raff o' rain," "ghaist," "the cleiks" (merest shadow). The section both begins and ends with a lament for the lost Eden—linked firstly with the image of the thistle, and lastly with the image of an empty skull. The deliberate repetition of "What forest worn to the backhauf's [worst half] this / What Eden brocht doon to a beanswaup [hull of bean]" at both the beginning and the end of the section draws attention to the framing technique that MacDiarmid often uses in these early sections. The statement of theme cups the paradox within its hands.

The centre of this section rests in the magnificent conclusion to "The Mortal Flaw" ("For nocht but a chowed core's left whaur Jerusalem lay / Like aipples in a heap!") and in the lyric that follows as an illustration of this "chowed core," the ugly nothing that resulted from the Fall. The suggestive image of the "chowed core" gains added poignancy from "The Tragic Tryst":

It's a queer thing to tryst wi' a wumman
When the boss o' her body's gane,   *trunk*
And her banes in the wund as she comes   *wind*
Dirl like a raff o' rain.   *rattle, streak*

It's a queer thing to tryst wi' a wumman
When her ghaist frae abuneheid keeks,   *above, peers*
And you see in the licht o't that a'
You ha'e o'r's the cleiks. . . .   *merest shadow*

(p 95)

The ambience is as mysterious as "O Wha's the Bride," but infinitely more tragic, while hovering more closely on the borderline between the horrible and the comic. The desolate monosyllables, their desolation deepened by the alliterative "r"s and "b"s, emphasize the empty shadow of past possibilities: "boss o' her body," "banes in the wund," "dirl like a raff o' rain." Only two words are given the privilege of more than one syllable: "wumman," warm and tangibly earthy (as in "Love"); "abuneheid," ghostly and removed (like the "mune"). These two words, linked by their syllabic uniqueness, represent the horrifying disparity between what is and what was. The "l"s that emerge in the final lines reinforce this disparity as the speaker moves from the evocative "licht" to the brutal "cleiks." Meanwhile his ironic restraint ("It's a queer thing") results in an avoidance of sentimentality, an insistent touch of humour, and a deepening of the emotional tone. MacDiarmid has never expressed more vividly the "beanswaup" that has emerged from the earlier Eden than he does in the climactic lines, "And her banes in the wund as she comes / Dirl like a raff o' rain," where one can hear the empty rattle of bone against bone. Her "banes," chattering gruesomely in this strangest of all sexual climaxes, reveal the true nature of the loss that mankind has suffered—the "chowed core" that is all that is left of the "aipples in a heap."

130

VII "The Spur of Love"—"Love Often Wins Free"

This section moves thematically from the fall of man to the possible redemption of mankind. Focus now rests on the "licht" that flows from the most meaningful sexual experience, rather than on the "cleiks" that provided the major focus in the earlier section. The inextricable tangle of man's state is transformed into the knot of true marriage, the philosophical bonding of the masculine and feminine principles. The earlier poems celebrating the power of women find clearer definition in relation to the explicit philosophical content of this section. The mystery and the elusive hints of possible illumination are now revealed as rays of light that come together in the blazing light of the vision presented here—the marriage of the speaker-poet with the universe.

As in so many of the sections, the thematic kernel is presented on a lower level of intensity than the lyrics that illustrate the theme. So here, "The Feminine Principle" presents lucidly, but on a lower poetic level, the theme of the merging of the masculine and feminine principles. Daringly the poet-speaker develops and expands the philosophical theme, moving from the relationship between himself and Jean, with a twist of Donnean logic and an almost Whitman-like faculty of absorption, into a marriage first with Scotland, and then with the entire world:

> Create oorsels, syne bairns, syne race.   *children*
> Sae on the cod I see't in you   *pillow*
> Wi' Maidenkirk to John o' Groats
> The bosom that you draw me to.
>
> And nae Scot wi' a wumman lies,
> But I am he and ken as 'twere
> A stage I've passed as he maun pass't,
> Gin he grows up, his way wi' her! .
>
> A'thing wi' which a man
> Can intromit's a wumman,
> And can, and s'ud, become
> As intimate and human.
>
> And Jean's nae mair my wife
> Than whisky is at times,
> Or munelicht or a thistle
> Or kittle thochts or rhymes.   *ticklish, bawdy*

> He's no' a man ava',   *at all*
> And lacks a proper pride,
> Gin less than a' the warld
> Can ser' him for a bride!   (p 97)

The bride figure, whether Jean or the mysterious woman of "Poet's Pub" or the moon-like goddess or the unearthly virgin who "cairries the bunch / O' thistles blinterin' white," is now revealed as a manifestation of the feminine principle: "a' the warld." The original sexual context is carried on into the philosophical theme, symbolic of something greater and more mysterious. MacDiarmid's philosophy here is basically a poetic philosophy, one which can only be diminished when "translated" into prose, as it is based on a leap of imagination ("intromit," for example), convincing within its own context but not amenable to other treatment.

The lyrics that surround the thematic kernel back up this poetic leap of imagination. The beauty of the vision is to be found in these lyrics which provide the *poetic* kernel, as they hover protectively and convincingly around the stated theme, revolving like moons around a sparsely illuminated earth.

Both "The Spur of Love" and "The Light of Life" identify knowledge and sight with the light shed by the woman in the act of love. While the title of each comes from one page in *Tertium Organum,*[36] MacDiarmid uses Ouspensky as a springboard into his own paradoxical vision. In their worship of an idealized woman-figure and in the humble attitude of the speaker towards this woman, these lyrics seem to belong in the courtly love tradition rather than in twentieth-century poetry. "The Spur of Love" even uses the cliché of courtly love: the woman has the power to darken the sky at noon or to brighten the sky at midnight. While the poem also draws heavily on Donne—the entire poem can be viewed as a Donne-like conceit—the result is surprising and original. The language helps. Just as Dunbar in "Done is a Battell" used traditional materials in an entirely original manner, so here MacDiarmid, partly through the novel combination of Lallans and this subject matter, achieves similar success:

> The munelicht is my knowledge o' mysel',
> Mysel' the thistle in the munelicht seen,
> And hauf my shape has fund itsel' in thee
> And hauf my knowledge in your piercin' een.

E'en as the munelicht's borrowed frae the sun
I ha'e my knowledge o' mysel' frae thee,
And much that nane but thee can e'er mak' clear,
Save my licht's frae the source, is dark to me.

Your acid tongue, vieve lauchter, and hawk's een,   *vivid*
And bluid that drobs like haill to quicken me,   *pricks*
Can turn the mid-day black or midnicht bricht,
Lowse me frae licht or eek frae darkness free.   *free*

(p 96)

Both Dunbar and Donne are obviously present. Lawrence presides. And there is none of the sentimentality that has been the bane of Scottish love lyrics. Robert Burns could never have written with such sharp focus—the whole would have been awash in sentiment before the second stanza. This sharp focus is reinforced by the imagery: the individual rays of moonlight, the prickles of the thistle, and the piercing suggestiveness of "acid tongue, vieve lauchter, and hawk's een." (Women's eyes are not usually compared to those of a *hawk*—or at least not if the speaker intends a compliment. Yet here the woman's eyes, penetrating, loving, and wise, are appropriately described in these terms). The long "ee" provides more reinforcement. All of the rhymes are based on this vowel, and the pattern of "ee"s predominates in most of the lines. A counterbalancing force emerges in the soft and gentle "l"s, "m"s, and "ch"s. The entire poem constitutes a blending, or at the very least a paradoxical balance, between sharp and gentle, masculine and feminine, culminating in the magnificently delayed climax:

Bite into me forever mair and lift
Me clear o' chaos in a great relief
Till, like this thistle in the munelicht growin',
I brak in roses owre a hedge o' grief. . . .   (p 96)

The obvious parallel between this climactic vision and the climax of the sexual act is achieved with great delicacy: the sexual act is elevated by the parallel, and the vision is made more human. We are reminded of the closing lines of "Love" ("Till clear and chitterin' and nesh / Move a' the miseries o' the flesh") as the "hedge o' grief" takes over the role of the earlier "miseries o' the flesh." The granted illumination is both climactic and poignant, disturbing in its implication, just like the final lines in

133

"Love." But now the roses, through their aural link with "chaos," represent the ultimate beauty and triumph of the vision. In addition, a typical MacDiarmid trick has been played. We are accustomed to the paradox of a rose with prickles; we are not accustomed to the paradox of a thistle with roses. The twisting of the conventional paradox is both striking and appropriately Scottish. The "hedge o' grief," meanwhile, through its suggestiveness, its lack of explicit definition, and its climactic position in the lyric, calls to mind the "miseries o' the flesh," the prickles of the Scottish thistle, and the agony of Christ's crown of thorns. This final stanza represents one of the finest moments in *A Drunk Man* with its perfect blending of vision and language.

"The Light of Life" picks up the "ee" pattern and presents it in muted fashion. The "l"'s predominate as the speaker focuses on the "licht" made possible by "The Spur of Love," and the "ee"'s which emerge forcefully in the first stanza are later heard only as echoes, and finally are forgotten entirely:

> Use, then, my lust for whisky and for thee,
> Your function but to be and let me be
> And see and let me see.
>
> . . .
>
> Whisky mak's Heaven or Hell and whiles mells baith,
> Disease is but the privy torch o' Daith,
> —But sex reveals life, faith!
>
> I need them a' and maun be aye at strife.
> Daith and ayont are nocht but pairts o' life.
> —Then be life's licht, my wife! . . .   (p 98)

The speaker here explains too much. He seems to be both too coldly logical and too gushingly sentimental. It is as if the poem is struggling to achieve the heights of "The Spur of Love" and falling short, perhaps because the philosophy of "The Feminine Principle" intrudes upon the experience and reduces it. The woman and the experience are *used* in a way which was not true in "The Spur of Love." Whether or not I am being unfair to MacDiarmid's intent here, the sequential arrangement of the poems pays tribute to his concept of the *Drunk Man* as one whole. The poems are not haphazard drunken meanderings. "The Light of Life" crystallizes the experience of "The Spur of Love" and the philosophy of "The Feminine Principle." At first glance, the two lyrics might seem to be roughly parallel or interchangeable, but to switch "The Spur of Love" and "The Light of Life" would be to do damage to the careful progression of thought and mood.

This conclusion is reinforced by the poem that follows, "Love Often Wins Free." Just as the "ee" pattern was gradually quenched by the "l"s, so here the "l"s must give way to less gentle consonants:

> Love often wuns free
> In lust to be strangled,
> Or love, o' lust free,
> In law's sairly tangled.
>
> And it's ill to tell whether
> Law or lust is to blame
> When love's chokit up
> —It comes a' to the same.
>
> In this sorry growth
> Whatna beauty is tint
> That freed o't micht find
> A waur fate than is in't? . . .   (p 98)

The tone is playful, a needed and welcome relief to the generally serious tone of the section. Once again MacDiarmid reverses expectation and undermines the carefully achieved effect that preceded this poem. The conviction of the ultimate beauty and value of the vision released by the sexual experience is suddenly and dramatically called into question. Humorously the speaker backs down, leaving the reader with an unanswered question, as earlier confidence is transformed into playful cynicism. The "licht" of "The Light of Life" has disappeared, and inexorably its partner "love" is trapped, first into "lust," and then into "laws," as love is "chokit up." The clipped monosyllables accentuate the victory of the prickles, whose inherent sharpness and vitality overcome the unearthly roses of "The Spur of Love." Once again MacDiarmid has thoughtfully arranged the sequential order of these lyrics. While "The Light of Life" could not possibly follow "Love Often Wins Free," the effect of "The Light of Life" is chastened and modified by the tone of the following poem. This particular section provides an impressive example of the care and skill with which MacDiarmid arranged the sequence.

VIII "Yank Oot Your Orra Boughs"—"The Form and Purpose of the Thistle"

This section marks a turning point in the sequence. From this section until the end of the entire sequence the long philosophical poems will predominate, and the short intense lyrics will fade largely from view, only to emerge in the final coda. A glance at the index of the 1967 edition of the *Collected Poems* verifies this impression in a somewhat mechanical manner. The sequence is not yet half-completed. So far I have treated in depth only thirty-five of the eighty-seven pages. And yet the total number of individual poems before this point in the sequence greatly exceeds the number of poems to follow. The poems in the sections before this point are also the most anthologized. The choice made by Craig and Manson in the *Selected Poems* is typical. Out of twenty pages devoted to *A Drunk Man,* fourteen are devoted to poems which appear before this point in the sequence, and a meagre six pages to the poems that follow.

Why this sudden development? We can look back to the first poem in the sequence for some justification:

> (To prove my saul is Scots I maun begin
> Wi' what's still deemed Scots and the folk expect,
> And spire up syne by visible degrees
> To heichts whereo' the fules ha'e never recked.   (p 63)

The lyrics that had proved so successful in *Sangschaw* and *Penny Wheep* ("what the folk expect") are about to give way to the "heichts whereo' the fules ha'e never recked," although the longer poems in *Penny Wheep* might have given some indication of the direction in which MacDiarmid is moving. Inexorably he is leaving behind the short Lallans lyric, and the attempted justification seems in the context almost desperate—as ironic perhaps as his previous outcry against a "bensil o' a bleeze." MacDiarmid himself, like the thistle, is caught between two opposing forces, the "ferlies" and the "bensil o' a bleeze." As the later sections of *A Drunk Man* make clear, he is about to opt for the "bensil," regardless of the sacrifices that must be made. His personal "crucifixion" as a poet gives added poignancy to the two sections that follow this turning-point, those sections dealing with the rose-prickles paradox and with the thistle as Christ crucified. The magical world that MacDiarmid entered through the "datchie sesames" of Lallans turns out to be as transitory as the

136

moment of vision, as subject to time as Eden. The short intense lyrics with their dense Lallans, their concentrated movement and tone, will now give way to the long poem written in a much less dense Lallans, or in English with a Scottish accent. Viewed in this light, *A Drunk Man* serves as a symbol for this turning point in MacDiarmid's poetry. What I have called the "poetic kernels" will become much less frequent and will emerge in the midst of thematic sections, rather than existing in dynamic juxtaposition with other poetic kernels.

At the same time, as Weston has noted, the speaker in *A Drunk Man* seems to sober up as the poem progresses.[37] Weston's insight can lead into a realization that the divine intoxication made possible by Lallans is fading; and the speaker leaves behind the poetic heights and searches for a different kind of height, a different structure, and a different frame of reference. From this point onward in the sequence the dynamic juxtaposition of different levels of approach will, on the whole, merge into one, the major exception consisting of the final coda. Much of the drama and the jarring conflict that stood at the heart of the sequence until now will be muted. The speaker is sobering up, and as he does so, MacDiarmid is leaving behind the "first fine careless rapture," which, unlike Browning's thrush, he will not (or perhaps cannot) recapture.

A retrospective glance at MacDiarmid's letter to Ogilvie reveals MacDiarmid's need for reassurance that what he is attempting is right. He looks both to Scott and to Ogilvie for this support:

> We both felt that the section I've been re-writing—which comes about midway in the book and should represent the high water mark, the peaks of highest intensity, could be improved by being recast and projected onto a different altitude of poetry altogether—made, instead of a succession of merely verbal and pictorial verses, into a series of metaphysical pictures, with a definite progression, a cumulative effect.[38]

The "definite progression" and the "cumulative effect" of the sections that follow will indeed be on a "different altitude of poetry altogether," but the peaks of highest intensity are not to be found in these midway sections—rather in the earlier crystallized lyrics, in the farewell coda, and in the sudden flashes of the old lightning.

In the later sections of *A Drunk Man* these sudden flashes of lightning are by no means negligible. At this point in his career MacDiarmid gives focus and intensity to his longer poems through these frequent and often surprising moments of illumination. A long poem suddenly jumps into focus, sharply defined and evocative. These sudden peaks of intensity occur frequently enough to make the longer poems as dynamic as the more concentrated lyrics, although the method is different. In his later poetry, however, these peaks will become much less frequent. The tendency to create a distance between the peaks, observable in this sequence, will increase in his later poetry. In this way, *A Drunk Man* can be viewed as the major turning point in MacDiarmid's poetry, just as this section marks the turning point in the sequence itself. Ironically his masterpiece represents both the culmination of his work in Lallans and the beginning of his movement away from Lallans, both the finding of a suitable form for his paradoxical vision and his inability to sustain that form, both the climax of his career and the beginning of his decline.

Iain Crichton Smith's theory that the psychological risks that MacDiarmid took at this time could not have been sustained without annihilation of the self goes a long way towards explaining why *A Drunk Man* had to be the turning point. Here MacDiarmid opens himself up more than ever before, exposing his vulnerability; and it is this experience and the anguish connected with it that cause him to draw back in the later poetry, to erect protective barriers around the self.

The turning point in the sequence, the eighth section, focuses on the rose-plus-prickles paradox of the thistle. The desperate nature of man's plight is revealed through the paradox of the roses and prickles, the essence of the thistle and the obverse side of the masculine-feminine coin. In "Yank Oot Your Orra [worthless] Boughs" the speaker's passionate realization of the hopelessness of the situation contrasts dramatically with his rising determination to break the bonds that hinder him. The chorus-like refrain, "Yank oot your orra boughs, my hert," breaks in at shorter and shorter intervals, in defiance of man's tragic plight which is revealed through a cluster of related images: "clytach" [nonsense], "Blottie O," "leprous chuns" [sprouts], "a jungly waste o' effort," "the thorter-ills [paralytic seizures] o' leaf and prick," "mongrel growth." Diseased, meaningless, and painful growth makes the roses' triumph seem heartless: "The roses like the saints in Heaven treid / Triumphant owre the agonies o' their breed, / And wag fu' mony a celestial heid." But while the speaker sympathizes with the agony of the rest of mankind, ultimately he takes the side of the aristocratic roses through his increasing determination to "yank oot your orra boughs." Paradoxically the brutal nature of this command (the clipped monosyllables, the violent "oot," the fierce "r"s) aligns him with the less sophisticated prickles rather than with the celestial roses, a paradox that reaches its climax in the final stanza. Here the subtle refinement of Mallarmé's French, its gentle sophistication and exquisite control are undermined by the brutality of the Lallans and the sharpness of *its* prickles:

> "Mon doute, amas de nuit ancienne s'achève
> En maint rameau subtil, qui, demeuré les vrais
> Bois même, prouve hélas! que bien seul je m'offrais
> Pour triomphe la faute idéale des roses."

> *Yank oot your orra boughs, my hert!* (p 101)

In "The Form and Purpose of the Thistle," the final poem in this short section, the violence of "Yank Oot" is left behind as the speaker moves into a more relaxed mood, a quieter consideration of the thistle and its purpose. Now he feels "a certain symp'thy wi' its orra ways," as he wonders what kind of God could have created such a paradox. In a very lovely stanza the speaker identifies the thistle as the meeting place of "contraries," an implicit parallel to the merging of the male and female principles in the preceding section:

The craft that hit upon the reishlin' stalk,	*rustling*
Wi'ts gausty leafs and a' its datchie jags,	*ghostly, secret*
And spired it syne in seely flooers to brak	*happy*
Like sudden lauchter owre its fousome rags	*disgusting*
Jouks me, sardonic lover, in the routh	*evades, abundance*
O' contrairies that jostle in this dumfoondrin' growth. (p 102)	

The jagged leaves and stalk are now "reishlin'," "gausty," and "datchie," as well as "fousome," and the roses are elevated to "seely" (happy, blessed, like the German "selig"), a less equivocal form of praise than the earlier comparison with angels wagging "fu' mony a celestial heid." Similarly the "jungly waste" is now "the routh / O' contrairies that jostle in this dumfoondrin' growth," as the speaker views the thistle with reverence rather than with condemnation. The stanza hovers over the contraries that make up the paradox of the thistle, just as the speaker, like a "sardonic lover," hovers between devotion and cynicism. The general effect of this hovering is mystery, a similar mystery to that presented in the love lyrics, the mystery which the speaker indicates is at the heart of all creation and in the god responsible for this "dumfoondrin' growth."

IX "Ballad of the Crucified Rose"—"The Fork in the Wall"

This section centres on the image of the crucifixion: the crucifixion of the thistle, of the hero Christ-figure, of mankind trapped in inexorable tension between flesh and spirit, and, I would claim, of MacDiarmid as a poet. The vision of "A Moment in Eternity," the great tree of life, quivering and shining, vibrant with energy, is once more present. Now the quivering is linked with pain as well as with joy, with the death spasm as well as with life, and with ugliness as well as with beauty: "The tree that fills the universe, / Or like a reistit herrin' crines" (like a dried herring shrivels up) (p 109).

I view this section as the central section of the sequence. It provides the magnet, the central core around which the rest of the sequence clusters. MacDiarmid's driving vision of the beauty of mankind's potential and the ugliness of mankind's achievement, the hopes of the spirit and the cynicism of the flesh, emerges here in the ultimate paradox: this crucifixion is both ugly and beautiful, hopeful and despairing, poised at the meeting place of life and death.

The most important poem in the section, the poem which itself is the quivering magnet, is "The Thistle's Characteristics," one of MacDiarmid's finest poems and the key poem of the entire sequence. It is introduced by "The Ballad of the Crucified Rose" which establishes the central motif of the crucifixion. In a footnote MacDiarmid links the ballad with the General Strike of May 1926, and it is his first explicitly political poem. Viewed in relation to the earlier "I Heard Christ Sing" of *Sangschaw* or to "The Thistle's Characteristics," the wider implications are soon evident. The hopes and the failure of the General Strike are the hopes and failure of all mankind. The speaker sees a rose "loupin' oot / Frae a camsteerie [perverse] plant." The rose grows miraculously, parallelling the movement of "The Bonnie Broukit Bairn":

> And still it grew until it seemed
> The haill braid earth had turned
> A reid reid rose that in the lift   *sky*
> Like a ball o' fire burned.   (p 104)

But the triumph is only temporary, and the rose shrivels up:

> Like grieshuckle the roses glint,   *embers*
> The leafs like farles hing,   *ash*
> As roond a hopeless sacrifice
> Earth draws its barren ring.   (p 105)

Typically MacDiarmid uses the image of lost light, glowing embers resolving into barren ash, to represent the disparity between what was and what is, the hopes of man contrasted with his failure. In a characteristically ironic reversal of expectation, the poem ends with a plea to God to forsake the thistle, rather than with Christ's cry, "My God, my God, why hast Thou forsaken me?":

> The bitter taste is on my tongue,
> I chowl my chafts, and pray   *twist my jaws*
> "Let God forsake me noo and no'
> Staund connoisseur-like tae!" . . .   (p 106)

While the power of this final stanza might first appear to reside in the reversal of expectation, its major impact results from a much more subtle movement: the identification of the speaker with the thistle-like Christ. The "I" of the first stanza who "saw" the rose is now the crucified rose itself, a transformation made possible by the experience of the poem.

This identification of the speaker with the crucified rose, with the Christ-like figure, and with suffering humanity, prepares the way for "The Thistle's Characteristics":

> The language that but sparely flooers
> And maistly gangs to weed;
> The thocht o' Christ and Calvary
> Aye liddenin' in my heid.   *moving*
>
> (p 106)

Here MacDiarmid has solved the problem of the long poem. The intensity of the lyric shines forth in the daring image or in the sudden upward movement, similar to the upward surge of many of his lyrics. These highpoints create a dynamism of their own, so that the poem seems to move from one summit to yet another. The characteristic highpoints are of two types, linked closely together by the insistent upward movement, the characteristic Dionysian thrust towards release, and by related imagery. For the first type of highpoint MacDiarmid daringly chooses the image of semen as the symbol of the paradoxical

141

mystery of man's plight. (He has already given a hint of this development in "The Splore," and he will later develop the image in "Harry Semen"). The energy, the wriggling life, and the promise of the sperm are contrasted with their failure:

> The wasted seam that dries like stairch   *semen*
> And pooders aff, that micht ha' been
> A warld o' men and syne o' Gods.   (p 107)

> As a' Earth's magic frae a spirt   *spurt*
> In shame and secrecy, o' dirt!   (p 107)

> O stranglin' rictus, sterile spasm
> Thou stricture in the groins o' licht
> Thou ootrie gangrel frae the wilds   *outré wanderer*
> O' chaos fenced frae Eden yet
> By the unsplinterable wa'
> O' munebeams like a bleeze o' swords!   (p 108)

> A black leaf owre a white leaf twirls,
> A grey leaf flauchters in atween,   *flutters*
> Sae ply my thochts aboot the stem
> O' loppert slime frae which they spring.   *clotted*
> The thistle like a snawstorm drives,
> Or like a flicht o' swallows lifts,
> Or like a swarm o' midges hings,
> A plague o' moths, a starry sky.   (p 109)

MacDiarmid is treating the image of semen in a parallel fashion to his treatment of the image of the thistle. The basic image is "translated" into a host of related images. Just as the thistle can be an octopus, or the top of a balmoral bonnet swallowed by an alligator, or a phallus, so semen can become a thistle, a snowstorm, a swarm of insects, a starry sky. While the ultimate meaning of the sequence, the release of sexual energy, emerges clearly in "The Thistle's Characteristics," the relationship between this theme and the image of the thistle is also clarified. The image of semen takes over the role of the thistle as *leitmotif* (once again a foreshadowing of "Harry Semen"). The semen *is* the thistle, Lawrence's life-force, Ouspensky's higher logic, the meeting-place of contraries, and the key to the paradox.

At the central point of "The Thistle's Characteristics" the speaker
links the mystery of the semen with the Christ-man, eternally crucified
between spirit and flesh. With anger, agony, and defiance, the speaker
rebukes the creator of this paradoxical crucifixion:

> The tug-o'-war is in me still,
> The dog-hank o' the flesh and soul,
> Faither in Heaven, what gar'd ye tak'   *made*
> A village slut to mither me,
> Your mongrel o' the fire and clay?
> The trollop and the Deity share
> My writhen form as tho' I were
> A picture o' the time they had . . .   (p 110)

"Slut," "mongrel," "trollop," and "writhen" brutally debunk the holy
mystery of the virgin birth. But suddenly the poem rises; and for one
brief, brilliant moment we breathe crystal-clear air as the almost Miltonic
grandeur of the conception emerges:

> When Licht rejoiced to file itsel'   *defile*
> And Earth upshuddered like a star.

The trembling quality of these lines brings together the pain and the joy
of humankind in this most miraculous of sexual climaxes, and provides
the second type of highpoint: the elusive and trembling enlightenment
that MacDiarmid had suggested in "The Watergaw," the flickering
moment when the paradox takes shape and when a perfect balance is
achieved. Life and death, joy and sorrow, flesh and spirit, man and God,
all tremble in precarious unity at those moments. At several points this
kind of unity is suggested:

> The thistle in the wund dissolves
> In lichtin's as shook foil gi'e way
> In sudden splendours, or the flesh
> As Daith lets slip the infinite soul.   (p 107)

These moments are isolated and transitory. Just as the "shook foil"
gives way to the "pickled foetus," so in the final lines the expansive
trembling moment is qualified and made more human:

> The nervous thistle's shiverin', like
> A horse's skin aneth a cleg,   *beneath, gadfly*

> Or Northern Lichts or lustres o'
> A soul that Daith has fastened on,
> Or mornin' efter the nicht afore. (p 112)

The mysterious paradoxical unity embraces the horse's wince at the insect's bite, the beauty of the Northern Lights, the trembling "watergaw" of death, and the *delirium tremens* of the drunk man himself. The shivering or "chitterin' " quality of these epiphanies is closely linked to the semen imagery and to the moment of sexual climax. At these moments all contraries are reconciled. The opposing forces of *A Drunk Man* suddenly reach their focal point, their moment of fulfilment, their paradoxical place of unity.

The poem that follows, "The Grave of All Mankind," opens with a similar view of the thistle: "*Shudderin'* thistle, gi'e owre, gi'e owre" (my italics). It moves, however, into a recognition of the emptiness that results from the vision, a foreshadowing of the final coda, and an echo of the earlier "thistleless fule":

> Nae man can ken his hert until
> The tide o' life uncovers it,
> And horror-struck he sees a pit
> Returnin' life can never fill! . . . (p 112)

The barren nature of this emptiness sets the tone for "A Stick-Nest in Ygdrasil," where the wooden cross of Christ and of mankind becomes a "forhooied [deserted] nest" in the tree of life, insignificant and worthless as the blind bird's nest in the introductory section of the sequence. Sporadically a hint of the precarious vision returns:

> And through a cylinder o' wombs,
> A star reflected in a dub, *puddle*
> I see as 'twere my ain wild harns *brains*
> The ripple o' Eve's moniplies. *intestines*
>
> (p 115)

But in the end the lifelessness and the stupidity of the wooden cross triumph:

> Aye, this is Calvary—to bear
> Your Cross wi'in you frae the seed,
> And feel it grow by slow degrees
> Until it rends your flesh apairt,

And turn, and see your fellow-men
In similar case but sufferin' less
Thro' bein' mair wudden frae the stert! . . .   (p 117)

The vision and the mysterious unity of the vision are called into question, and never more brutally than in the closing poem of the section, "A Fork in the Wall." It marks a return to a denser and more brutal Lallans. When MacDiarmid moves away from the lyric into the longer poem in *A Drunk Man,* his language alters perceptibly. Dense Lallans gives way to English with a Scottish accent and an odd word of dialect. Consider, for example, the ending of "A Stick-Nest" quoted above. With a few minor alterations and with very little loss of effect ("wudden," with its dull Lallans thud, is the major exception), this stanza could be converted into King's English. "The Fork in the Wall," however, depends much more on a Lallans that cannot be lifted out of the poem, a Lallans that is one of the most violent ingredients in the lyric:

I'm fu' o' a sticket God.	*stuck*
THAT'S what's the maitter wi' me.	
Jean has stuck sic a fork in the wa'	*spell for couvade*
That I row in agonie.	*roar*
Mary never let dab.	*let on*
SHE was a canny wumman.	*careful*
She hedna a gaw in Joseph at a'	*hold on*
But, wow, this seecund comin'! . . .	(pp 117-18)

The power of the spirit and the miraculous union of God with man, as symbolized in the virgin birth, are converted here into brutally fleshly terms. This "seecund comin' " is a coming of the flesh, a blasphemous and unholy parallel to the coming of the spirit, and its violence is accentuated by the initial stressed syllable in the second line ("THAT'S," "SHE") and the internal rhyme of "row" and "wow"—a shreik of unmitigated pain. The prayer of the "Crucified Rose" has been answered. God has departed, and the flesh reigns supreme, agonized and brutal, and with added poignancy because of the intervening vision of unity. The balance of the paradox, an uneasy and precarious equipoise, has been upset.

145

X "The Goal of Scottish History"—"Farewell to Dostoevski"

In this section the speaker-poet takes his place in world literature in an attempt to make a unity out of the "contrair" qualities of Scotland and mankind and to redress the upset balance of the paradox. In "The Goal of Scottish History," the speaker's path leads through Melville, another "Scottish" Christ, "bleedin' like the thistle's roses," to Dostoevski: "My whim (and mair than whim) it pleases / To seek the haund o' Russia as a freen' / In workin' oot mankind's great synthesis." The speaker continues with his plan in "Letter to Dostoevski" where once again Melville's spirit will be an intermediary between the speaker and the towering figure of the Russian giant. Burns, Melville, and the speaker, by a trick of poetic logic, together plough the depths of the Scottish soul, together turn from wife and child, together break free from the fetters that restrain them:

> Lowsed frae the dominion   *freed*
> O' popular opinion,
> And risen at last abune
> The thistle like the mune
> That looks serenely doon
> On what queer things there are
> In an inferior star. . . .   (p 124)

The major thematic tension of this section resides in the conflict between vision and all that surrounds the vision, just as the major thematic tension resides in the movement between trembling poetic heights and the intermediary logical connections. The earlier sections of *A Drunk Man* were structured on clashing moments of intensity. By this point in the sequence the tension is less a brutal yanking asunder and more a slow pull away from the peaks of intensity, a pattern that MacDiarmid will later develop in "Harry Semen." For example, a somewhat mundane passage will lead into a moment of breathless vision:

> And this, I ha'e nae doot,
> This road'll bring aboot.
>
> The munelicht that owre clear defines
> The thistle's shrill cantankerous lines
> E'en noo whiles insubstantialises

> Its grisly form and 'stead devises
> A maze o' licht, a siller-frame,
> As 'twere God's dream frae which it came,
> Ne'er into bein' coorsened yet. . . .   (p 125)

The climactic "A maze o' licht, a siller-frame" rings out purely and clearly before the tone slowly drops away. And similarly:

> The thistle canna vanish quite.
> Inside a' licht its shape maun glint,
> A spirit wi' a skeleton in't.
>
> The world, the flesh, 'll bide in us,
> As in the fire the unburnt buss. . . .   (p 127)

For one brief, hovering moment, "A spirit wi' a skeleton in't," the vision shines forth, only to fade again as the poem moves onward.

MacDiarmid is obviously both aware and in control of what is happening:

> These are the moments when my sang
> Clears its white feet frae oot amang
> My broken thocht, and moves as free
> As souls frae bodies when they dee.
> There's naething left o' me ava'   *at all*
> Save a' I'd hoped micht whiles befa'.   (p 126)

The moments of liberation and of vision coincide with the peaks of poetic intensity: the "sang." Their contrary is no longer the brutally intense lyric, but the "broken thocht," the passages of tortuous philosophical speculation from which the speaker-poet occasionally wins free in a moment of pure vision.

The importance of these moments of vision is emphasized by a growing desire that the vision might be true: "Be like the thistle, O my saul"; "I wad ha'e Scotland to my eye / Until I saw a timeless flame / Tak' Auchtermuchty for a name"; "Be thou the licht in which I stand / Entire in thistle-shape as planned"; "Syne liberate me frae this tree"; "O for a root in some untroubled soil, / Some cauld soil 'yont this fevered warld"; "And let my roses drap." Just as for Hart Crane, the truth of the vision becomes more and more of a necessity for the speaker. As in Crane's poetry, the shining vision resides in the vision itself, not in the prayer that it might be true. Indeed the prayer provides a major point of tension, an agonizing undercutting of the vision, and an insistence upon the tenuous link between the vision and the world of man.

Nevertheless, despite the undercutting, the confusion, the horrible tangle of logical thought, and the yawning gap between the speaker and Dostoevski, the vision does persist, and past and future come together in the climactic lines:

> *I ken nae Russian and you ken nae Scots.*
> *We canna tell oor voices frae the wund.*
> *The snaw is seekin' everywhere: oor herts*
> *At last like roofless ingles it has f'und.*   hearths
>
> *And gethers there in drift on endless drift,*
> *Oor broken herts that it can never fill;*
> *And still—its leafs like snaw, its growth like wund—*
> *The thistle rises and forever will! . . .*
>
> The thistle rises and forever will,
> Getherin' the generations under't.
> This is the monument o' a' they were,
> And a' they hoped and wondered.   (p 135)

Just as earlier in the sequence, the phallus had risen in defiance of Jean's absence and in the presence of the "strange Goddess," so the thistle rises here, indomitable, inexplicable, and insistent on its own vitality. When vision seems impossible, the thistle rises and gathers to itself all the contraries that had seemed far apart; and once again the paradox forms. Despite the speaker's failure to reach Dostoevski, despite his failure to see Scotland's destiny as part of the destiny of the world, "the thistle rises and forever will," secure in the timeless world of paradox.

XI "The Barren Tree"—"The Great Wheel"

This section presents the ultimate and climactic vision, the only vision that can justifiably be compared to the medieval dream vision, namely "The Great Wheel," the wheel of the universe, of creation, and of time. This vision is preceded by several poems that present a formidable array of forces counter to the vision and a recapitulation of themes presented earlier in the sequence—emptiness, barrenness, death, and the "owre sonsy rose" whose victory is based on subjugation and inhumanity.

The most powerful poem in this introductory section is "In the Keel of
Heaven," another return to the intensely focused lyric, free of lengthy
expostulation and tortuous thought, and packed with evocative Lallans.
In almost every line the unifying imagery of twisted, entangling coils
builds in intensity, reinforced by repetition and the strong alliterative
patterns:

> Maun I tae perish in the keel o' Heaven,
> And is this fratt upon the air the ply   *fretwork*
> O' cross-brathed cordage that in gloffs and gowls   *dark and light*
> Brak's up the vision o' the warld's bricht gy?   *spectacle*
>
> Ship's tackle and an eemis cairn o' fraucht   *unsteady, cargo*
> Darker than clamourin' veins are roond me yet,
> A plait o' shadows thicker than the flesh,
> A fank o' tows that binds me hand and fit.   *coil of rope*
>
> What gin the gorded fullyery on hie   *frosted foliage*
> And a' the fanerels o' the michty ship   *flapping parts*
> Gi'e back mair licht than fa's upon them ev'n
> Gin sic black ingangs haud us in their grip?   *entrails*

(p 139)

MacDiarmid provides here a lyric equivalent of the entangling
suffocating thought of the previous sections, the blackness from which
the light of vision emerges. The entangling coils are also sexually
suggestive, and the line of demarcation between logical thought and
instinctive disgust becomes increasingly blurred. The darkness here is
overwhelming. The "l"'s, normally gentle in MacDiarmid's lyrics, are
now, by association with menacing alliterative pairs ("gloffs and
gowls," "fullyery"-"fanerels"), like wriggling eels, bent on entrapping
and restraining. Even the seemingly innocuous "ship's tackle" through
the aural link with "fanerels o' the michty ship" and "black," and the
suggestive link with the other images ("a plait o' shadows"), plays its
part in the creation of an atmosphere of menace and unchecked evil. This
atmosphere results in the climactic and despairing question to which the
only possible answer, given the evidence of the poem, must be, "It
matters not."

The "demoralisin' dearth / O' onything worth while on Earth," as
presented in these introductory poems and with additional force in "The

149

Keel of Heaven,'' prepares the way for the climactic vision at a time when vision seems impossible or worthless, a typical reversal of expectation and an illustration of the central paradoxical movement of the sequence. Out of one extreme its ''contrary'' emerges. The entire sequence rounds itself out, ironically when we least expect it, and with double irony as the very first line of ''The Great Wheel'' takes us back to the first line of the sequence: ''I'm *weary* o' the rose as o' my brain,'' cf. ''I amna' fou' sae muckle as *tired—deid dune*'' (my italics). While the speaker-poet has moved in a circle, now he begins with the experience of the sequence behind him. Appropriately the title of the poem is ''The Great Wheel,'' and the major image representing the entirety of creation, including a place for Scotland and humanity, is that of the endlessly turning wheel. Within this wheel all contraries are caught, separate yet united within its movement, like the grooves of a gigantic gramophone record:

And see I noo a great wheel move,
And a' the notions that I love
Drap into stented groove and groove? *appointed*

. . .

Then suddenly I see as weel
As me spun roon' within the wheel
The helpless forms o' God and Deil.

. . .

Upon the huge circumference are
As neebor points the Heavenly War
That dung doon Lucifer sae far, *dashed*

And that upheaval in which I
Sodgered 'neth the Grecian sky
And in Italy and Marseilles.

. . .

And Jesus and a nameless ape
Collide and share the selfsame shape
That nocht terrestrial can escape? (pp 142-4)

This unity in diversity emerges as the speaker's ultimate need:

"Whatever Scotland is to me, / Be it aye pairt o' a' men see / O' Earth and o' Eternity." To poetry falls the task of bringing about this unity: "The function, as it seems to me, / O' Poetry is to bring to be / At lang, lang last that unity," a claim which the entire sequence attempts to justify through its paradoxical movement and theme.

The turning point in the vision occurs in the brilliantly comic section where the speaker becomes aware of the company he keeps, the other Scots sharing his particular groove:

> I felt it turn, and syne I saw
> John Knox and Clavers in my raw,   *row*
> And Mary Queen o' Scots ana',   *also*
>
> And Rabbie Burns and Weelum Wallace,
> And Carlyle lookin' unco gallus,   *very indifferent*
> And Harry Lauder (to enthrall us).   (p 148)

The speaker's bitterly comic outrage leads into a realization of the ultimate irony: "Ye maun choose but gin ye'd see / Anither category ye / Maun tine [lose] your nationality." In order to break the "livin' tomb" which both Scotland and humanity inhabit, the speaker must relinquish both his Scottishness and his humanity. He must leave one side of the paradox forever.

And so the vision ends in a dichotomy, in an unanswered question, an ironic backing away from the decision, and in a summoning up of the image of Jean whose embrace will welcome the speaker back to the everyday world:

> But aince Jean kens what I've been through
> The nicht, I dinna doot it,
> She'll ope her airms in welcome true,
> And clack nae mair aboot it. . . .   *talk*
>
> (p 150)

To a certain extent the summoning up of Jean is an evasion of the issue, an attempt to avoid the pain of decision. Equally well, however, the speaker's turning to Jean is a positive affirmation of his sexuality, his Scottishness, and his human qualities; and thus it serves as a refusal to obey the command to "tine your nationality." It represents an insistence upon the part of the speaker on maintaining the paradox without which he would not be human.

XII "The Stars Like Thistle's Roses Flower"—"Yet Ha'e I Silence Left"

The paradox of this ending is preserved in the final section where once again the speaker calls upon the figure of Jean in an ironic undercutting of the dilemma: "—'And weel ye micht,' / Sae Jean'll say, 'efter sic a nicht!' " The poems that have preceded Jean's final unanswerable comment—"The Stars Like Thistle's Roses Flower" and "Yet Ha'e I Silence Left"—present the dichotomy in a totally different manner. The ironic distance which the speaker preserved in "The Great Wheel" is left behind. The speaker's anguish in the face of his condition—the positive and negative emptiness left by the vision—emerges purely in the lyrical language and the suggestive images.

In the first lyric, light and empty darkness are counterbalancing forces. "Stars" surround "sterile" nothingness, and "bitter blasts" attack the speaker's anguish and his hopes ("fain," "hert," "hain," "licht," "shinin' "):

> The stars like thistle's roses floo'er
> The sterile growth o' Space ootour,   *all over*
> That clad in bitter blasts spreids oot
> Frae me, the sustenance o' its root.
>
> O fain I'd keep my hert entire,
> Fain hain the licht o' my desire,   *keep*
> But ech! the shinin' streams ascend,
> And leave me empty at the end.
>
> For aince it's toomed my hert and brain,   *emptied*
> The thistle needs maun fa' again.
> —But a' its growth 'll never fill
> The hole it's turned my life intill! . . .   (p 150)

The empty hole of this final stanza, its emptiness reinforced by the long "oo" and the yawning "fa' " and "a'," is not entirely empty. The paradoxical coin flips over, and in the following poem the nothingness becomes a mysterious and wonderful silence, pure in a way that is uncannily reminiscent of the "virgin womb" of the bride with the "thistles blinterin' white." Loneliness, fear, death, and God are left behind; they dwindle in importance before the mysterious silence, the

152

"croon o' a'," "wha's deed owre often and has seen owre much." The reaction to the vision of the great wheel becomes in turn an even more mysterious vision:

> Yet ha'e I Silence left, the croon o' a'.
>
> No' her, wha on the hills langsyne I saw
> Liftin' a foreheid o' perpetual snaw.
>
> No' her, wha in the how-dumb-deid o' nicht   *midnight*
> Kyths, like Eternity in Time's despite.   *appears*
>
> No' her, withooten shape, wha's name is Daith,
> No' Him, unkennable abies to faith   *except*
>
> —God whom, gin e'er He saw a Man, 'ud be
> E'en mair dumfooner'd at the sicht than he.
>
> —But Him, whom nocht in man or Deity,
> Or Daith or Dreid or Laneliness can touch,
> *Wha's deed owre often and has seen owre much.*
>
> O I ha'e Silence left.

The mysterious inhumanity of perpetual snow, eternity, her "withooten shape, wha's name is Daith," and "Him, unkennable abies to faith" quails in an increasingly inevitable manner ("No' her," "No' her," "No' her," "No' Him") before the triumphant "*But* Him, whom *nocht* in man *or* Deity, / *Or* Daith *or* Dreid *or* Laneliness can touch" (my italics). And the tentative "*Yet ha'e I* Silence left" becomes the radiantly affirmative "*O I ha'e* Silence left" (my italics).

Just as in "O Wha's the Bride," the magic and mystery are skilfully woven. Attaching too limited an interpretation breaks the spell (e.g., Daiches's theory that this silence is "the silence of the man who has lost speech in experience," or Weston's theory that it represents the "collective dumb experiences of all mankind"[39]). The power of this silence is mysterious, its value convincingly and awesomely portrayed in the language, and we need go no further. In the lyric itself the mystery of the silence *deepens* in the paradoxical "wha's deed owre often and has seen owre much"—just as the mystery of the bride deepened in the paradoxical "seed o' a' the men that in / My virgin womb ha'e met." If we attempt to elucidate the mystery any further than it is elucidated in the poem, we shall be restricting its suggestiveness. The power of this

153

silence rests in its paradoxical suggestiveness and in its lack of clear definition.

While this silence is broken by Jean's final comment, its value seems to spread throughout the poem and throws a new light on the entire sequence. Some sort of peace (and the sequence up until now has never been peaceful), some mysterious purity, and some ultimate unity are reached. The quiet affirmation reinforces all the tentative affirmations of the previous sections. There is a gentle peacefulness about the paradox here, a quiet acceptance, a reverent wonder that reconciles all contraries. *This* moment of epiphany remains, as none of the others does, holding together lost Eden, present suffering, and future paradise in an eternal moment of paradox.

The "thing as a whole" that MacDiarmid was "mainly concerned with" is more of a whole because of this moment of peaceful affirmation. The tension is at last relaxed, and the paradox accepted.

The struggle is over, and the vision remains.

CHAPTER FIVE

'Shadows that Feed on the Light'

To Circumjack Cencrastus

The indications in *A Drunk Man* that MacDiarmid had reached a turning point are confirmed by the quality and the nature of the work that followed. While the coda of *A Drunk Man* had suggested that the struggle was over and the vision remained, MacDiarmid's next volume reversed the situation. The vision has been lost, and the struggle remains, more painful than the dynamic balance of the previous work. The balance of the paradox has been upset. Lallans has failed MacDiarmid; and with the departure of the vision and the language, the strength and confidence of the voice are lost. Undoubtedly this failure in confidence must be linked to the psychic risks and anguish that stand behind the *Drunk Man*. Never again, with the exception of "Harry Semen," would MacDiarmid open himself to such an experience.

To Circumjack Cencrastus was advertised by Blackwood's in 1926 (the year of *Penny Wheep* and *A Drunk Man*), but it did not appear until 1930. The four intervening years were both busy and stormy. The lapse in time between *A Drunk Man* and *Circumjack* gives some indication of the turmoil in Grieve's life at this period and stands in contrast to the speed and energy that attended his earlier work. Not only was he becoming increasingly involved in active political work and in the Scottish literary movement, he was also undergoing a personal crisis of immense proportions. Each of these three factors has a bearing on *Circumjack* and on the very obvious differences between it and *A Drunk Man*. Despite these differences, Edwin Muir compared it with *A Drunk Man:* "It is in its own erratic way a sort of whole; like *A Drunk Man Looks at the Thistle,* it is an essay in a very eccentric form which Hugh M'Diarmid has made his own, and may be called the long poem that is not a long poem." [1] But *Circumjack* does not merit this comparison. It is very much less "a sort of whole" than *A Drunk Man,* much less structured and much more erratic. It is more of a ragbag collection, tenuously containing the garnerings of these years, and the image of the curly snake fails to bring these elements into an ordered and meaningful relationship with each other.

MacDiarmid's increasing political concern is much in evidence. From 1925 to 1928 Grieve had served as an Independent Socialist member of the Montrose Town and Parish Council. His early belief in Socialism (he had joined the Independent Labour Party in 1908) carried over into his new interest in Scottish Nationalism, the political movement that parallelled the literary movement in Scotland. In 1927 Grieve was a member of the Scottish National Convention. A founder member of the National Party, he received and accepted the party's invitation to stand as their candidate in Dundee in 1928. This resulted in his active participation in lectures, meetings, and "weekend schools," although he finally withdrew when it became evident, according to the *Scots Independent,* that "he would not get in." [2]

This increasing political concern seems to be linked both to the Scottish literary movement and to MacDiarmid's personal crisis as a poet. In "My Quarrel with the Rose" of *A Drunk Man,* he had given the first explicit hint of a link between English political domination and the shoddy quality of Scottish verse. "The Parrot Cry" of *Circumjack* develops and personalizes this theme. It opens with:

> Tell me the auld, auld story
> O' hoo the Union brocht
> Puir Scotland into being
> As a country worth a thocht.　　　　　　　　　　(p 154)

And the speaker speculates that:

> It's possible that Scotland
> May hear its ain voice speak
> If only we can silence
> This endless-yatterin' beak.　　　　　　　　　　(pp 155-6)

Within the context of *Circumjack* the "blackbird or the mavis," the Scottish bird who is silenced by the "painted foreigner," is identified with the speaker: "I am the mavis o' Pabal / Back on the tap o' the hill." This mavis is attempting to recreate the glories of its earlier song: "And I'll sing as I sang in the past / —If singin' depends upon will." We can interpret this as a metaphor for MacDiarmid's attempt to raise Scottish poetry again to the level it had achieved in the work of Dunbar, or we can interpret it on a more personal level, a *cri de coeur,* lamenting the loss of his initial poetic drive and placing the blame on the shoulders of the English parrot. Both interpretations seem valid, especially in the face of his waning use of Lallans as a poetic language. The Lallans of these poems is much more like English than the Lallans of *Penny Wheep* or *Sangschaw* or the early sections of *A Drunk Man.* Scottish politics seem to attempt, somewhat unsuccessfully, to fill the gap.

Grieve's Socialism is as intimately linked to his poetry as his Nationalism is. The figure of the speaker's boss, like Pound's Mr Nixon, advises, "Cut oot this poetry stuff, my lad." MacDiarmid moves from this into an explicit indictment of the system: "Curse on the system that can gi'e / A coof [fool] like this control o' me," and

> For sae the will to ignorance o' his kind,
> Their line o' least resistance, ruins life
> As wha maun tine through foul disease   *lose*
> The heich ideas wi' which he's rife. . . .   (p 186)

And so the *system* is responsible for the loss of "heich ideas," just as the "clung-kite" family of the speaker, starving because of the system, forces him to remain the " 'Review' reporter still," rather than the Christ-like figure of *A Drunk Man:* "Ech, weel for Christ: for he was never wed / And had nae weans [children] clamourin' to be fed!" (p 187). The evils of society pose a direct threat to the speaker's aims and efforts and thwart his growth. MacDiarmid's political concerns, as they appear in *Circumjack,* appear as almost desperate attempts to explain why the mavis o' Pabal is "wantin' / A wee thing in strength and skill." The pinnacle of achievement reached by the fledgling who "wi' worms like this in its wame / Nae airels sall lack" is now in the past, and MacDiarmid's failure to recapture its "slee and sliggy sang" is transposed into an indictment of the failures of society.

The superiority of the "slee and sliggy sang" over the system emerges, however, with the ring of truth in "Better One Golden Lyric." The earlier confidence shines through, in ironic contrast to the *Circumjack* theme of the dependence of song upon the system: "Better a'e gowden lyric / Than a social problem solved." For a brief moment the poet is once again one of the "unacknowledged legislators of the world":

> Better a'e gowden lyric
> The mob'll never ken

For this in the last resort
Mak's them less apes, mair men,
And leads their leaders albeit
They're owre blin' to see it.

Better a'e gowden lyric
Than Insurance, Bankin', and Law,
Better a'e gowden lyric
Than the Castle's soarin' wa';
Better a'e gowden lyric
Than onything else ava!   *at all*   (p 198)

Although the triumphant tone and the expanding, soaring movement are characteristic of the early lyrics, they are exceptional within *Circumjack,* and the poem appears almost as an ironical note to MacDiarmid's fulminations against "Insurance, Bankin', and Law," the established system. If we flip the coin, MacDiarmid's political concerns appear as the ironic reversal of the earlier confident vision. Now there is a desperate need to improve the poetry, rather than the poetry improving the system as "Better One Golden Lyric" claims it can.

While Grieve was becoming more and more active in politics, he was also becoming more and more active in the Scottish Renaissance movement. *The Scottish Chapbook* was succeeded by *The Scottish Nation, The Northern Review,* and *Contemporary Scottish Studies* (a 1926 collection of articles Grieve had published in *The Scottish Educational Journal* attacking most of the accepted literary figures of Scotland). Short stories in Lallans, articles, propaganda, and literary criticism poured forth from his pen. In 1927 he was instrumental in forming the Scottish branch of P.E.N. In 1928 he attended the Tailltean Games in Dublin where he met the leaders of the Irish Renaissance. Gogarty took him round the pubs which he and Joyce had frequented as medical students. MacDiarmid introduced Yeats to the Social Credit theories of Douglas ("I do not know whether I could call him an apt pupil, but he listened very attentively and now and again lured me into more detailed discussion of certain aspects of the matter"), and to some bawdy lines from Burns's *The Merry Muses,* a poem which Yeats "declared one of the finest obscene poems he had ever heard, a verdict enthusiastically endorsed by Dr. Oliver St. John Gogarty."[3] In 1929, as honorary secretary of the Scottish P.E.N., MacDiarmid was a delegate to the conference in Vienna.

Meanwhile his concept of the aims of the Scottish Renaissance was gradually changing. The original programme in *The Scottish Chapbook* had supported writers in English, Lallans, and Gaelic. Increasingly, however, MacDiarmid now looked to Gaelic as the Ur-language of the Scots. In 1927 he asserted that the "Scottish Renaissance movement is even more concerned with the revival of Gaelic than of Scots."[4] In 1929 he was claiming that the revival of Scots was only a "half-way house"[5] in the movement from English to Gaelic—and in *A Drunk Man* he had already recorded his contempt for half-way houses. Gaelic came to represent to MacDiarmid what Lallans had represented before: a means of re-establishing contact with a more elemental, more pure, and more vital world, in order to create a new Scotland and a new literature. Once again he tries to move back to a pre-Fall Eden, in this case a purely Celtic Scotland, in order to reach a future paradise:

> I took him to the islands
> Where the wells are undefiled
> And folk sing as their fathers sang
> Before Christ was a child.   (p 167)

To MacDiarmid Gaelic represents something very pure, "undefiled," an untouched Eden.

Theoretically he links Gaelic to more than just Scotland and Scottish literature. The movement towards Dostoevski in *A Drunk Man* and the parallel between Scotland and Russia are continued in the concept of synthesis that MacDiarmid is developing in the late twenties and early thirties. This concept is essentially paradoxical in its insistence upon the uniting and balancing of contraries, and it provides yet another example of the characteristic movement of MacDiarmid's mind. The repossession of the Gaelic Eden soon becomes a necessary step in the re-creation of civilization, a grand concept indeed. By 1931 he had fully developed the theory, only emerging in *Circumjack,* that "the old balance or conflict between the North and the South has been violently disrupted by the emergence of Russia and the Soviet concept of things. That constitutes a third side; where is the fourth to come from—not from England; but whence else if not from Gaelic culture—the fourth side upon which European civilization can re-establish itself."[6] By forming this quadrilateral paradox, MacDiarmid unites the Gaelic language, European civilization, politics, and literature, all in an attempt to create a new world by repossessing the lost Eden. While the concept of a balance between Russia and Scotland belongs in the *Drunk Man* frame of reference, the Gaelic element is new. Undoubtedly his 1928 visit to Ireland helped to suggest this development, a method of uniting the Irish and Scottish Renaissances in a common struggle to bring balance, order, and synthesis to Europe.

The results of this theory have an immediate effect on MacDiarmid's poetry and produce a major problem of language. The densest Lallans of the early lyrics was not different in nature, only in degree, from the language that Grieve had spoken as a child. While he mocked those who found "insuperable difficulties" in his Lallans, he must surely have been aware that the movement from English to Lallans would be easier to accomplish, both for the reader and for the poet, than the movement from Lallans to Gaelic. Grieve's knowledge of Gaelic as a child appears to have been minimal, a smattering picked up from Highland relatives; and the Gaelic parts of *Circumjack* consist therefore of phrases, quotations, and references, *not* whole poems written in Gaelic. Grieve was in no position to make this choice. A sympathetic reader, meanwhile, with a minimal exposure to Dunbar or Burns as background and with a glossary as a crutch, can *hear* the Lallans lyrics and understand them too. A line in Gaelic, however, does provide an almost "insuperable difficulty." Unless one has been a student of Celtic or has had a Gaelic background, one does not know how to pronounce the line, let alone find its meaning. One cannot recognize a noun, an adjective, a verb, or even a participle. One backs away, both humbled and infuriated by MacDiarmid's display of knowledge. Few clues lead into these lines. They remain a mystery, both tantalizing and annoying. One line of Gaelic appears more esoteric than an entire lyric in Lallans.

Duncan Glen notes that "it is tempting to suggest that MacDiarmid's interest in Gaelic stems from an unspoken realisation of the failure of the Scots revival—but the facts show that he was stressing the importance of Gaelic while at the height of his Scots period."[7] The date he cites as proof, however, is 1927, a time when the "height of his Scots period" has passed, if we view the central sections of the *Drunk Man* as the turning point. There is very little dense Lallans in *Circumjack*. While MacDiarmid seems to have adopted Gaelic lines as a substitute for Lallans lyrics, Gaelic cannot provide what Lallans provided. The theory behind the adoption of Gaelic is much more grandiose, the results much less impressive. Either because of psychological reasons or because he had exhausted the possibilities of Lallans as he saw it, MacDiarmid had largely stopped writing in Lallans at this point. His language is now, almost entirely, English with a Scottish accent and with a smattering of Gaelic lines, phrases, and references. When in "MacDiarmid's Curses" (p 186), the speaker laments, "Curse on my dooble life and dooble tongue, /—Guid Scots wi' English a' hamstrung," we are much more aware of the poet's language as a bastard form of English. This holds true through most of *Circumjack*. Rather than progressing, as he claimed, further away from English to Gaelic, he has ironically taken a step closer to English, the professed arch-enemy of both the poet and Scotland.

Gradually MacDiarmid was losing his confidence about resurrecting Lallans and Scottish literature. Some private letters to William Soutar, a fellow Scottish poet, detail this. While these letters belong to the early thirties, *Circumjack* and the move towards Gaelic give evidence that the earlier confidence was missing before this time. In 1931 he wrote: "I am quite clear that I am not now nor likely to become—whatever potentialities I may have had in the past—the man to repopularize Scots." And in 1932, "I have been in regard to Scots a thoroughly bad influence on you and others and . . . my own practice in regard to the synthetic business is so purely individual and inimitable that it justifies in my case alone—so far—what in other cases simply clutters up the verse with unvivified and useless words."[8]

It takes a great deal of strength and confidence to hold a paradox together. The addition of Gaelic to the paradoxical vision of synthesis and the suggestion that the "old balance or conflict between the North and the South has been violently disrupted" indicate that the essential balance of the paradox as it appeared in *A Drunk Man* has been "violently disrupted." And not so much by Russia (a factor easily incorporated into the paradoxes of *A Drunk Man*), but by some inner psychic disturbance that makes the old balance no longer possible: "my dooble life and dooble tongue." The most striking element in *Circumjack* is the fading of the vision, and this too must be linked to the personal crisis in Grieve's life. Something in the four years between *A Drunk Man* and *Circumjack* has made the earlier paradoxical vision of synthesis no longer possible. The voice of hope and innocence that was one of the essential ingredients in *A Drunk Man* is drowned out by the voice of despair, of self-disgust, of bitterness, and of elegiac yearning for the lost vision; and it seems probable that the personal crisis was the major factor: "But I am as a man wha's love is deid" (p 188). The extent to which MacDiarmid's vision depended upon the relationship between Grieve and his wife Margaret is revealed through what happens to the vision when that love is no longer an unquestioned reality. The speaker's earlier tributes to his wife (the figure of Jean in *A Drunk Man*, the woman of "The Spur of Love" and "The Light of Life") now appear as indications of the dependence of MacDiarmid's vision. She is the *sine qua non*, the essential ingredient, and as he had indicated in the early lyrics, it is she, the "luvin' wumman," who provides the "searchin' licht" of MacDiarmid's vision.

Very little is known about this personal crisis. Glen provides the bald facts:

> In 1929 he left Montrose and went to London as acting editor of *Vox,* "The Radio Critic and Broadcast Review" edited by Compton Mackenzie. . . . *Vox* lasted only some three months. For MacDiarmid began a period of personal tragedy. After a short spell of unemployment, he went to Liverpool as Publicity Officer of the Liverpool Organisation. . . . He went alone, however, as his wife refused to leave London. After a far from sober year in Liverpool he lost his job and returned to Edinburgh. Almost at once, however, he went back to London to accept responsibility for his broken marriage and was divorced early in 1932. Fortunately for the well-being of MacDiarmid—and of Scottish literature—he met and married Valda Trevlyn.[9]

Although Glen dates the beginning of Grieve's "period of personal tragedy" as early 1930, obviously Grieve's personal troubles had begun before this date. They came to a head in early 1930 with the refusal of his wife to accompany him to Liverpool, and much agony must have preceded his separation. (Undoubtedly the psychic stress behind *A Drunk Man* is an early indication of the approaching crisis).

MacDiarmid himself made few public statements about this period in his life, but the obvious pain with which he approached the subject and the results evident in his poetry bear eloquent witness to its traumatic effect. In *Lucky Poet* he tackles the subject in a direct fashion only twice: "After . . . one most unfortunate interlude in London, and a subsequent year in Liverpool (equally unfortunate, but for other and more painful reasons, and owing perhaps to a considerable extent to my own blame), I have been desperately anxious not to leave Scotland again"; "My story . . . is the story of an absolutist whose absolutes came to grief in his private life (leading to a whole host of slanders responsible for the bad name he has now been given, as a dipsomaniac, wife-beater, and Heaven knows what else)."[10] This crisis, at any rate, was one of immense importance and long-lasting effect. As late as 1934 he was still shaken by it. In the summer of that year, when he was living with Valda and their young son Michael in the Shetland Islands, he seems to have undergone a nervous breakdown of sorts. His close friend David Orr, who was the doctor on Whalsay and who had been instrumental in arranging the Grieves' move to the Shetlands, describes his condition: "physically he was poorly, but in addition there was a certain disorientation, which we later surmised was due to a summation of numerous subconscious 'insults' arising from domestic difficulties a few years previous."[11]

Whatever the precise nature or hidden details of this period in Grieve's life, its effects are there in *Circumjack*. Shadows, dark roots, and mire threaten the light of the earlier vision, and the tone is one of despair, self-disgust, and mourning:

> A burn may dream o' a warld aince mair
> O' water and licht and nocht beside,
> But has ayc as faur to gang as it's gane,
> And a burn in the dark roots' clutch'll bide.

> Tint in a windhaw or siller swirl   *lost*
> Bigger and blacker the roots strike back.   (p 152)

And,

> Sib to dewdrop, rainbow, ocean,
> No' for me their hues and motion.
> This foul clay has filed me till   *defiled*
> It's no' to ken I'm water still.   (p 183)

The trembling moment of vision is past, and the "shadows . . . feed on the licht for aye." Light no longer penetrates darkness; darkness feeds on light, its victory all the more total because of the remembered vision of the past. The word "aince" echoes through these poems. The burn may dream "aince mair," but the "dark roots clutch," and the speaker can "nae mair reply to fire." No moon illuminates this volume, the thistle no longer unites opposites, and "bigger and blacker the roots strike back."

The fading of the vision is transposed into an awareness of the falsity

of the original vision. The vision has betrayed the speaker, has led him to
hope when he should have despaired:

> Nae wonder if I think I see
> A lichter shadow than the neist
> I'm fain to cry: "The dawn, the dawn!
> I see it brakin' in the East."
>   But ah
>   —It's juist mair snaw!   (pp 165-66)

The emptiness of the final vowels ("ah," "snaw") and the despair that
accompanies them stand in poignant contrast to the foolish but human
excitement of "The dawn, the dawn!" The light of the earlier vision is
now no more than a "lichter shadow" which the speaker admits, "I
think I see."

The precarious balance between darkness and light achieved in *A
Drunk Man* has been disturbed, and with it the concept of synthesis that
stands at the centre of the earlier vision. The gap has been increased, and
the powers that separate are stronger: "I doot it needs a Hegel / Sic
opposites to fuse" (p 155), and

> The trouble is that words
> Are a' but useless noo
> To span the gulf atween
> The human and 'highbrow' view.   (p 173)

And it is a *fool* who can dream of the uniting of contraries and the
paradoxical moment of synthesis, in the image of circumjack cencrastus,
the curly snake:

> A fool sings "O it's braw to see
> The mortal coil come adder-like
> Oot o' the heather at yin's feet
> And owre the glintin' water strike
> In corkscrew style and instant glide
> Frae sicht again on yonder side.
>
> "Wad that the Zeitgeist, progress, a'
> The warld's perplexities thegither
> Micht as sma-bookit slide across   *shrunken*
> Oor vision in the sunny weather,
> And leave the gowden warld ahint
> Withoot a single crinkle in't." . . .   (p 158)

The vision of paradoxical synthesis is now the vision of a fool, no longer the vision of a drunk man; and it is a vision that is hoped for, rather than experienced: "Wad that."

As the gap between the two sides of the paradox increases, the speakers search for a more desperate solution—a clean, clear-cut, violent separation which would resolve the agony with one blow, divide the paradoxical elements, and destroy the painful link between them. It is tempting to parallel this movement with Grieve's separation from his wife and to link it up with his increasing political concern to cut Scotland free from England. The parrot must be killed in order to set free the "native Scottish bird":

> And gin that disna dae, lads,
> We e'en maun draw its neck
> And heist its body on a stick
> A' ither pests to check. (p 156)

The speaker's poetry, whose function in *A Drunk Man* was "to bring to be / At lang, lang last that unity," now becomes a weapon to kill, to separate, and to cleave the paradox in two:

> Scots steel tempered wi' Irish fire
> Is the weapon that I desire. (p 197)

> If there's a sword-like sang
> That can cut Scotland clear
> O' a' the warld beside
> Rax me the hilt o't here,   *reach*

> For there's nae jewel till
> Frae the rest o' earth it's free,
> Wi' the starry separateness
> I'd fain to Scotland gie. . . . (p 201)

Synthesis has failed, and separation must take its place.

The role of sexuality has correspondingly altered. The representatives of the male and female principles coming together in the sexual act constitute another side of the vision that is now dying or dead. Sex becomes something despised, or remembered, or imagined, just as the vision of synthesis is something despised ("A Fool Sings"), or remembered ("I wha aince in Heaven's height"), or imagined ("A burn may dream o' a warld aince mair"). Sex is relegated to the same position that Lallans occupies, a half-way house: "While sex and ither hauf way stages / Perish wi' the barbarous Ages" (p 175). The dark roots strike back as "whiles through a high-falutin' o' love / I hear my body mockin' my talk" (p 152). The balance between disgust and wonder that trembled in "Love" is no longer possible.

Jean, the drunk man's "Light of Life," does not appear in these poems, but her ghost is present: a remembered and lost love, merging with the dreamed-up figure of Valéry's Athikte:

> Athikte I dreamt that you were here
> Lyin' by me like a wumman in the daurk.
> I heard the breathin' o' the seven seas
> Faint as the matins o' a licht-lost lark,
> —Or was it my ain happy hert that passed
> My hearin', and was tint in sleep at last . . .   *lost*
> Athikte, I thocht I kent I didna ken
> Which o's was you and which me, then.
> The haill warld pillowed on my shouder, licht.
> As gin I'd been the sun by nicht.
>
> Athikte I dreamt that you were here
> But I am as a man wha's love is deid.
> She comes in a' her beauty to his bed
> But when he wauks, the toom nicht's there insteed   *empty*
> Sae a' the poet's moods I hae
> Look in the cruel licht o' day
> As silly as an effort to
> Cuddle a ghaist my airms gang through.
> And ilka sang is like a moon
> That hings, a bonny aught, at noon. . . .   (pp 187-88)

The sun at night is the dream; the moon at noon the reality. The vision is tentative ("I thocht I kent I didna ken"), both dreamed and remembered. And the lark is "licht-lost," the song "a bonny aught." The vision and the poetry are recognized as interdependent, both of them the ghosts of the "wumman in the daurk," the lost love who appears only in dreams and memories. In *A Drunk Man* this woman was a "licht," the source of the paradoxical vision, and the speaker awoke from the dream of the great wheel to the reality of Jean. Now he awakens from the dream of Athikte to the "toom nicht" and to an awareness of her and his poetry as a "ghaist my airms gang through."

The elegiac tone that is dominant in this volume is linked to the lost love, the lost vision, and the lost poetry. It is also closely linked to Grieve's memories of Langholm, the lost Eden of his boyhood. As the balance of the paradox becomes upset, MacDiarmid turns to the memories of Langholm, just as he turns towards Gaelic, in order to re-establish contact with an earlier and more vital world in an attempt to give back to the paradox the balance that has been destroyed. Even the title of *Circumjack* comes from Langholm—a serpentine path near the town which was known as the "Curly Snake." Langholm, like the Garden of Eden itself, has its own serpent. As late as 1955 MacDiarmid wrote of the path known as the "Curly Snake": "It has always haunted my imagination and has probably constituted . . . the ground-plan and pattern of my mind." [12] The characteristically paradoxical movement of his mind (back to a repossession of Eden in order to move with the curly snake into a new world of gods) is revealed in *Circumjack* as a movement back to Langholm. Paradoxically too, when the origins of this basic thrust are most in evidence, as in *Circumjack,* the future Eden seems most uncertain. The failure of Grieve's marriage seems to lead back to Langholm, to a re-examination of the source, and it shatters the earlier confidence that had, perhaps unconsciously, used Langholm as a base.

In prose writings nearer to the time of *Circumjack* he suggests a connection between Langholm and his marital problems, with the figure of a child serving as the link. When he quotes in *Lucky Poet* the autobiographical poem dealing with his father's death and with his relationship with his Langholm relatives, he adds: "I wrote these verses at a time when I realised, with terrible distress, that, against my will, the ties between my wife and two children, Christine and Walter, were about to be broken no less completely than I had allowed the ties between myself and my relatives in Langholm and elsewhere to break." [13] The separation between himself and his wife has been transposed here into a consideration of the separation between his wife and children, and linked to Grieve's own childhood, his father's death, and his memories of Langholm. His personal crisis has thrown him back to recollections of the earlier crisis (his father's death), and to Langholm—the ultimate source. In "My Native Place," an essay filled with recollections of Langholm and published in 1931, he writes:

In all my published poetry there is, I think, but one lyric in *A Drunk Man* ["The Crying of the Fair"] and a few lines of allusion in *To*

Circumjack Cencrastus [the title and "Losh! They'd ha' put me a brass plate up / In Langholm Academy"] devoted to it. And yet, within the past year or two I have found myself . . . caught up in happy recollections of it. . . . One of the main reasons for this, probably, is the fact that my own children are domiciled in London, and that I cannot but compare the quality of the childhood available to them with my own childhood's happy playground.[14]

Once again MacDiarmid has linked his children's position (a partial disguise at least) with his childhood memories. He continues:

But for myself—and perhaps for them, if a return to Langholm or any like spot (and there is no like spot—no spot quite like) is impossible—if ever I go "out of the world and into Langholm again", it will only be in dreams or in my poet's craft in which, perchance, I may yet find words for some of the felicities I remember and to which (despite all my subsequent divergence of interest and effort) the texture of my spirit must owe incomparably more than I can ever repay or acknowledge.[15]

Whatever the precise psychological reasons behind this reaching back to Langholm, *Circumjack* attests to the upsetting of the paradoxical vision of synthesis and to a link between this lost vision and Grieve's memories of his lost childhood. The fading of the vision has resulted in the elegiac tone that predominates: "Lourd on my hert as winter lies / The state that Scotland's in the day" (p 165); "But I'm lanely, and flute as I will, / There's nae sign o' a mate to be seen" (p 154); "El Rey de Escocia no es nada" (p 179); "I wha aince in Heaven's height" (p 183); "Strangers are in my true love's hame" (p 197); "And hoo should I forget the Langfall" (p 200); "And yet you mind, dear, on the bridal hill" (p 201); "But I am as a man wha's love is deid" (p 188); "And weel I mind ane came / And kindled in oor lyart hills / What look't like livin' flame" (p 201). Langholm and the lost Eden that is associated with it are linked to this, present in more ways than the "few lines of allusion" that MacDiarmid recognizes.

Whenever MacDiarmid writes in prose about Langholm, he emphasizes the importance of the three rivers that flow through the town, and these rivers provide him with the major motif of *Circumjack*—the image of water. This image does more to unite the sequence than the image of the curly snake. Like the thistle, water is an intermediary between darkness and light, the host of each. It appears sometimes as tears, or as a "watergaw," a much more painful image than light *per se*. And in the waters of *Circumjack,* darkness is usually a powerful force.

MacDiarmid has written that his first experience of the world, an experience he does not remember but that has been related to him, was being carried outside as an infant in his mother's arms to see "the Esk frozen over so hard that carts and horses could go upon it for twenty miles as upon a road."[16] From the very first, water is a medium—subject, like the thistle, to almost magical metamorphoses. His Langholm memories continually emphasize this:

> My earliest impressions are of . . . strange and subtle relationships of light and water—
>
> > The recurrent vividness of light and water
> > Through every earthly change of mood and scene,
>
> and of a multitude of rivers, each with its distinct music and each catering in the most exciting way for hosts of the most stimulating and wholesome pleasures. . . . These were, indeed, the champagne days . . . on the Esk, the Wauchope, and the Ewes.[17]

Once again, water is subject to metamorphosis, an integral part of his "enchanted" childhood days.

And so, as in Grieve's mind the vision fades and the memories of Langholm stir, in the poetry of MacDiarmid light and darkness struggle for dominance in the image of water. The "jostling of contraries" of the thistle and the "chitterin' licht" of the vision are transformed into a terrible struggle where darkness is usually victorious. Three distinct states emerge: the victory of darkness; the victory of light, nearly always qualified as belonging to the past or to the future or to the elusive Gaelic culture; and an in-between stage where light and darkness battle together in the waters of the poet's craft.

Darkness is victorious in the "shaddows that feed on the licht for aye." One side of the paradox threatens to consume the other. While the burn may dream of a world of "water and licht and nocht beside," the roots will strike back "bigger and blacker." The speaker is now "buriet in the mire" to such an extent that "it's no' to ken I'm water still." Darkness gives way to light for a brief moment before its final victory:

Water nor licht nor yet the barley field
That shak's in silken sheets at ilka braith,
Its lang nap thrawin' the quick licht aboot
In sic a maze that tak's and gies at aince
As fair oot-tops the coontless ripplin' sea.
There's nae chameleon like the July fields;
Their different colours change frae day to day
While they shift instantly neath the shiftin' licht
Yet they're owre dull for this, stagnant and dull;
And even your een, beloved, and your hair
Are like the barley and the sea and Heaven
That flaw and fail and are defeated by
    The blind turns o' chance.   (pp 199-200)

MacDiarmid has moved far beyond the confident vision of the "breists like stars." The "blind turns o' chance" have darkened the speaker's love: "the barley and the sea and Heaven." The parallel between "the barley and the sea and Heaven" and "flaw and fail and are defeated" pinpoints the movement from darkness to light. The "chitterin' licht" of the earlier vision has become the "shiftin' licht" that makes a chameleon of the July fields and of the remembered sexual act.

When light is victorious, its victory is qualified. In the Gaelic culture, an untouched Eden, the speaker finds what he is searching for:

I took him to the islands
Where the wells are undefiled
And folk sing as their fathers sang
Before Christ was a child.   (p 167)

The wells of the islands and of the Gaelic culture are "undefiled," because they have bypassed European civilization completely. Because of their purity, these wells offer, like Christ, a hope for the salvation of mankind. Eden before the Fall, Christ, and the world of childhood gather in these waters. By going back into the past, the speaker can regain the vision of light and pure water, an essential component in the paradoxical vision. And by going forward into the future, moving directly to the future paradise, the speaker can reach a similar vision:

But a' the stream o' consciousness
In maitter as in a tunnel lost
'll yet win free and jaw   *wave, spurt*

170

> Owre the world's edge tost
> Like a gowden waterfall.   (p 173)

The soaring movement of these lines and the image of the flooding
waterfall suggest that this vision is sexual in origin—as does the word
"jaw." Despite the absence in *Circumjack* of a woman comparable to
Jean and despite the speaker's renunciation of "maitter," the vision of
future fulfilment is still dependent upon a sexual metaphor; and this
makes the link between the present and future very tenuous indeed. The
elegiac tone of the volume as a whole militates against such a leap of
imagination, a movement that was much more convincing within the
framework of *A Drunk Man*. There the relationship between past,
present, and future was intricate, complex, and binding. Now the upset
balance of the paradox makes the clutching of the dark roots too
powerful, and the relationship between present and future remains
unclear.

The vision which concludes *Circumjack,* "My Love Is to the Light of
Lights," is as precarious as the golden waterfall. The first three stanzas
suggest that this love is a woman, similar to the mysterious bride in her
ability to eradicate the past:

> My love is to the light of lights
> As a gold fawn to the sun
> And men, wha love ocht else, to her
> Their ways ha' scarce begun.
>
> For God their God's a jealous God
> And keeps her frae their sight
> He hasna had her lang eneuch
> Himsel' to share his delight,
>
> And kens gin he'd been worth his saut
> He'd ha' made her first, no' last,
> Since but a'e glimpse, a'e thocht, o' her
> Discredits a' the Past.   (p 202)

But the speaker's love undergoes an unexpected transformation. This
woman is not a woman of flesh and blood at all. She is one side of the
paradox without the other:

> My love she is the hardest thocht
> That ony brain can ha'e,

> And there is nocht worth ha'en in life
> That doesna lead her way.

This transformation is both undercut and supported in the final stanza by an elusive image of water and light with implicit sexual connotations:

> My love is to a' else that is
> As meaning's meaning, or the sun
> Men see ahint the sunlight whiles
> Like lint-white water run. . . .   (p 203)

The sexual metaphor links water and light in a convincing metamorphosis, but it detracts from the identification of "my love" with the "hardest thocht"—especially when considered in relation to "Strangers are in my true love's hame," and "I am as a man wha's love is deid." The elegiac tone of the volume casts a shadow on this triumphant vision. The background that could make the vision credible is missing, both in this lyric and in the volume as a whole. Meanwhile, the obvious difficulty that MacDiarmid is having with language contributes to the shaky confidence. The first line, "My love is to the light of lights," leads us to expect standard English (otherwise "licht o' lichts"), as does the second, "As a gold fawn to the sun," while the third suddenly gives the speaker a strong Scottish accent. This strange feeling of the speaker being caught between two languages continues in the second stanza where "sight" and "delight" continue the English pattern, despite the "ocht" and "thocht" of the surrounding stanzas. The disconcerting feeling caused by this continues, especially in the climactic stanza where "ahint the sunlight" rings uneasily as Lallans mixed with English. The insecurity of the voice does nothing to support the already shaky vision.

The combination of light and water is more convincing when darkness is also present, however agonizing the paradoxical relationship between them may be. The vision of the fool is beautiful, and more beautiful *because* the speaker realizes its folly: "And leave the gowden warld ahint / Withoot a single crinkle in't." But these *were* the champagne days, the July fields are a chameleon, and it is a fool who wishes that all the world's perplexities "micht as sma-bookit [shrunken] slide across / Oor vision in the sunny weather."

The passage describing the dream of Athikte holds darkness and light together in excruciating tension:

> I heard the breathin' o' the seven seas
> Faint as the matins o' a licht-lost lark.　　　　　　　　(p 187)

Although the lark is "licht-lost," it is singing, and the song, faint as it may be, is like the "breathin' o' the seven seas." The "haill warld" is "pillowed on my shouder, licht, / As gin I'd been the sun by nicht," with the lovely pun on "licht" (weightless, filled with light). The beauty of the vision is accentuated by its loss—which indeed is an ingredient in the vision itself ("licht-lost," "faint")—and by the awakening to the "toom [empty] nicht's there insteed," empty rather than weightless, and dark as the hell to which the speaker returns.

The fading of MacDiarmid's vision does not necessarily detract from the power of his poetry as these lines bear witness. However the damage to Grieve's psyche that led to the upset paradox and gave to darkness a consuming power, coupled with the problem of language and linked to his developing literary and political activities, makes this a tortured volume. It lacks the power, the intensity, and the discipline of *A Drunk Man*. Athikte has become a "connached [spoiled] mermaid," and the "bride that cairries the bunch / O' thistles blinterin' white" dissolves into the "hardest thocht / That ony brain can ha'e."

With the departure of the vision and the bride, MacDiarmid has become the "mavis o' Pabal, / A pool cut aff frae the sea." And the song of the "licht-lost lark" is only a faint memory of the "breathin' o' the seven seas" and of the richly suggestive lyricism of *A Drunk Man*.

CHAPTER SIX

'Labradorite Crystals'

Scots Unbound and *Stony Limits*

If in *Circumjack* MacDiarmid had become the "mavis o' Pabal, / A pool cut aff frae the sea," *Scots Unbound and Other Poems* (1932) represents an attempt to bring the sea back to the pool, and *Stony Limits and Other Poems* (1934) an attempt to find another sea. The problem of language that was so noticeable in *Circumjack* remains largely unresolved. These volumes bear witness that the damage to Grieve's psyche has created problems of language, form, emotion, and control, and each of these is linked to the upset balance of the paradox. Only with great pain, difficulty, and risk, can MacDiarmid regain the lost vision.

The imagery becomes colder, and frequently the emotion is so "chilled" that we are left with an empty shell of language. At other times, the emotion is almost out of control, dancing along the razor's edge of madness. It is to language that MacDiarmid turns in order to redress the upset balance. But although he concentrates a great deal of effort on finding a language to bolster up the lost vision, language on its own cannot restore the paradox. When he finds the courage to face the agony of his loss and to accept the disparity between past and present, the paradox takes shape and the words come to him. Rarely does this happen when he is concentrating on experimentation with language. Despite his attempts to recover the lost voice of *A Drunk Man* and to find a new voice, neither of these voices is as strong or as confident as the voice he once possessed.

In 1953 in the introduction to the second edition of *A Drunk Man*, MacDiarmid recognized in a rare moment of candour the effect the crisis in his personal life had had upon his poetry: "Crises in my personal life deflected me from following up the "*Drunk Man*" line myself."[1] In the 1967 introduction to *A Lap of Honour* he more characteristically compares himself with Heine in his effort "to break up the unity of the lyric and introduce new material . . . on different levels of significance."

He concludes: "It took Heine years of agonised effort to find the new form he needed, and his later work, in which he did find it, never won a measure of esteem like that secured by his early work. So it is in my case."[2] All this talk of form omits any mention of language, a much more crucial issue in the light of the success of the *Drunk Man* which combined new form with the old voice. MacDiarmid's own "years of agonised effort" are evident both in *Scots Unbound* and in *Stony Limits,* and the effort is aimed almost entirely at coping with the problem of language. As he notes in his introduction to the "combined edition" of 1956,

> Both were largely experimental, the first [*Scots Unbound*] in an extended use of *synthetic Scots* but also of modern scientific terminology, and the second [*Stony Limits*] in an endeavour to employ recondite elements of the English vocabulary. Each in its different but complementary way marked steps in the transition from my earlier volumes of lyrics toward my later "world view" poems.[3]

More importantly, each marks a stage in MacDiarmid's attempt to find a suitable language, a replacement for the unsatisfactory "dooble tongue" of *Circumjack*.

In 1923 when MacDiarmid expounded the theory behind the adoption of Lallans as a poetic language, he revealed the rather shaky logical conection between the language of the early lyrics and the new languages with which he was experimenting in the early 1930's: "if the next century is to see an advance in mental science equal to that which last century has marked in material science, then the resumption of the Scots Vernacular is . . . inevitable."[4] In *Scots Unbound* he is attempting to recover the language of *A Drunk Man,* "the extended use of synthetic Scots," and to inject into it "modern scientific terminology"—perhaps in an attempt to hide his lack of confidence with the language he had previously used with such power and ease. Realizing consciously or unconsciously his failure to recapture the lost voice, he turns in *Stony Limits* to an "extended use" of "modern scientific terminology" and other "recondite elements of the English vocabulary." The Scots vernacular must finally give way to the language of material science, an unexpected, yet strangely logical step.

The language of *Scots Unbound* also marks the desire to "go out of the world and into Langholm again." The return to the images of Langholm (in *Circumjack*) moves into a return to the language of

175

Langholm, dense "synthetic Scots." The most experimental poem in the volume is "Water Music," which is framed by a stanza that takes us "out of the world and into Langholm again" and invites comparison with Joyce's experiments with language:

> Wheesht, wheesht, Joyce, and let me hear
> Nae Anna Livvy's lilt,
> But Wauchope, Esk, and Ewes again,
> Each wi' its ain rhythm till't.   (p 270)

The poem is a strange and uneven *tour de force,* carried along by an insistent rhythm and by a somewhat irregular movement through the alphabet, no doubt helped along by *Jamieson's Dictionary*. A's ("Archin' here and arrachin' there, / Allevolie or allemand") give way to b's ("Brent on or boutgate or beschact / Bellwaverin' or bornheid"). Roughly midway through the poem two stanzas takes us from p to t:

> And 'twixt the pavvy o' the Wauchope,   *bustle*
> And the paspey o' the Ewes,   *dance*
> And the pavane o' Esk itsel',   *dance*
> It's no' for me to choose.
>
> Be they querty, be they quiet,   *lively*
> Flow like railya or lamoo,   *satin, wool*
> Only turn a rashmill or   *toy mill*
> Gar a' the country tew   *toil*
>   (p 272)

The tone is frolicsome, delighting in the onomatopoeic qualities of Lallans, but an important ingredient seems to be missing. Emotion—the tenderness of "The Watergaw" or "Bonnie Broukit Bairn," or the violence of "The Looking Glass"—has departed, leaving an empty shell of language for its own sake. We can marvel at the skill, we can hear the rushing water, but we are not moved in any deep way. When the speaker concludes, somewhat weakly,

> Lappin' on the shirrel,   *turf*
> Or breengin' doon the cleuch,   *charging, ravine*
> I can listen to the waters
> Lang—and no' lang—eneuch   (p 273)

we feel a sort of relief that he has finally called a halt. The farewell stanza which repeats "Wheesht, wheesht, Joyce," punctuates the poem, but leaves the reader still unsatisfied, conscious of the disparity between MacDiarmid's use of Lallans in his early lyrics and the showmanship of this poem.

"Tarras," the one other poem that displays the "extended use of synthetic Scots," is much more successful in its ability to move the reader. Its structure, language, and tension are reminiscent of "Gairmscoile." Both poems present a vision of primitive and savage sexual strength, and the primal qualities of Lallans reinforce the vision. In "Gairmscoile," the speaker indicated at the beginning that it is "deep in the herts o' a' men" that these monsters lurk. In "Tarras," the speaker indicates in the first line a different point of reference: "This Bolshevik bog! Suits me doon to the grun'!" He continues:

> Little the bog and the masses reck
> O' some dainty-davie or fike-ma-fuss.   *fastidious*
> Ho for the mother of usk and adder
> Spelderin' her in her coal and madder   *sprawling*
> Faur frae Society's bells and bladder.   (p 274)

Just as the major tension in "Gairmscoile" rested on juxtaposition of twentieth-century Freudian insight with ancient vision and language, so here the major tension rests on the juxtaposition of Marxist ideology with ancient vision and language. The reference and the relationship having been established (as in "Gairmscoile"), the speaker moves into a presentation of the vision itself—sexual union between man and the essential earth, with not a trace of sophistication or gentleness about her:

> And drulie water like sheepeik seeps   *muddy, grease*
> Through the duffie peats, and cranglin' creeps,   *spongy, winding*
> Crowdles like a crab, syne cowds awa',   *crawls, floats*
> Couthless eneuch, yet cuttedly tae . . .   *tartly*
>   (p 274)

The winsome alliteration of "Water Music" pales in comparison with the brute strength of the language here—the savage long "ee," the relentlessly harsh "c"'s and "r"'s, the howl of "ow" and "ou."

The contrast between sexual union with the earth and sexual union with a woman (and the implicit contrast between the primal strength of Marxism and Capitalistic degeneracy) emerges not only from the language, but also from dramatically suggestive imagery, rhythmic movement, and rhyme:

177

Ah, woman-fondlin'! What is that to this?
Saft hair to birssy heather, warm kiss   *bristly*
To cauld black waters' suction.
Nae ardent breists' erection
But the stark hills!

The strength of the "birssy heather" and the "cauld black waters' suction" and the erection of the "stark hills" (stripped of all pretension, naked in the sexual act) makes "woman-fondlin' " seem trivial and insignificant, sentimental and "fond." The speaker continues:

In what dry-gair-flow   *where two hills join*
Can I pillow my lowin' cheek here   *burning*
Wi' nae paps' howe below?   *hollow*
What laithsome parodies appear
O' my body's secrets in this oorie growth   *weird*
Wi' its peerieweeries a' radgie for scouth   *smallest things ready*
And the haill ratch and rive o' a warld uncouth?   *for freedom*

The climactic "ratch and rive" (wrenching and tearing) parallel the progression from p to "railya" and "rashmill" in "Water Music." But here the effect is more than just an intellectual exercise; it is the inevitable result of the "peerieweeries a' radgie for scouth," the earth heaving in orgasm, and the movement of the line heaves in sympathy.

The language used by MacDiarmid in this poem contributes far more than any logic could to the parallel between Marxism and Tarras. The language is a basic ingredient in the vision, *the* convincing factor, just as the language of "Gairmscoile" was a basic ingredient in its vision. "Water Music" and "Tarras," however, are the only two poems in the volume that experiment purely with the extended use of synthetic Scots. The others are either short lyrics, or a mixture of languages. For example, the title poem, a "Divertissement Philologique," uses Lallans, English with a light Scots accent, scientific vocabulary, and abstruse words and phrases from other languages:

Bestail, grains, vins, fruictz.
Haithi, timrjan, thaurnus, blowans.
Fani hugs, Hwaiwa us siggis?
Silence, come oot o' him!
Keep oot, che' vor ye![5]

The footnotes illuminate these lines to a certain extent: Rabelais, the Wufilic Gospel, Christ's words to the unclean spirit in the synagogue at Nazareth, and a quotation from *Lear*. The effect that remains, however, is one of incantation, like the disciples speaking (rather comically) in tongues at Pentecost. As in "Water Music," the sound is impressive, but emotional movement and purpose are missing, and the whole soon becomes tedious.

In one magnificent lyric, "Milk-Wort and Bog-Cotton," MacDiarmid succeeds in recapturing the voice of the early lyrics. While he claimed that the whole volume was "experimental," two of the most successful poems are recapturings of earlier voices and techniques, rather than experiments. "Tarras" goes back to "Gairmscoile," and "Milk-Wort and Bog-Cotton" goes back to the early Lallans lyrics for its language, tone, structure, movement, and control. In this lyric MacDiarmid manages to re-create the paradox and to re-establish the balance, while recognizing its immensely precarious nature. The poem centres on the paradox of light and darkness, the dependence of light on darkness, and the terrible suffering that is the price men must pay for "licht." The theme can be interpreted on many levels: the relationship between genius and suffering; a Marxist awareness of human misery; a harking back to the lost vision; a description of the human condition. Both the open-endedness which keeps the mystery of the vision intact and the initial presentation of a compelling image are characteristic of MacDiarmid's early work, but the pain that holds the paradox together belongs very much to this period in his writing:

> Cwa' een like milk-wort and bog-cotton hair!   *come away*
> I love you, earth, in this mood best o' a'
> When the shy spirit like a laich wind moves   *low*
> And frae the lift nae shadow can fa'   *sky*
> Since there's nocht left to throw a shadow there
> Owre een like milk-wort and milk-white cotton hair.   (p268)

The central image, "een like milk-wort and bog-cotton hair," is as suggestive and dream-like as the "breists like stars" of the bride of *A Drunk Man*, and the first stanza moves lazily and dreamily around this image, just as the "laich wind" and the "shy spirit" move slowly around the woman-earth. Milk-wort is a blue flower, hence its association with eyes, but the insistent connotation is one of whiteness and maternity. Similarly bog-cotton is a silky plant, hence its association with hair, but once again the insistent connotation is one of whiteness and maternity, reinforced by the transformation to "milk-white cotton hair." The image itself contains the mystery—a strange, beautiful, virginal (white, "shy spirit") woman who is a mother. The rhythmic balance of the line ("een like milk-wort and bog-cotton hair") cups the mystery in its hands, just as the first and last lines gently contain and define the paradox.

The second and concluding stanza consists of a prayer that this vision might not be transient, counterbalanced by a painful awareness of the impossibility of this prayer:

> Wad that nae leaf upon anither wheeled
> A shadow either and nae root need dern   *hide*
> In sacrifice to let sic beauty be!
> But deep surroondin' darkness I discern
> Is aye the price o' licht. Wad licht revealed
> Naething but you, and nicht nocht else concealed.   (p 269)

The pain of this stanza stands in moving contrast to the dreamlike quality of the first stanza. Thematically it grows from the hint of the second line in the first stanza: "I love you, earth, *in this mood* best o' a'," with its suggestion of transience. Structurally it grows from the "een" of the first and last lines of the first stanza. The piercing "ee," which in the first stanza was shrouded in gentleness, is now developed as a climactically darkening sound. Each line of the second stanza increases the darkness and the pain of the long "ee": "leaf," "wheeled," "need," "be," "deep," "revealed," "concealed." Simultaneously the "l" of "milk-wort," "milk-white," "lift," and "licht" is counterbalanced and finally vanquished by two ominous trios ("deep"-"darkness"-"discern" and "naething"-"nicht"-"nocht," with "nicht," through association, appearing as a negative as well as a dark power). The control, the poise, the discretion, and the emotional subtlety of this lyric seem, in the context of *Scots Unbound,* like a voice from the past. It is much more moving than any of the more superficially intellectual poems in the volume, with their Joycean experiments in language or their scientific terminology. Here MacDiarmid has succeeded in recapturing the voice and the skill of the early lyrics, but now this voice is exceptional, rather than characteristic. Meanwhile, the pain through which the paradox takes form is an indication of the courage required by MacDiarmid to recapture the lost voice and to face the disparity between what was and what is.

While MacDiarmid had gone "out of the world and into Langholm again" in his attempt to recapture the lost voice, he has also returned to Langholm in his use of the image of water, once again the major *leitmotif,* but now it is presented almost exclusively as an element linked to metamorphosis or creative movement. For example, in "Water Music" the present participles that hold the poem together create the impression of water continuously in motion, just as the present participles of "A Moment in Eternity" presented light as continuously in motion. The onward-rushing rhythm contributes to the effect of rushing water. The water in "Tarras" also moves, more slowly but just as inevitably, with sudden bursts of speed that vary the movement of the poem. In "Cheville" the water is the water of the Great Flood, "towering like God over the spirits of men," so that the stream appears as a "tiger-cub torrent," representative of the same kind of terrible power as Blake's tyger. This power is related, however, to destruction rather than to creation (the point of view in Blake's lyric), and the speaker hovers between pity for those destroyed and admiration for the power that destroyed them: "Seeing, and sorry for, all drowned things, sorry / Yet with, *cheville,* a sense of God's glory" (p 276).

The admiration and fear of a power before which man seems to "outgrow / His mortality in huge recognition" (p 276) is an indication of the new role that pre-Fall Eden is assuming in the paradoxical vision. The clear purity of the earlier Eden (the bride in *A Drunk Man,* or the Gaelic culture "where the wells are undefiled") has been muddied, disturbed, and made more fearsome. The increasing strength of darkness has cast a shadow over the early, elemental world, as the balance of the paradox moves in favour of the dark powers. It is still possible to plunge to the depths of the pool of humanity in order to emerge transformed, but the bottom of the pool is muddy. By going beyond woman, back to the bog of Tarras, one resurrects a primal strength before which the modern world seems weak, and this strength will crush anything in its grasp. The gentle innocence of Eden is no longer possible.

As a result of this development, the movement back into the past in order to reach future paradise no longer seems either as simple or as desirable as it once did. A cold detachment seems to accompany the muddying of the vision. For example, the theme is presented in a strangely detached and ironic manner in "Dytiscus," where once again the image of water as the source of man, the medium through which he may reach metamorphosis, is basic. The source is much less pure, however, and the future triumph much less attractive. Each item in the paradox (past, present, and future) has become paradoxical:

> The problem in the pool is plain.
> Must men to higher things ascend
> For air like the Dytiscus there,
> Breathe through their spiracles, and turn
> To diving bells and seek their share
> Of sustenance in the slime again
> Till they clear life, as he his pool
> To starve in purity, the fool,
> Their finished faculties mirrored, fegs,
> Foiled-fierce as his three pairs of legs?
> Praise be Dytiscus-men are rare.
> Life's pool still foul and full of fare.
> Long till to suicidal success attain
> We water-beetles of the brain! (p 277)

The controlled and distanced irony is a new tone for MacDiarmid and one of the most successful experiments in *Scots Unbound*. It is far removed from the violence that characterized his disgust before this: "Lap up your ugsome aidle wi' the lave." The emotion is there, but it is firmly controlled, almost Popean in its cleverness and sophistication, and colder than the unmitigated rage of some of his earlier work. The detachment of the scientist seems to be the pose, a clinically ironic attitude. The speaker of "Dytiscus" could never feel the excitement of the speaker in "Sea Serpent" when he sees "the spirit o' God gaed dirlin' through't / In stound upon stound o' pride." The sense of pulsating life, warm energy, and raw emotion has departed from MacDiarmid's work at this time, and the speaker is able to stand back and observe ironically: "Praise be Dytiscus-men are rare. / Life's pool still foul and full of fare." The bitterness comes through with vigour, but it has been tempered and filtered by the intervening irony.

The lack of warm emotion evident in this scientific attitude is also noticeable in the imagery of this volume. A chill pervades the air. In "Antenora" the speaker describes the state of Scotland in terms of frozen water, ice which must be thawed:

> The stream is frozen hard. Going by
> This wintry spectacle I descry

<blockquote>
How even Edinburgh folk may be
In Scotland, not Antenora, yet,
Not traitors to their land, condemned
To a frore fate in Cocytus' pit,
But seasonably Scottish in their way,
And thaw, though hellish slow, some day!   (p 284)
</blockquote>

The state of Scotland is something that "I descry," rather than feel, and the emotion surfaces only in the final line, "though hellish slow," where the speaker's pain is camouflaged by the ironic pun on "hellish."

The need to warm and to break the curse of coldness emerges in another strange poem—"Why I Became a Scottish Nationalist." The metaphor of warming up a cold woman in the act of love is appropriate to a description of MacDiarmid's attempts to revitalize Scotland, but the emotion that lies behind the poem is as cold as the woman described. The speaker wants his "smeddum to prove / In scenes like these," and compares himself to Pushkin:

<blockquote>
My time for flichty conquests by,
Valuing nae mair some quick-fire cratur'
Wha hurries up the ways o' natur'.   (p 276)
</blockquote>

By implication, he cares nothing for the woman, nor for Scotland, but only for the challenge of this cold struggle:

<blockquote>
But wi' nae raptur, cauldly there,
Open but glowerin' callously,
Yet slow but surely heat until
You catch my flame against your will
And the mureburn tak's the hill.   annual burning of the moor
    (p 276)
</blockquote>

Victory in the face of all odds is the irresistible bait. The speaker's cold approach and his deliberate manipulation of the woman indicate how far MacDiarmid has moved from the youthful vision of "Consummation" and "A Moment in Eternity." In these earlier poems the speaker was set alight by the flame of the woman and by a god-like spirit. Now, like a distant god himself, he glories in his victory over the woman and over Scotland.

The coldness of the speaker's approach, noticeable in "Dytiscus," "Antenora," and "Why I Became a Scottish Nationalist," is at its most effective when linked explicitly to grief or loneliness, as in "Of John Davidson." The emotions aroused by Grieve's memories of his father's death and Davidson's death (darkness, grief, loneliness) give this poem an impact which the other "cold" poems lack. There is nothing warm here, but the emptiness and the coldness are human qualities, human reactions to death:

> I remember one death in my boyhood
> That next to my father's, and darker, endures;
> Not Queen Victoria's, but Davidson, yours,
> And something in me has always stood
> Since then looking down the sandslope . . .　　　　(p 284)

The distance maintained by the speaker throughout locks in tension with the undercurrents of emotion: the simple but telling "and darker," the surge of emotion in the final lines,

> On your small black shape by the edge of the sea,
> —A bullet-hole through a great scene's beauty,
> God through the wrong end of a telescope.　　　　(p 284)

The relentless stresses of "smáll bláck shápe" and "greát scéne's beáuty" hammer out the speaker's grief. MacDiarmid in the two penultimate lines accustoms the reader's ear to a link between a group of three stresses and a group of two. This expectation contributes to the power of the climactic line with the strong monosyllabic "God" that draws to itself the weight of two stresses through its relation to the three-stress "wróng énd of a télescope." And the power of image itself, "God through the wrong end of a telescope," God reduced to a "small black shape," "a bullet hole," the drowned body of John Davidson, wrests the movement away from the matter-of-fact restrained surface.

This coldness, both of tone and of imagery ("nae ardent breists' erection / But the stark hills' "), is the dominant feature of *Stony Limits* (1934), the volume that follows. In the spring of 1933, through the help of some friends concerned about his physical and psychological health and the damage resulting from an overindulgence in drink, Grieve had moved with his wife Valda and their young son Michael to a small cottage on Whalsay, one of the smaller Shetland islands. These islands are the most northerly part of Scotland, roughly on the same latitude as Bergen in Norway, isolated, bare, and very different indeed from the "almost tropical luxuriance of nature" in Langholm. The setting and the company of a friendly geologist led MacDiarmid to a new language and a new image: the language of science (untouched by any mellowing influence of Lallans) and the image of the stone. There is little warmth in either. It seems as if human emotion has failed MacDiarmid, and he turns away from the language of vulnerability to the language of impersonal facts, from the world of human beings to the world of stones. An inexorable coldness and loneliness accompany this move. The need to thaw moves into a delight in inhuman coldness. The ancient Eden that must be explored in order to reach the future paradise becomes, appropriately, the world of the stones, a world that has not changed, that has not suffered, that has not been "ruined."

Thus in *Stony Limits,* even in the sections that deal with Langholm, an inhuman coldness predominates. The Esk is "vivid and impulsive in crystalline splendour / Cold and seething champagne" (p 205), and the speaker-poet describes his task as "Mid the elemental enemies—cold, ravening brine— / The intellectual flame's survival I sing" (p 207). When faced with such relentlessly inhuman forces, the intellect has a chance of survival, the emotions none:

> Hot blood is of no use in dealing with eternity.
> It is seldom that promises or even realisations
> Can sustain a clear and searching gaze.
> But an emotion chilled is an emotion controlled;
> This is the road leading to certainty,
> Reasoned planning for the time when reason can no longer avail. [6]

With this changing viewpoint, an unblinking acceptance and intellectual appreciation of the stones of the world, the speaker requires a new art and bids farewell to his old kind of poetry:

> No more of sound, the least part!
>
> . . .
>
>   knowing well
> The greater risk of taking no risks,
> Creating no ecstasies, changing the mights
> Of old safe ecstasies to counters, discs,
> Transports reduced to play-level?
> The problematic, the murderous, element
> Of all art eschewed; no mad leap taken
> Into the symbol . . .
>
> . . .

185

No restless eager poem that speaking in
A thousand moods achieves a unity,
No wracking indispensable energy,
Only emotions forgotten in tranquillity.   (pp 206-7)

This poetry must be as coldly beautiful, as inhumanly beautiful as the stones that it describes; and as the allusions to the theories of Wordsworth and Coleridge make clear, the search must be scientifically and Classically ordered, rather than Romantic.

Obviously Lallans could not fit into this scheme: "There are no twirly bits in this ground bass."[7] Muir was correct in his insistence upon the emotional power of Lallans—the language of the child, rather than the language of the stone. By 1933 MacDiarmid was concentrating more and more on English and on the need to stretch *its* limitations, rather than on Lallans and the movement back to Gaelic: "A concerted effort to extend the general vocabulary and make it more adequate to the enormous range and multitudinous intensive specializations of contemporary knowledge is long overdue."[8] Paradoxically, while the poet searches for "contact with elemental things" in a "simple and sterner, more beautiful and more oppressive world, / Austerely intoxicating,"[9] he leaves behind the "elemental" language of *A Drunk Man*, a language that intoxicates in too warm a fashion. The word "intoxicating" indicates, however, that the Romantic impulse is still present in his work, and that he is still searching for "ecstasies." He wishes an appropriate language, "adamantine and inexorable," and he finds it in the language of science:

Hatched foraminous cavo-rilieva of the world,
Diectic, fiducial stones. Chiliad by chiliad
What bricole piled you here, stupendous cairn?[10]

Any "recondite elements" of the English vocabulary or the international vocabulary of science are fuel to this cold fire:

She did not change her epirhizous posture
But looked at me steadily with Hammochrysos eyes
While I wondered what dulia might be her due
And from what her curious enanthesis might arise.[11]

While there is a remoteness and a coldness about this new language, it does not necessarily guarantee emotionless poetry. A suggestive image or a rising movement wrenches the poem away from the objective, scientific plain of neutral language: "Or caught in a dark dumosity or even / In open country again watching an aching spargosis of stars,"[12] where "spargosis" draws to itself a painfully beautiful stretching movement, similar to Hart Crane's "sigh of stars." MacDiarmid's delight in dictionaries and in exotic vocabulary tends to push this new language to its extreme and to test its limits, just as he had quickly set himself the task of testing the limits of Lallans. The result is paradoxical, because as MacDiarmid pushes it to the extreme, the language becomes *less* austere and *less* elemental. An aureate quality enters, a quality that is inappropriate to the "simpler and sterner" world. And MacDiarmid, perhaps unconsciously but with a poet's ear, turns to "simpler and sterner" language. Just as in "A Moment in Eternity," the lines "I shone within my thoughts / As God within us shines" rang out climactically and clearly, so in this new poetry of "synthetic English" the highpoints are often composed of similar moments, direct and simple English: "I must begin with these stones as the world began," "This is no heap of broken images," "The stones will reach us long before we reach them," "We must reconcile ourselves to the stones, / Not the stones to us," "I grasp one of them and I have in my grip / The beginning and the end of the world," "There are plenty of ruined buildings in the world but no ruined stones."[13] The stones themselves link the present with the time when "the world began," and instinctively MacDiarmid uses unsophisticated, non-Latinate language to parallel this link with an elemental world. The stones themselves have not been touched by the Fall, but the Eden they represent is cold, inhuman, and distant. In direct and simple words the cold inhumanity and the uncompromising quality of the stone world appear convincingly, much more so than in the aureate "diallage of the world's debate, end of the long auxesis."[14] The starkness of "I must get into this stone world now" is more stone-like than "glaucous, hoar, enfouldered, cyathiform."[15] The "forgotten shibboleths" that MacDiarmid sought and found in Lallans were more elemental than the shibboleths of science, and instinctively MacDiarmid is aware of the limitations of this new language. At the climaxes of the early lyrics the Lallans often became more dense ("the haill clanjamfrie"), whereas at the climaxes of these poems, as in "A Moment in Eternity," the language becomes simpler, starker, and closer to standard English.

"The Skeleton of the Future," for example, uses the language of geology to establish the cold and inhuman beauty of the ancient world of the stones, of the future, and of Lenin's vision which provides the link between past and future. Its climax, however, depends upon a simpler English:

> Red granite and black diorite, with the blue
> Of the labradorite crystals gleaming like precious stones
> In the light reflected from the snow; and behind them
> The eternal lightning of Lenin's bones.　　　　　　(p 204)

The sharp "ite" of "granite," "diorite," and "labradorite" suggests both the hardness and the coldness of the stones. "Labradorite," however, suggests something else: Labrador, perhaps Crane's "North Labrador," "a land of leaning ice" that "flings itself silently into eternity," and the concept of the frozen paradise suggested in "A Moment in Eternity." The cold sophisticated beauty of these "crystals gleaming like precious stones" becomes something simpler, something even less human, "the light reflected from the snow," and moving even further back, "the eternal lightning of Lenin's bones," a strange and daring image. The concept of "eternal lightning" is mysteriously paradoxical. Lightning is associated with the gods, hence the appropriate nature of "eternal lightning" in a description of the god-like Lenin. At the same time, lightning is usually, by its very nature, sporadic, flashing and dying, flickering; and this lightning comes from Lenin's bones, the legacy of a mortal. Within the context of the poem, "eternal lightning" is a steady, cold gleam—like the gleam of the precious stones and the light from the snow. For a brief moment the paradox takes shape once more. The inhuman and indestructible beauty of Lenin's vision emerges through the relationships established between the crystals, the snow, and Lenin's bones, a relationship made possible by language, association, and the image of light. The magnitude of his influence emerges from the realization that the "eternal lightning of Lenin's bones" maps out the "skeleton of the future." This playing about with focus and proportion is as dramatic as "God through the wrong end of a telescope" or the shifts of focus in the early lyrics.

The control of this poem results in a successful merging of the languages of science and vision, largely because of the superb "labradorite" and the climax which is built upon a starker and more emotion-packed language than the language of science. "Labradorite" links these two vocabularies in a uniquely successful manner—no other word would suit. Such control and such disciplined skill, however, are not always so obvious. More and more MacDiarmid gets carried away and fails to impose limits, and more importantly, he fails to realize the effect of this. (The failure in *A Drunk Man* to impose restraints resulted in dramatic and exciting effects. This same tendency in *Stony Limits* has disastrous results). This is especially true when the language is experimental English, "modern scientific terminology" or "recondite elements of the English vocabulary." And so:

> What logodaedaly shall we practise then?
> What loxodromics to get behind the light?
> Glistening with exoskeletal stars we turn in vain
> This way and that and but changing perigraphs gain,
> Parablepsies, calentures, every curséd paranthelion.[16]

The line lengthens. Distillation and concentration disappear. A very loose iambic pentameter shepherds the line along, as the break with Lallans accompanies a break with formal control. Sometimes this loosening-up results in great rhythmic sweeps:

> I am only that Job in feathers, a heron myself,
> Gaunt and unsubstantial—yet immune to the vicissitudes
> Other birds accept as a matter of course; impervious to the effects
> Of even the wildest weather, no mean consideration in a country
>   like this;
> And my appetite is not restricted to any particular fare.
> Hence I am encountered in places far removed from one another
> And widely different in an intimately topographical sense
> —Spearing a rat at the mouth of a culvert at midnight
> And bolting an eel on the seashore in the halflight of dawn . . .

(p 264)

The rhythmic control behind these lines is not very formal, but there is a control—a movement similar to the slow pulsing of the waves or the beat of a heron's wing, punctuated by the stabbing rhythm of the last two lines as the bird devours its prey.

The emotionless quality of many of the poems was to be counterbalanced in *Stony Limits* by two important pieces—"Ode to All Rebels" and "Harry Semen"—that were deleted from the first edition on the publisher's insistence. "Ode to All Rebels," as Buthlay has noted, is the "longest *sustained* flight (about 800 lines) that MacDiarmid has achieved since the *Drunk Man*."[17] "Harry Semen," meanwhile, is

189

undoubtedly one of the finest poems MacDiarmid has written. The exclusion of these poems from *Stony Limits* may have calmed the publisher's fears, but at the very least did a disservice to the work as a whole. The "strong, forceful style"[18] of these poems, based on a language that falls midway between dense Lallans and standard English, is an important counterbalance to the "synthetic English" of most of the volume. (The other poems in Scots are of a lower quality). In addition, the released emotion in these poems, an emotion that goes to the verge of madness, not only counterbalances the lack of emotion in the experimental poems, but helps to explain why MacDiarmid was forced psychologically into a chilling of emotion: "an emotion chilled is an emotion controlled."[19] Both "Ode to All Rebels" and "Harry Semen" present emotions that are almost out of control, and indicate the extent to which the paradox has been upset. In *Stony Limits* MacDiarmid seems to split into two poets: one whose emotion is almost out of control; and one who has "chilled" his emotion to such an extent that not a shred remains in a vulnerable position.

Paradoxically both of those poems where the emotion is almost out of control have a more controlled structure than most of MacDiarmid's work at this time. "Ode to All Rebels," like the *Drunk Man,* is a sequence based upon sections whose "handrails" have been removed. The first section deals almost exclusively with sexuality and the link between sexuality and poetry. In a wave-like motion the speaker compares Kate and Jean, the two women he has lost, one through death and one through divorce. Sexuality, disease, and death are tied together in one pathological knot. The atmosphere becomes increasingly nightmarish as the speaker remembers an experience in medical school ("As I fingered the vagina lyin' afore me / —Carcinoma o' the uterus—while o'er me / Swept the thocht: 'Darlin' the neist may be you' "), or as he speculates on the "secret joy" with which his woman bound up a cut on his finger:

> I thanked her kindly and never let on,
> Seein' she couldna understand,
> That she wished me a wound faur waur to staunch
> —And no' i' the hand![20]

The openly confessional and pathological aspects of this section are new developments for MacDiarmid. We are reminded of Sylvia Plath's "Two

Views of a Cadaver Room'' and "Cut.'' The speaker seems closer to madness than any of the previous speakers, and bears witness to the enormous psychological turmoil that MacDiarmid was suffering at this period in his life. Meanwhile the form has become more controlled, almost as if control of either form or emotion were essential to him at this time.

This section sets the stage for the three that follow. In the second section the personal nightmare that results from the loss of Kate and Jean becomes the representative of the world nightmare: the senseless wars, the "agonies and abominations 'yont a' tellin','' and the miseries of the slums: "I am the woman in cancer's toils, / The man withoot a face."[21] The third section moves in the opposite direction. Just as the personal nightmare led into world nightmare, so the personal vision leads into world vision as the paradoxical synthesis forms once again:

> I see the slack mooth and gogglin' een
> Ahint this glory and ken them for mine
> Nor if I could wad I tine for a meenut
> Divine in human or human in divine.
> O dooble vision fechtin' in the glass!
> Noo licht blots oot sic last distinctions o' class.
> O magical change. O miracle.
> I am suddenly beyond mysel'.
> Reid, white, and square,
> Tearin' the soul to rags.[22]

And this in turn makes possible the final section which considers the relationship of the poet-speaker with the world, leaving out the intermediaries of Kate and Jean. The "haill warld" that was lost when Kate and Jean were lost must be regained, or at least the speaker must attempt, like the madman or God, to regain it: "Insane enough, with you [God] so near, / To want, like you, the world as well!"[23]

Although this sequence is vastly inferior to *A Drunk Man,* it provides *Stony Limits* with a counterbalancing force not only to the cold language of science and the lack of formal control, but also to the coldness of the imagery. Human beings, rather than stones, are the focus here: the pitiful frailty of the flesh, the obstinate stupidity of their minds, and their irrepressible animal lusts. As the coffin bearing the body of the speaker's wife is lowered to the grave:

> A thocht I mind ha'en
> Even as frae lowerin' the coffin I raze
> Conscious o' my nature in a wud amaze   *mad*
> And strauchtened up my muckle animal frame
> That kent what it wanted and kent nae shame
>   And stood in a burst o' sun
>   Glowerin' at the bit broken grun'.[24]   *ground*

The human body, whether "kindlin' aince mair" or riddled with disease, is the central image. Kate's eyes were "sea-green," Jean's "sky-blue," and so "I could cry / I'd mairriet the sea and syne the sky / And seen the ane gang dry / And the ither / Curl up and wither / Like a floo'er and die."[25] The warm humanity, the couthy language, the confessional vulnerability and pain are an important contrast to what happens in the rest of the volume.

Midway between the pathological nightmare of some of the sections of "Ode to All Rebels" and the austere restraint of "Dytiscus" lies "Harry Semen," a precarious balancing act on the edge of madness: "and the difference 'twixt / The sae-ca'd sane and insane / Is that the latter whiles ha'e glimpses o't / And the former nane" (p 247). There is a daring madness about the speaker's three visions, his swirling white worlds of semen, and Ginsberg's obscenities seem juvenile in comparison. The earlier sexual visions ("O Wha's the Bride," "In the Peculiar Light of Love," "The Thistle's Characteristics," "The Spur of Love") are like stepping stones leading to this supremely daring confrontation between the speaker and semen. He recognizes the mystery, and, in his madness, faces the god. The holiness and the miraculous purity of the visions appear in the three central images (the woman's body, the flowering cherry tree, the snowstorm), in the *leitmotif* of whiteness, and in the suggested context of the virgin birth : "Sae Joseph may ha'e pondered." Just as the colour white brings together connotations of both virginity and semen, so MacDiarmid incorporates once again in his vision the contraries of beauty and ugliness, wonder and disgust, creation and waste, man and god. He has at last found an image similar to the thistle in its power to unite contraries, and he develops fully the image that stood, along with the thistle, at the centre of *A Drunk Man*. Once again the paradoxical vision reaches a kind of epiphany. By stepping to the edge of madness, the speaker is able to face the paradoxical synthesis, which in *A Drunk Man* he reached by stepping to the edge of drunkenness.

The poem hovers between extremes, sometimes yoking them together forcibly and shockingly, sometimes moving smoothly from one to the other. The poise of this poem and the delicately controlled balance provide another point of tension as form and madness struggle together for dominance. The free flowing form of the verse is deceptively casual. Control is evident in the unifying imagery, in the rhythmic movement from vision to vision, and in the cyclical structure. The final stanza with its introductory line, "Sae Joseph may ha'e pondered," establishes this cyclical effect. The reader returns to the first line of the poem with the new context of the virgin birth brought to bear upon the entire poem. Meanwhile the concluding climactic vision is itself cyclical, framed by "Sae Joseph may ha'e pondered," and presenting a whirling, encompassing snowstorm that envelops the universe and draws the themes of intense sexual experience and vision together in the new theme of the conception of mankind's saviour:

> Sae Joseph may ha'e pondered; sae a snawstorm
> Comes whirlin' in grey sheets frae the shadowy sky
> And only in a sma' circle are the separate flakes seen.
> White, whiter, they cross and recross as capricious they fly,
> Mak' patterns on the grund and weave into wreaths,
> Load the bare boughs, and find lodgements in corners frae
> The scourin' wind that sends a snawstorm up frae the earth
> To meet that frae the sky, till which is which nae man can say.
> They melt in the waters. They fill the valleys. They scale the peaks.
> There's a tinkle o' icicles. The topmaist summit shines oot.
> Sae Joseph may ha'e pondered on the coiled fire in his seed,
> The transformation in Mary, and seen Jesus tak' root.
>
> (p 248)

The movement from vision to vision, culminating in this one, parallels MacDiarmid's own development. While the final vision is one of cold, perfect, inhumanly beautiful consummation, the first one presents a warm, human, and vulnerable woman:

> Hoo mony shades o' white gaed curvin' owre
> To yon blae centre o' her belly's flower?
> Milk-white, and dove-grey, wi' harebell veins.
> A'e scar in fair hair like the sun in sunlicht lay,
> And pelvic experience in a thin shadow line;
> Thocht canna mairry thocht as sic saft shadows dae.
>
> (p 247)

The Scottish accent and the Lallans words, meanwhile, form an integral
part of the vision: the long "a" sounds ("shades," "gaed," "blae,"
"grey," "hare," "veins," "hair," "mairry," "dae"), the alliteration of
"blae," "belly," and "harebell" (a Scottish flower), and the soft
gentleness of the "ch"s and "s"s in the climactic line.

The second and intermediary vision moves from a flowering cherry
tree to precious stones, and finally to the cold and perfect stars, while the
language moves from Lallans ("flooerin' gean") to English with a light
Scottish accent:

> But this is white, white like a flooerin' gean,
> Passin' frae white to purer shades o' white,
> Ivory, crystal, diamond, till nae difference is seen
> Between its fairest blossoms and the stars
> Or the clear sun they melt into,
> And the wind mixes them amang each ither
> Forever, hue upon still mair dazzlin' hue.
>   (p 248)

As the coldness increases in the final vision ("snawstorm," "bare
boughs," "tinkle o' icicles"), the Scottish accent becomes less and less
integral. The climactic effect of "They melt in the waters. They fill the
valleys. They scale the peaks. / There's a tinkle o' icicles. The topmaist
summit shines oot" depends upon rhythm and imagery, the suspense-
filled climbing of the mountain and the breathless movement towards
orgasm, and hardly at all upon Lallans. Changing "o' " to "of,"
"topmaist" to "topmost," and "oot" to "out" would have very little
effect. In contrast, "Thought cannot marry thought as such soft
shadows do" is a woefully inadequate substitute for the lovely "Thocht
canna mairry thocht as sic saft shadows dae."

Because of the structure of the poem (the cyclical effect, the movement
from tortured thought and disgust—"sick-white onanism"—to vision, a
movement that is repeated three times) and because of the unifying image
of white semen, the first vision (warm, emotional, and linked to Lallans)
is an ingredient in the final cold, inhuman vision of consummation. It
forms the first step towards this vision. The framing puzzlement of
Joseph and his "coiled seed" joins with the vision of the woman's body
as a humanizing influence upon the climactic vision. The "topmaist
summit" of the tinkling icicles began with a contemplation of "yon blae
centre o' her belly's flower," and moved through the "flooerin' gean"

(possibly a pun on "Jean") to "crystal, diamond" and to the final transcendent moment of consummation.

The poise of this poem is unique in MacDiarmid's work. It dares to step to the threshold of madness, yet retains artistic control. The snowstorm of the vision swirls around it, and yet the speaker can step back to see clearly: "Sae Joseph may ha'e pondered." Conscious control seems to have been left behind as the poem moves relentlessly towards the climax of the "topmaist summit," only to be reintroduced in the deliberate movement from the summit to the eternal circle. The poem is like a spring, wound up, released, and rewound, with the visions emerging climactically at the moments of release.

In the rest of *Stony Limits* MacDiarmid opts for either formal control plus lack of emotional control ("Ode to All Rebels"), or emotional control plus lack of formal control. "Harry Semen" provides a strange halfway house, a moment of precarious balance where both formal and emotional control seem almost about to be sacrificed, yet never are. The "mad leap into the symbol" is as powerful here as it was in the *Drunk Man,* and at times even more powerful because of the risks taken. It is a supremely successful poem.

This balancing act, however, is, within the context of *Stony Limits* and *Scots Unbound,* even more precarious than it appears when considered in isolation. Only with great difficulty, pain, or danger, is MacDiarmid able to resurrect the old paradox, to put together the broken pieces. The upset balance that manifested itself in *Circumjack* has created enormous problems of language, control, and emotion. And the poetry itself reveals the "fatal division" and the lack of unity that succeeded the earlier balancing act of *A Drunk Man*.

The islands that make up these poems are, like the islands of "Harry Semen," "each inhabited / Forever by a single man." Only at very rare moments—and at the risk of madness—is it possible to see "a dooble vision fechtin' in the glass."

CHAPTER SEVEN

'Politics is Bairns' Play'

First Hymn to Lenin and *Second Hymn to Lenin*

MacDiarmid's Marxism restores some of the balance to the paradox and helps to recreate the "dooble vision fechtin' in the glass." In the poetry of the thirties it provides an essential link between the world of stones and the world of human beings. Without it MacDiarmid's poetry of this period would be cold and lonely in the extreme.

His political career has been as consistently paradoxical as his poetic career. The central and paradoxical vision of synthesis has absorbed readily and eagerly into itself the various elements which in any other mind would rest uneasily beside one another. His early description in *Annals of the Five Senses* of an ideal society where "class should be bound to class by the fullest participation in the treasure of the one life," of "new kingdoms of the spirit" where "the Infinite would have a worship and an abiding city,"[1] has remained with him throughout the twists and turns of his political career, twists and turns that have been made necessary by the parties involved, rather than by MacDiarmid himself. The paradoxical leap of imagination that joins the present moment to eternity, man to the more than human, permeates all of his political thought and explains his reluctance to be content with any one restricting mould. It also explains the uneasiness felt by the various parties when confronted with a paradoxical identification between their ideology and that of another party. MacDiarmid's central vision can reconcile contraries while the world of party politics stands aghast.

To the central vision of a New Jerusalem as presented in *Annals*, MacDiarmid adds, step by step, the Socialism of his pre-war days, a fierce conviction of the senselessness of war, the economic theories of Douglas, a Scottish Nationalism that is part of a grand cultural campaign, and an acceptance of Marxism that is as intimately linked to his insistence upon the full development of man's potential as his Scottish Nationalism is. None of these ingredients ever disappears—to the embarrassment of the parties involved. In 1931 when the publication of "First Hymn to Lenin" in *New English Poems* revealed that MacDiarmid was a Marxist, although he had not yet joined the Communist Party, he saw himself as both a nationalist and an internationalist, and his position has changed very little since then. As he summed up in 1957,

> I am a Nationalist because life as we know it is always specific—specific in time and place. It is of where and when it is, and of no other where or when.
>
> I am a Communist because life is always, and has always been, individual. There is no question of a universal, because any attempt at definition of life must start out with the concept "individual", otherwise it would not be life.
>
> And Communism, I am convinced, is the only guarantee of individuality in the modern world. . . . Socialist society alone offers a firm guarantee that *the interests of the individual will be guaranteed.*[2]

One must begin with the individual, whether the peculiar genius of a country or the peculiar genius of a man. Both must be free to grow, and national independence together with the Communist removal of "breid-and-butter" problems can make this freedom possible. Both are steps towards "new kingdoms of the spirit."

While Nationalism offered a hope for individual development and freedom from foreign influence and while Communism offered freedom from economic restrictions, the combination of these two approaches must have been irresistible to MacDiarmid. Both the Nationalist and the Communist parties, however, have been unwilling to condone his yoking together of political theories, and as a consequence his political career *seems* to move erratically from one to the other, while the man remains faithful to both. In 1933 he was expelled from the National party for his Comunism, and in 1934 he joined the Communist Party. In 1937, almost predictably, the Communist Party expelled him for his nationalistic views. He appealed the case and was reinstated, only to be expelled in the following year for continued nationalistic activity. In 1944 he joined the Scottish Nationalist Party. In 1945 he stood as their candidate in Kelvingrove. In 1948 he left the Scottish Nationalist Party, and in 1950 stood as an Independent Scottish Nationalist in the Kelvingrove election. When he rejoined the Communist Party, he did so in 1957, at a "time of trouble," when "one must cleave to one's friends," just after the

Hungarian rising.[3] His driving vision of unity and fulfilment reconciles paradoxically all the petty counterclaims of the two political parties. Just as the thistle yoked together a "routh o' contraries," so MacDiarmid can easily accommodate both Nationalism and Marxism—with room to spare.

The Marxist vision of a New Jerusalem where man would be freed from all that thwarts his growth brings MacDiarmid back to the world of humankind. The world of stones is balanced by the world of humans—suffering, disease-ridden, crippled, legless, killed in insane wars, obsessed with "squalid little needs"—and this world is very far away from the fulfilment that at present is merely a potential. The entrance of Marxism as a component in MacDiarmid's vision revives and makes human the bleak loneliness of the world of stones. Horror, pity, rage, and bitterness emerge from the juxtaposition of man's misery with man's potential, viewed in the light of Marxist solution. The balance of MacDiarmid's vision is partly restored, and the paradox takes shape under a new guise.

Marxism somehow releases in MacDiarmid the emotion which, at this period in his life, is either missing (the experimental poems) or almost out of control ("Ode to All Rebels," "Harry Semen"). The speakers in *First Hymn* and *Second Hymn* are in general much more emotional than the speakers in *Scots Unbound* and *Stony Limits,* and it is an emotion which, although controlled, is by no means "chilled." One speaker can cry out in sympathetic agony: "Sae to my bosom yet a' beasts maun come, / Or I to theirs,—baudrons [cats], wi' sides like harps, / Lookin' like the feel o' olives in the mooth" (p 288). Disgust, anger, and courage (an almost horrifying amount of each) burst forth in "What maitters 't wha we kill / To lessen that foulest murder that deprives / Maist men o' real lives" (p 286). A similar vortex of emotion whirls in "Are the living so much use / That we need to mourn the dead" (p 304), and "Would you resembled the metal you work with, / Would the iron entered into your souls" (p 315).

Apparently linked to this emotional release is a lack of experimentation with language. The experiments in language are confined to *Stony Limits* and *Scots Unbound.* By contrast, in *First Hymn* the language is standard English with a strong Scottish accent and an occasional Lallans word (as in *Circumjack*). In *Second Hymn* the language is standard English, with the exception of the title poem whose language is similar to that of *First Hymn.* Even the lyrics from "Ode to

All Rebels'' that have been included in *Second Hymn* have been anglicized.

These two characteristics, the emotional involvement of the speakers and the lack of experimentation with language, seem to go hand in hand, especially when we consider the dates of the two volumes in relation to *Scots Unbound* and *Stony Limits: First Hymn* was published in 1931; *Scots Unbound,* 1932; *Stony Limits,* 1934; *Second Hymn,* 1935. While the two *Hymns* frame the experimental volumes and seem to suggest that the ''synthetic English'' business took place between 1931 and 1934, the impression they give is false. MacDiarmid was by no means finished with synthetic English or polyglot, as many of his later poems bear witness. The thesis that he is moving from Lallans to standard English via synthetic English holds up only if we limit our attention to these four volumes. How then can we explain the pattern?

With the exception of a few poems in *Stony Limits* and ''Tarras'' in *Scots Unbound,* explicit Marxist references are confined to *First Hymn* and *Second Hymn.* In MacDiarmid's writing of this period there is an almost schizophrenic separation of elements. Marxist vision, emotion, formal control, and conventional language form one group, while lack of vision, lack of emotion, lack of formal control, and unconventional language form the other. The precise chronological order of these poems is largely irrelevant. The separation takes place ultimately in MacDiarmid's mind, and more and more the language experiments appear as a desperate attempt to compensate for the ''chilled'' emotion and lack of vision. No doubt this separation derives ultimately from the psychic injury caused by Grieve's divorce. Without Marxism, however, the damage would have been much greater, as *First Hymn* and *Second Hymn* suggest. Without these volumes and the Marxist vision that stands behind them, MacDiarmid's poetry of the thirties would be cold, lonely, and inhuman. Marxism gives him an emotional strength and courage that would otherwise be missing. Without it the central paradox would probably have collapsed completely.

In *First Hymn to Lenin,* indeed, the Marxist vision appears almost as an excuse for the poet's exploration of his own history and of the relationship between *his* genius and the past. Through Lenin and through the parallel between the speaker, Lenin, and Christ (similar to the parallel between the speaker, Burns, and Christ in the *Drunk Man*), MacDiarmid is able to go back to Langholm without the protection of an experimental language. In such poems as ''Charisma and My Relatives,''

"The Seamless Garment," "Water of Life," and "Excelsior," the Muckle Toon with its "perfect maze o' waters" is a continual point of reference. And with it comes an acceptance of the relatives and family that Grieve had left behind him. The Marxist awareness of the suffering of man is linked to an acceptance of man as he is, and to a recognition of the relationship between the speaker and his "kin," just as an appreciation of Lenin's genius is linked to an examination of his own genius.

Thus, while the title of this volume is *First Hymn to Lenin,* Lenin appears mainly as a point of reference, a link between the speaker and his relatives. For example, in "The Seamless Garment," the speaker is able to talk to his cousin Wullie *because of* and *through* Lenin:

> You are a cousin of mine
>   Here in the mill.
> It's queer that born in the Langholm
>   It's no' until
> Juist noo I see what it means
> To work in the mill like my freen's.   (p 290)

This first stanza leads into a somewhat patronizing attempt to explain Lenin to the millworker and to link the Marxist vision to the poet's task. The millworker, the poet, and Lenin are united through their individual attempts to create a "seamless garment."

This poem has troubled me for many years. Lavish praise has been heaped upon it, but there is something about the smug modesty of the speaker that is uncharacteristic of MacDiarmid and unappealing, while the basic conceit of the "seamless garment" is a little too neat in its application to Lenin, Rilke, Wullie, and the speaker. Lenin's presence is much more effective in his absence, in a poem such as "At My Father's Grave," where although Lenin is not an active ingredient in the poem, the Marxist vision and frame of reference have given MacDiarmid strength to tackle directly and explicitly the theme of the death of Grieve's father. Just as the figure of Lenin enabled the speaker to reach his cousin, so the Marxist background of *First Hymn* enables the speaker to contemplate his father's death. There is no easy resolution here as there was in "The Seamless Garment," for all the speaker's talk of "integrity," and the greater pain that bursts forth to link the living man's mind with the father's death makes this a greater poem:

> The sunlicht still on me, you row'd in clood,   *wrapped*
> We look upon each ither noo like hills
> Across a valley. I'm nae mair your son.
> It is my mind, nae son o' yours, that looks,
> And the great darkness o' your death comes up
> And equals it across the way.
> A livin' man upon a deid man thinks
> And ony sma'er thocht's impossible.   (p 289)

The power of this poem resides in the sense of suppressed emotion that bursts forth in two wave-like motions ("like hills / Across a valley"; "your death comes up / And equals it"). The rolling enjambment and the stretching movement that it suggests unite father and son for a brief moment, despite the straining tension and separation suggested by the image of the two hills, one sunlit, the other "row'd in clood," and by the stark and moving simplicity of "I'm nae mair your son." MacDiarmid recognized that the power of direct statement in poetry was a peculiar quality of the Scots language, and in a later essay has cited, as an example of what he considers the most powerful line in Burns's poetry, "Ye are na Mary Morison."[4] The striking aural similarity between "I'm nae mair your son" and "Ye are na Mary Morison" may have led to an emotional appreciation of the Burns line, or the aural memory of Burns's line may have suggested the form that MacDiarmid's line takes. Certainly the emotional reverberations in the restraint of "I'm nae mair your son" are a powerful ingredient in the lyric.

The dull "d"s, associated with the father in the first line ("row'd in clood") thud tragically in the "darkness o' your death" and the "deid man," in contrast to the "sunlicht" and the quivering "l"s, "n"s, and "s"s that run throughout the poem and parallel the unifying movement of the two enjambments. Because of the heavy Scots accent "sunlicht" is more gentle and "deid man" more desolate than their English equivalents. Similarly the Scottish accent makes possible an aural link between "the sunlicht still" and "sma'er thocht's impossible," a link that would be impossible in standard English. Rhythm, language, movement, and imagery support each other here, as they do in the best of MacDiarmid's work.

"At My Father's Grave," like the other poems in *First Hymn,* is concerned with the source and with the relationship between present and future to that source. In these poems MacDiarmid comes as close as he

201

ever does to intellectualizing his basic drive, the attempt to recapture the past in order to reach the future. Lenin himself is seen as a "mair than elemental force" in the introductory poem, linked through this aspect to the other poems that emphasize "memories o' the Flood": "vivid recollection o' trudgin' that / Crab-like upon the ocean-flair" (p 293); the "ancient memory" (p 294); "the instinct in the seas / And jungles we were born in" (p 296); and of course the "perfect maze / O' waters . . . aboot the Muckle Toon" (p 293). Characters from Grieve's boyhood make their appearance: his cousin Wullie, the boys with whom he played as a child, and the "Waterside folk" who through their continuous connection with the "perfect maze" of waters inhabit a more ancient and vital world,

> Their queer stane faces and hoo green they got!
> Juist like Rebecca in her shawl o' sly.   *slime*
> I'd never faur to gang to see doon there
> A wreathéd Triton blaw his horn or try,
> While at his feet a clump o' mimulus shone
> > Like a dog's een wi' a' the world a bone.   (p 297)

The delightful appearance of the Triton, a Classical allusion that is rare in MacDiarmid's poetry, is superb. While the Triton is suitably "wreathéd," he remains firmly associated with a less sophisticated world through the Scottish "blaw," the undercutting "or try," and his closeness to the mimulus, a savage and ancient plant.

This final stanza of "Excelsior" and the lyric "At My Father's Grave" provide the moments of highest intensity in this volume. As a whole, *First Hymn* is a personal autobiographical exorcism, an attempt to re-establish contact with the Langholm relatives, no matter how painful such an attempt may be. The pain emerges powerfully in "At My Father's Grave," and horribly in one of the stanzas in "Charisma and My Relatives":

> Sae to my bosom yet a' beasts maun come,
> Or I to theirs,—baudrons, wi' sides like harps,   *cats*
> Lookin' like the feel o' olives in the mooth,
> Yon scabby cur at whom the gutter carps,
> Nose-double o' the taste o' beer-and-gin,
> > And a' my kin.   (p 288)

The initially sympathetic tone which, through the piled-up images of the skinny cats, the bitter taste of the olive, and the diseased, revolting dog, moves into one of deep disgust, horrifies when the final ingredient is added: "And a' my kin." The technique is almost Swiftian. The reader is aware of the full horror and the terrible implications *after* he has finished the train of thought and has paused to understand it. A reader who doesn't pause to let the implications develop and who rushes on to the next stanza will miss the entire point.

Significantly there is neither a mother-figure nor a brother-figure in any of these poems, although "a' my kin" presumably includes both. And the tone of the stanza quoted above, moving from sympathy to disgust is similar to the tone of the 1927 short story "Andy" at the point where the speaker sees his brother's mind and feels "wae" (sad) for him, while recognizing the full disgust of the "fell clarty [extremely filthy] road." Similarly the grossly physical effect of the images (the sight of the skinny cats, the taste of the olives, the smell of the beer and gin) is reminiscent of the disgust associated with Andy's physicality, as opposed to the sensitive dreaminess of the narrator. Andy and his mother are never far distant in *First Hymn*.

Second Hymn to Lenin also uses Lenin as a major point of reference. The personal exorcism involved in the return to Langholm is over, but the emotion that was released through the combination of Marxism and Langholm remains, despite the emotionless tone of the intervening *Scots Unbound* and *Stony Limits*. The sympathy and the disgust felt by the speaker at the sight of the "baudrons, wi' sides like harps" and "a' my kin" become a sympathy and a disgust for all mankind. There is an authority and a conviction behind MacDiarmid's voice here. The poems are focused clearly. The emotions surge against the formal limits of the lyrics. The tension is often almost excruciating, and the irony is Sassoon-like in its bitterness. Voice, confidence, and subject matter back each other up—as they have in general failed to do since the *Drunk Man*. Without a doubt, *Second Hymn* is the most exciting, masterful, and sustained volume since the early lyrics and *A Drunk Man*. Yet John Speirs is the only critic to have noticed this. Speirs claims that in *Second Hymn* Grieve has "really found himself," and he draws attention to the phenomenon of "anger finding direct, naive expression," to the influence of Yeats, to the lack of complexity in contrast to Yeats, and to the individuality of the voice.[5] While Speirs grossly underestimates MacDiarmid's early poetry, he speaks truth in his estimation of the quality of *Second Hymn*. While less impressive than the early work in

Lallans, it is the finest volume since *Drunk Man*. It fails to match it, but it comes closer than any of the other subsequent volumes. Why then has no other critic drawn attention to the superior quality of *Second Hymn?*

In many ways MacDiarmid has been a victim of his own propaganda. The issue of Marxism, blazoned forth in the title, is usually the first path down which critics of *Second Hymn* wander, despite the fact that in the title poem the speaker gives poetry an almost Shelleyan position of authority over politics: "Ah, Lenin, politics is bairns' play / To what this maun be!" *Second Hymn* is very different in both quality and approach from *First Hymn,* but the ingredient of the Marxist vision and the similarity of the titles have helped to obscure the very real differences between them. The emotions aroused by the relationship of Marxism and poetry have meanwhile prevented a careful exploration of that relationship as presented in the poems themselves.

Secondly, the issue of language is also distracting, and especially so when linked to MacDiarmid's own propaganda on the subject. He had frequently attacked the inadequacy and the sterility of standard English, just as he had frequently suggested the necessity of a new language—whether a revival of the Ur-languages of the Scots or the creation of a new scientific language. *Second Hymn,* however, with the exception of the title poem, uses standard English. Those critics who had loyally supported his experiments in different languages and had defended him against hostile criticism suddenly found themselves up the proverbial creek. For them it was much easier to ignore *Second Hymn* and its embarrassing regression to standard English. Meanwhile those who had thought of MacDiarmid as a mad Scotsman were hardly likely to start taking him seriously when he began to write in standard English. The title that emphasized Lenin's godlike qualities branded him a mad Scotsman still.

Even as sympathetic a critic as Kenneth Buthlay dismisses *Second Hymn* as a "gathering together of interim work," concentrates on the move from Lallans to English, and complains about the propaganda involved. He treats together "some of the poems" in *Stony Limits* and *Second Hymn,* a combination that gives the impression that the quality of *Stony Limits* and *Second Hymn* is similar:

> . . . they are, firstly, badly-written propaganda and, secondly, crude and oversimplified in their message. They tell us only about Bad Guys and Good Guys; their values "stand out in black and white" precisely

because they are crudely conceived; and they do not utilise more than the barest fraction of the talents of the man who wrote them.[6]

Buthlay's original qualification that he was speaking of "some of the poems" is forgotten in the onslaught, and the impression given of the quality of *Second Hymn* is abysmal. After reading Buthlay, only a confirmed Marxist or a MacDiarmid addict would tackle *Second Hymn*.

Part of the blame for this hostility must lie in Buthlay's rejection of an explicitly Marxist vision as a valid ingredient in poetry—there are "Good Guys" and "Bad Guys" in Pound's poetry too—and partly the blame must rest on MacDiarmid's prose propaganda and on a narrow interpretation of two lines that Buthlay uses in support of his judgement: "In short, any utterance that is not pure / Propaganda is impure propaganda for sure."[7] These two lines are not one of the moments of highest intensity in *Second Hymn,* and they unfortunately lend themselves to the specious claim that MacDiarmid is writing propaganda—and oversimplified propaganda at that. An examination of some of the other lines in *Second Hymn* quickly dispels this impression.

The title poem establishes the link between Lenin and the poet. Both are concerned with the whole, the "haill art," the full development of man's potential. While poetry is the "greatest poo'er amang men," Marxism promises to free "oor poo'ers for better things" by removing the "breid-and-butter" problems that stand in the way: "politics is bairns' play / To what this maun be!" (p 303). This, regardless of what Buthlay claims, is no crude conception. Romantic it may be, but crude propaganda it is not.

The central theme of the volume is the relationship between the human race as it is now and the human race as it could be. The "genius" of the poet and of Lenin link the two together and form a bridge between the present and the future. Genius is the symbol of the paradox, and Lenin the "barbarian saviour of civilization" (p 298). Suffering is an essential ingredient in the formation of the paradoxical vision. And so, in "On the Ocean Floor":

Now more and more on my concern with the lifted waves
  of genius gaining
I am aware of the lightless depths that beneath them lie;
And as one who hears their tiny shells incessantly raining
On the ocean floor as the foraminifera die.

(p 303)

There is no crude simplification here. Genius and suffering are both ingredients in the paradoxical vision. The "lifted waves" are associated through alliteration and metre with the "lightless depths," and each is dependent on the other. The last two lines with their "tiny" monosyllables focus on all the little deaths, the infinite number of little sufferings, while at the same time they suggest that a creative as well as a destructive process is at work. The word "raining" suggests both the tears of suffering and the generative process of life—the rain that makes the flower possible. Similarly the "foraminifera," splendidly polysyllabic in its surroundings, brings all the little sufferings together to suggest a great creative movement. In its suggestive link between science and vision, "foraminifera" is similar to "labradorite." Its Latin root suggests "hole-maker," while its sound suggests both "form" and "man." This word links paradoxically the tiny shells with the "lifted waves of genius," and gathers them together to make out of their combined suffering a new creation. The ocean floor makes the waves possible, and the paradox takes shape in the "foraminifera."

A similar relationship is suggested in "O Ease My Spirit." Here the physical and the spiritual come together in the vision of synthesis, another version of the basic paradox:

> And quicken me to the gloriously and terribly illuminating
> Integration of the physical and the spiritual till I feel how easily
> I could put my hand gently on the whole round world
> As on my sweetheart's head and draw it to me.   (p 305)

The paradox emerges in the relationship between "gloriously and terribly" (parallel to the shells-and-waves relationship), in the "physical and the spiritual," and in the change of focus from "whole round world" to "sweetheart's head." Simultaneously the movement of the verse (the encompassing embracing enjambment) includes both world and head, and supports the paradox.

There is no "impure propaganda" in these lines, no simplification, and no crude conception such as Buthlay suggests. Instead, the framework of the Marxist vision has made possible a return to the authentic and moving tenderness of the early lyrics. The language is different now, and the specially gentle qualities of Lallans no longer support the vision, but much remains: the tenderness; the dramatic switch of focus as the speaker moves from one side of the paradox to the other; and the evocative parallel between the movement of the verse and the movement of the thought.

Many of the lyrics focus on the thwarted lives and the terrible suffering that form one side of the paradox: "their tiny shells." The tone is one of bitter outrage, Sassoon-like irony, and anger that "foulest murder" of man's potential still exists in a world where the "barbarian saviour of civilization" has shown how such senseless suffering could be eliminated. The Marxist vision stands implicitly behind these poems as a point of contrast, a symbol of what could be.

MacDiarmid's technical control is effective. The "naive" expression of anger that Speirs noted seems to struggle against the formal limits, this movement in itself a symbol of the frustration felt by the speaker as his anger hammers against an unresponding wall of inhumanity. Often the tension builds to a climax in the final lines where the anger emerges purely and clearly, a movement that is reminiscent of the soaring moment of vision in the early lyrics. For example, in "At the Cenotaph" the ironic restraint of the introductory "Are the living so much use / That we need to mourn the dead?" is gradually left behind as the emotion mounts and as the questions rapidly follow one another until the final outpouring of anger and disgust:

> *Keep going to your wars, you fools, as of yore;*
> *I'm the civilisation you're fighting for.* (p 304)

Even more masterful is the control in "In the Children's Hospital":

> Now let the legless boy show the great lady
> How well he can handle his crutches.
> It doesn't matter though the Sister objects,
> "He's not used to them yet," when such is
> The will of the Princess. Come, Tommy,
> Try a few desperate steps through the ward.
> Then the hand of Royalty will pat your head
> And life suddenly cease to be hard.
> For a couple of legs are surely no miss
> When the loss leads to such an honour as this!
> One knows, when one sees how jealous the rest
> Of the children are, it's been all for the best!—
> But would the sound of your sticks on the floor
> Thundered in her skull for evermore! (p 311)

The irony mounts and mounts in increasing tension as the speaker adds one terrible element after another: the overriding of the Sister's objection that he cannot manage the crutches yet; the bestowal of the royal pat that is meant to compensate for the loss of two legs; the jealousy of the other children, and the realization that there is a whole ward full of Tommies, and then the memory of the title, a whole hospital full. Meanwhile as the irony increases, the rhyme scheme alters. The stumbling awkward feminine rhymes ("crutches"-"objects"-"such is") parallel Tommy's "desperate steps." As the fury of the speaker mounts, the rhymes become more proud and more terrible in their strong monosyllabic echoes ("miss"-"this," "rest"-"best"), climaxing in the thundering stresses of "But would the sound of your sticks on the floor / Thundered in her skull for evermore." The full violence of the speaker's rage is unleashed, no longer bound by restricting irony nor by the weakness of a feminine half-rhyme. The pure violence of the early lyrics and of *A Drunk Man* finds a new voice, language, and form.

The peculiarly pure blending of violence and gentleness that was so characteristic of his early work appears now when he brings together the themes of genius and the suffering from which it emerges. For example, in "The Two Parents" the speaker feels for his son both irritation and tenderness, and when he contemplates the difference between himself and his wife, he hovers between contempt, disgust, affection, and envy at her ability to sink to that "dread level of nothing but life itself." This is a much quieter poem than "In the Children's Hospital," but the movement from tone to tone and the blending of one tone with another are more sophisticated.

> I love my little son, and yet when he was ill
> I could not confine myself to his bedside.
> I was impatient of his squalid little needs,
> His laboured breathing and the fretful way he cried
> And longed for my wide range of interests again,
> Whereas his mother sank without another care
> To that dread level of nothing but life itself
> And stayed day and night, till he was better, there.
>
> Women may pretend, yet they always dismiss
> Everything but mere being just like this.   (p 314)

The relationship between genius and "that dread level of nothing," as it is presented in this poem, is anything but crude simplification. There are no "Good Guys" and "Bad Guys" here, but a man and a woman and a child, each with a different need and a different potential. The line "And stayed day and night, till he was better, there," in its slow gentle unwinding movement, its quiet reconciliation of disgust and tenderness, and its appropriateness (partly through the rhyme on the climactic "there"), is exquisite in its control and in its release of emotion.

A similar paradoxical hovering between disgust and tenderness appears in "Lo! A Child Is Born." As in "The Two Parents" the blending of tones is more gentle than in the early lyrics, quieter in its effect. The title suggests a miraculous kind of birth, and the first few lines reinforce this impression: the stones themselves are "instinct with hope," and the entire house shelters the birth. This leads in a lovely change of focus to the image of the world as a woman about to deliver a child, and the loving peace of the initial lines changes into a meaningless jumble of noise:

> There is a monstrous din of the sterile who contribute nothing
> To the great end in view, and the future fumbles,
> A bad birth, not like the child in that gracious home
> Heard in the quietness turning in its mother's womb,
> A strategic mind already, seeking the best way
> To present himself to life, and at last, resolved,
> Springing into history quivering like a fish,
> Dropping into the world like a ripe fruit in due time—
> But where is the Past to which Time, smiling through her tears
> At her new-born son, can turn crying: "I love you"?
>
> (pp 311-12)

The disgust of "future fumbles" and "bad birth" moves easily into its contrary, the quiet wonder at the "child in that gracious home," and the movement builds through the suspense-filled pauses to the moment of birth. This climactic moment brings together the contraries of the fish and the fruit. There is a lightness and a movement about "springing into history quivering like a fish." There is a rich heaviness and stillness about "dropping into the world like a ripe fruit in due time." The motion of the first is a joyful leap into the air; and the motion of the second is a slowly perfect fall. The paradox of these two movements continues as MacDiarmid reintroduces the theme of the parallel birth—that of the future. The speaker's poignant question—a Yeatsian kind of ending—emphasizes the relationship between past and future, pain and joy: Time is "smiling through her tears." The enormous disparity between what could be and what is rings out painfully in the unanswered question. It pulls the reader back into a recognition that the miraculous birth is still to come, and forces the paradox apart, while the counterbalancing force of Time's tears pulls it together. There *has* been a miraculous birth in which the reader has taken part, despite the speaker's reminder that it is still to come. The vision remains.

The quiet poise and control of these poems are a remarkable development for MacDiarmid to have made. In contrast to the early work, there is a lack of madness and of the daring, extravagant leap into the symbol. But the vision of the paradoxical synthesis is achieved once more, and with it come the peculiar blendings of emotion and tone. In comparison with the early work in Lallans, the quality is inferior and the tones are muted. Lenin's vision, however, gives back to MacDiarmid some of the earlier confidence. He is never able to regain the primal ferocity, the strength, and the heartbreaking gentleness of the early work, but the Marxist vision helps him to move part of the way towards it.

Meanwhile the Marxist framework helps the focus and the bringing together of the vision of a New Jerusalem with a bitter awareness of how far men are from realizing the vision. The tension that results from this paradox quivers in these poems, a faint remembrance of the earlier "chitterin' licht." The paradoxical vision had been almost overwhelmed by Grieve's psychological difficulties, by the emotionless experimentation with language, and by MacDiarmid's entry into the world of stones. In *First Hymn,* however, he was able to go back to Langholm and explore the sources of the paradox. And in *Second Hymn* he is able to put parts of the paradox together again.

Lenin is the revitalizing power in this period—much less potent than Dunbar had been, but bringing with him a quiet confidence. While Lallans with its special elemental qualities and its primal power has departed, Lenin sustains MacDiarmid, so that although "much is taken, much abides." Through Lenin he is able to regain some of the poise, some of the control, and an echo of the earlier greatness.

CHAPTER EIGHT

'Different Birds in Different Places'

POETRY SINCE 1935

After the publication in 1935 of the *Second Hymn to Lenin* MacDiarmid produced very little poetry that matches the *Second Hymn* in quality. The years between 1935 and his death in 1978 were difficult, although there must have been some measure of satisfaction for Grieve in the gradual recognition of Hugh MacDiarmid as the grand old man of Scottish letters and as a poet of international stature.

There was little sign of this in the late thirties. He must have felt very isolated on the Shetland Islands, far from the early hopes of the Scottish Renaissance, expelled from both the Communist and Nationalist Parties, barely managing to feed his wife and child. In addition, the effects of his personal crisis persisted. By 1955 he was able to compare the crisis and its effects upon his poetry to Hofmannsthal's:

> . . . the cause of my new departure, the crisis which so completely altered the nature of my work, can hardly be better expressed than by Francis Golffing's passage regarding Hofmannsthal: "What happened to the young Hofmannsthal . . . will never be known in full. . . . A crisis as complete, as desperate, as one is likely to find in the annals of poetry; and Hofmannsthal saved himself as best he could. To this writer, at least, he was saved in more ways than one. Not only did he rise whole from the vortex of unbeing, but the new path he now chose to pursue spelt his salvation as a poet."
>
> Something similar may yet be said of me.[1]

The late thirties, however, gave little indication of such a possibility. There was little interest in his work, neither the early Lallans poems nor the experimental pieces. An indication of the dashed hopes of this period was the formation of the "Hugh MacDiarmid Book Club," whose only publication (*Scotland: and the Question of a Popular Front against*

Fascism and War) led directly to his 1938 expulsion from the Communist Party for "Nationalist deviation."

While the war years did little to sustain the paradoxical balance he had achieved in *Second Hymn,* they did move him geographically away from the "world of stones"—to Glasgow where he was trained as a precision fitter. He worked in the copper shell band department of Mechans of Scotstoun until an industrial injury forced his transfer to the Merchant Service. He became a deck hand and later a first engineer on a Norwegian boat, the *Gurli,* that serviced naval ships on the Clyde. 1948 and 1950 saw abysmal failures in the two Kelvingrove elections, once as a Scottish Nationalist and once as an Independent Scottish Nationalist, and it was not until the early fifties that the first indications of a growing reputation appeared—in the award of a Civil List Pension and in a trip to Russia. By 1951 Grieve was settled in his cottage in Biggar, modern conveniences installed by some loyal friends, and subsequently the honours poured in.

1957 was a specially momentous year: the rejoining of the Communist Party, the honorary LL.D. from Edinburgh University, the honorary membership of P.E.N., and the trip to China. In 1959 he toured Czechoslovakia, Bulgaria, Rumania, and Hungary, giving the Burns Centenary lectures. In 1963 he accepted the William Foyle poetry prize and refused the freedom of Langholm, an act that must have given him great satisfaction. In 1964 he made political waves by standing against Sir Alec Douglas Home in the Kinross election, and in 1967 he gave a poetry reading at the Y.M.H.A. in New York. He had won the long fight to make himself an international reputation, and ironically the honours arrived long after the great poetic achievement of *A Drunk Man,* the book on which he had staked his reputation: "if, as such, it does not take its place—sui generis—one of the biggest things in the range of Scottish literature, I shall have failed."[2] Ironically too, the honours arrived during the years when MacDiarmid insisted on the value of his later poetry, disparaged his earlier work in Lallans, and called attention to "the folly of differentiating between prose and poetry."[3] Even more ironically, the praise was bestowed, with a very few exceptions,[4] to his early poetry.

MacDiarmid's belief in the "folly of differentiating between prose and poetry" is exactly the problem that lies at the heart of the later verse, and both the belief and the problems that it causes originate probably in the "crisis as complete, as desperate, as one is likely to find in the annals of poetry.'' Unlike Hofmannsthal, MacDiarmid did not rise ''whole from the vortex of unbeing.'' Instead he rose as a ''divided bird,'' and only in a few rare instances (*Second Hymn,* individual lyrics in the later writing, small sections of longer poems) is he able to bring the two halves of the paradox together again, to form one song, complete in itself. The rest is fragmentary, disjointed, unemotional, or with embarrassingly excessive emotion. A lack of proportion, a failure to impose limits, an arrogance, and a self-indulgence characterize the later poetry.

A poem entitled ''The Caledonian Antisyzygy'' summarizes the unfortunate division in MacDiarmid's work. The speaker begins by considering the despair of his friends who plead with him for a choice between Lallans and English, for consistency, and for the ''true lyric cry'' rather than ''chopped-up prose.'' He moves into a typically pompous, professorial address, as irritating as much of MacDiarmid's later poetry:

> Fatal division in my thought they think
> Who forget that although the thrush
> Is more cheerful and constant, the lark
> More continuous and celestial, and, after all,
> The irritating cuckoo unique
> In singing a true musical interval,
> Yet the nightingale remains supreme . . .   (p 477)

If MacDiarmid had ended the poem at this point, the reader's annoyance at the ''irritating cuckoo'' of MacDiarmid's ''chopped-up prose'' would be well justified. Nothing so far has given any grounds for the speaker's implication that his song resembles the ''supreme'' nightingale. But the poem continues, and, as it continues, the broken paradox grows whole:

> The nightgale whose thin high call
> And that deep throb,
> Which seem to come from different birds
> In different places, find an emotion
> And vibrate in the memory as the song
> Of no other bird—not even
> The love-note of the curlew—
>
>   can do!   (p 477)

Here MacDiarmid gives us poetry, not ''chopped-up prose,'' and his *ear* knows the difference, even if his mind claims there is none. The effect of these lines depends upon the relationship between image, metre, language, movement, and *line*, as the previous "lines" fail to do. The "thin high call" of the nightingale slows down the movement through the three strong stresses that vibrate with the bird's song. The three parallel stresses in the following lines slow it down even further: "And that deep throb." Because of the shortness of this line in relation to the lines that preceded it, the stresses lengthen and gather to themselves a greater weight. From this moment on, the verse builds, through syntax and line, to the climactic "can do!" Enjambment plays a crucial role. The "different birds / In different places" are separated by the break in the line that emphasizes the distance between them. The following enjambments move the poem higher and higher, and the reader must follow the song of the bird beyond the emotion, beyond the memory of the vibration, beyond the songs of other birds, and finally beyond the climactic "love-note of the curlew." The "chopped-up prose" of the earlier sections now appears as the other side of the paradox: the song of the other birds that provides a setting for the song of the nightingale. Each becomes more extreme through the juxtaposition with its contrary. It almost seems as if we are back momentarily in the world of the drunk man:

> These are the moments when my sang
> Clears its white feet frae oot amang
> My broken thocht, and moves as free
> As souls frae bodies when they dee.   (p 126)

The paradoxical vision emerges slowly and painfully from the tortured thought.

These moments of illumination, however, are rare in the later poetry. When they occur, they coincide with the moments of highest intensity, moments when turning the line into prose would damage it enormously. The tendency, observable in *A Drunk Man,* to create distances between the moments of intensity increases, and MacDiarmid seems unaware of just how boring these bricks between the cement can be. Long passages, often pages and pages, resemble the "irritating cuckoo," "unique" enough in its interval, but without a "true musical" appeal.

It almost appears as if MacDiarmid is attempting to replace the lost quality by sheer volume. The catalogue becomes one of his favourite techniques, and paradoxically it attempts to replace the "datchie sesames" of his earlier vision where *one* Lallans word provided an entry

into a new world. Now words are piled on top of each other with the
hope that if there are enough, a new world will take shape. At the same
time, the short intense lyric with multiple connotations gives way to the
catalogue where the speaker gives a host of examples, and hopes they will
form one whole. What has been lost is the enormous suggestiveness of
the early lyrics, where each reader voyages on his own strange sea. Now
the "poetry of fact" attempts to control the reader's imagination, and
piles everything in his lap whether he wants it or not:

> Ah, fain would I follow if I could
> The *Imtheacht na Tromdhaimhe* proceedings of Great Bardic Assembly
> Of the whole round world!)
> *Ashugi, akyni, zhirshi, bakhshi,* and other folk singers,
> Creators of the new heroic epodes of to-day.
> The Turkic poems of Hussein Bozalgonly of Tauz,
> Uzbek and Darginian songs,
> The songs of Suleiman Stalksky, the singer of the
>   Daghestan people,
> The blind old *kobyar*, Ostap Vyeryesai,
> And Timofei Ivanitch, the old *skazitel*,
> Who knew all the songs of all Russia.
> The songs of the *akyn* Kenen of Kazakhstan
> (Kazakhstan in renaissance, strengthened by its new "iron
>   roads"). . . . (p 360)

The "thin high call / And that deep throb" of the nightingale are worth
hundreds of pages of catalogues like this. MacDiarmid seems incapable
of imposing restraints in these catalogues, just as in "Ode to All Rebels"
he was unable to impose emotional restraints. In these catalogues the
emotionless tone of the self-indulgent lecturer is the major feature.
Almost the only emotion they arouse in the reader is one of irritation. As
Buthlay notes, "The very boasting in such passages is aimed at attracting
the attention of the reader, if only by way of irritation, because the
structural device itself is patently incapable of sustaining his interest."[5]

Naturally MacDiarmid has found a theory for what he is doing. He
had formulated it as early as 1936 in an essay he wrote on "Charles
Doughty and the Need for Heroic Poetry." It is a brilliant example of the
characteristically paradoxical nature of his mind, as ancient Celtic music,
modern Marxist vision, and a need to recreate the epic merge into one
theory:

He [Wagner] knew (as Charles Doughty knew) that we were coming to another of the quantitative—as against accentual—periods in culture. . . . (It is this question of quantity as against accent that distorts to most Scots the nature of our pibrochs of the great period. These knew no "bar". They were *timeless* music—hence their affiliation with plainsong, with the neuma. . . . Unbarred music—quantity music—expresses itself in pattern repetition; hence the idea that the Celt has no architectonic power, that his art is confined to niggling involutions and intricacies—yet the ultimate form here is not symphony; it is epic.) It is epic—and no lesser form—that equates with the classless society.[6]

But the epic has to have a *form,* and a form with meaning, as Wagner would have been the first to admit. MacDiarmid had already had trouble in structuring *A Drunk Man* (the help provided by F. G. Scott, the continued insecurity about its structure, the attempt to disguise its structure through the "logic of drunkenness" theory and the fulmination against "handrails"). Quantity in itself does not make an epic. None of the work after *A Drunk Man* is as well structured on a grand scale as *A Drunk Man* had been. The structure of *Circumjack* had been shaky, and the only other structured sequence consists of "Ode to All Rebels" where emotional control is almost entirely missing.

What followed in the years after 1935 was a series of fragments, parts of greater wholes that were promised, but that never materialized fully. Both in *The Islands of Scotland* (1939) and *Lucky Poet* (1943), prose works which display a weak sense of form, MacDiarmid included fragments, snatches of work in progress (where appropriate or where inappropriate), the surrounding prose giving an impression of structure. Early in 1939 MacDiarmid announced the total length of *Cornish Heroic Song for Valda Trevlyn* as "some 60,000 lines," and very little of this has appeared. *In Memoriam James Joyce* (1955) was supposed to be the first section of *Mature Art* or *A Vision of World Language*—the titles of the work kept changing, and it was difficult to keep track of what MacDiarmid planned. *Impavadi Progrediamur* (whose title was at one time changed to *Haud Ferrit*) was to be the second section, but unpublished save in snippets.[7] In conclusion, the years between 1935 and MacDiarmid's death provided the critic with a series of fragments (whose structure was often weak and sloppy) and grand promises of a greater whole whose structure could not be judged as it had not been published.

The *Cantos* of Ezra Pound seem "organised to the last degree" in comparison with this amorphous and elusive epic. As in the "Author's Note" to *A Drunk Man,* MacDiarmid appeared to be attempting to disarm the critic in advance.

The inevitable conclusion of all this evidence is that his sense of structure, weak to begin with when faced with a large amount of material to organize, disintegrated. The presentation of these "fragments" is an attempt to disguise his inadequacy in the structuring of an epic work, and his theory about the need for a heroic poetry in this new "quantitative" period in culture is designed to back up his practice with a grandiose theory—and to make what he is writing seem desirable and an act of will, rather than one of necessity.

The *Complete Poems,* published shortly after MacDiarmid's death, gives implicit recognition to this failure. In his introduction, MacDiarmid admits defeat: "I have simply abandoned the whole project [*Impavadi Progrediamur*]. . . . Other large-scale projects, such as 'Clann Albann' . . . and the complete 'Cornish Heroic Song for Valda Trevlyn', were either abandoned or subsumed in other works, and are not recorded here."[8]

In addition, the great reliance in these works upon other people's writings would appear to indicate that MacDiarmid had largely exhausted his own poetic impulse. More and more he mines the work of others (dictionaries, scientific textbooks, any arcane pieces of material) to provide material for his "poetry of fact." He has become an arranger, a selector, rather than a poet in these writings, and an arranger who lacks a sense of structure:

> Such an understanding dawns
> On the lay reader when he becomes
> Acquainted with the biochemistry of the glands
> In their relation to diseases such as goitre
> And in their effects on growth, sex, and reproduction.
> He will begin to comprehend a little
> The subtlety and beauty of the action
> Of enzymes, viruses, and bacteriophages,
> Those substances which are on the borderland
> Between the living and the non-living.   (p 338)

The theme of this section is almost identical to that of "The Watergaw": the "borderland / Between the living and the non-living." The "subtlety and the beauty of the action," however, were manifest in the "chitterin' licht" of the rainbow, while here the speaker only talks about them, as if the mere mention of the words "subtlety and beauty" were enough to create them.

I would rather not dwell on MacDiarmid's obvious failures in the later poetry. The basic problem seems to be a lack of proportion and of perspective that has damaging results on the poetry. In these writings MacDiarmid is very much a "divided bird." He has lost the balance he achieved in *A Drunk Man* and in *Second Hymn*. Occasionally, however, the "divided bird" becomes whole again, and "that deep throb" sounds through the "thin high call." The paradox takes shape once more, all the more poignant because of the shattered world from which it emerges, the mass of accumulated data that obscures the "bonnie lowe o' eternity."

Such a precarious moment of paradoxical balance is to be found in the hawthorn section of *In Memoriam James Joyce* (1955). The speaker prays that the only consistency in his poetry may be like "that of the hawthorn tree," with its haws shining more and more brightly:

> And when the leaves have passed
> Or only in a few tatters remain
> The tree to the winter condemned
>   Stands forth at last
>   Not bare and drab and pitiful,
> But a candelabrum of oxidised silver gemmed
> By innumerable points of ruby
> Which dominate the whole and are visible
> Even at considerable distance
> As flame-points of living fire.
> That so it may be
> With my poems too at last glance
> Is my only desire.
> All else must be sacrificed to this great cause.
> I fear no hardships. I have counted the cost.
> I with my heart's blood as the hawthorn with its haws
> Which are sweetened and polished by the frost!   (pp 400-01)

The paradoxical relationship between suffering and beauty ("Our sweetest songs are those that tell of saddest thought") is reminiscent of *Second Hymn,* while the symbol that represents the paradox, the hawthorn tree transformed by winter's frost into an eternal beauty, is like two earlier trees—the tree in "A Moment in Eternity" and the thistle. This tree unites contraries, as the thistle did, but the ambience that surrounds it is one of quiet wonder, similar to the atmosphere at the end of *A Drunk Man* in "Yet Ha'e I Silence Left." The straining agony of the other sections of *A Drunk Man* has no place in the purity of this vision, a marriage between the thistle's power to unite contraries and the gem-like eternity and calm of the tree in "A Moment in Eternity."

The structure is strong and carefully controlled: the narrowing down of the line as the hawthorn is stripped of its leaves, as it "stands forth at last," and the triumphant expansion of the line, parallel to the movement in "Bonnie Broukit Bairn," as the beauty of the hawthorn is revealed. The magnificent polysyllables and the rising emotion of the lines build towards the climactic moment of the first section, the "flame-points of living fire." The quiet prayer, "That so it may be / With my poems too at last glance / Is my only desire," is linked to the image of the hawthorn through an intricate interweaving of rhyme, "be"-"ruby," "glance"-"distance," "desire"-"fire." The rhyme scheme of this whole introductory section is delicate and complex, like the interweaving boughs of the hawthorn itself, the "candelabrum of oxidised silver," and it suggests a precariously lovely relationship between the speaker and the tree.

This relationship is clarified and made more poignant in the climactic quatrain where the red haws are identified with the speaker's "heart's blood":

> All else must be sacrificed to this great cause.
> I fear no hardships. I have counted the cost.
> I with my heart's blood as the hawthorn with its haws
> Which are sweetened and polished by the frost!

The control here is magnificent: the traditional rhyme scheme that reinforces the identification between the heart's blood and the haws; the metrical and aural link between "heart's blood" and "hardships"; the alliterative link between these two and the "hawthorn"; the way in which "cost" seems to emerge from "cause" and "haws"; the simple directness of "I fear no hardships. I have counted the cost," similar in its moving simplicity to "I'm nae mair your son"; and the wonderful paradox of the last line, the sweetness and the polish bestowed by the frost. The climactic power of this last line is partly dependent upon an old MacDiarmid trick, as effective here as ever, and proof that his ear can still be as sure as it once was. In the three preceding lines he has accustomed our ear to four stresses per line ("else"-"sacrificed"-"great"-"cause," "fear"-"hardships"-"counted"-"cost," "heart's"-"blood"-"hawthorn"-"haws." The climactic line provides only three major stresses, and as a result the movement of the line slows and each of the stresses gains added weight: "Which are sweetened and polished by the frost!" The control is exquisite, and the paradoxical moment of unity is once again present, a precious moment—as its crystal purity is swallowed up almost immediately by the "cotton wool" of what follows:

> See how these haws burn, there down the drive,
> In this autumn air that feels like cotton wool,
> When the earth has the gelatinous limpness of a body
>   dead as a whole
> While its tissues are still alive! (p 401)

The "gelatinous limpness" forms a fine point of contrast to the "candelabrum of oxidised silver," but the "different birds / In different places" confusion soon takes over. Moments such as this have become rare, separated from other moments of intensity by long passages that are prosaic, irritating, and boring.

Occasionally the old confident voice rings out again in the poetry after 1935, and when it does, it is often a humorous one—a welcome relief indeed to the long humourless catalogues. The humour is more delicate than the violent black humour of the early lyrics, but when it appears, it brings with it a vitality and a confidence that have otherwise been missing. Mostly these poems are parts of the unpublished *Haud Ferrit (Impavadi Progrediamur)* which occasionally resembles *Second Hymn* in its quality, its irony, and its control—a much greater amount of control than in most of the poetry of this period. The distancing of humour and irony enables MacDiarmid to find his way back to the paradox.

For example, in "Glasgow 1960," irony and humour make possible a new vision of Glasgow, and bring together the contraries of philistines and highbrows. The poem begins quietly with no hint of what will develop:

> Returning to Glasgow after long exile
> Nothing seemed to me to have changed its style.
> Buses and trams all labelled "To Ibrox"
> Swung past packed tight as they'd hold with folks. (p 430)

The speaker assumes that they are on their way to a football match, but when he inquires about it, the Glaswegian answers:

> . . . "Where in God's name are *you* frae, sir?
> It'll be a record gate, but the cause o' the stir
> Is a debate on 'la loi de l'effort converti'
> Between Professor MacFadyen and a Spainish pairty."
> I gasped. The newsboys came running along,
> "Special! Turkish Poet's Abstruse New Song.
> Scottish Authors' Opinions"—and, holy snakes,
> I saw the edition sell like hot cakes.

The incongruity of this vision, brought into contrast with the reality of Glasgow through the speaker's ironical wonder, works wonderfully, especially in the timing of the last two lines, where the two suspense-filled pauses, caused by the naive expression of amazement ("and, holy snakes,"), build suspense towards the ridiculous punch-line. The lightness of touch here shows a new ability to see the humour in the disparity between vision and reality, and this humour provides a new means of linking contraries.

One of the most humorous passages that has developed from this new method of uniting contraries is the "Tutti-Frutti Forgle" passage in "Esplumeoir," another poem in *Haud Ferrit*. Here eternity does not appear as the "bonnie lowe" that flickered in the servant girl's bed, but in a modern, materialistic way:

> Or pit it like this—Eternity's
> Twa doors frae the corner a'whaur
> A sma', demure white biggin'   *building*
> Wi' shutters and a canopy.
> The canopy's royal blue
> And it says *Eternity*
> In discreet soap-glass letters
> On ilka-side. Under the canopy
> You walk up and the front door
> Is a' mirror wi' a cool strip
> O' fluorescent light on top.
> You push the pearl button,
> And listen to the delicate chimes

And adjust your tie in the mirror
And fix your hat—but the guy
Ahint the bullet-proof mirror
Sees a' that too,
Only you canna see him.
The guy ahint the mirror
Is Tutti-Frutti Forgle,
A muckle nigger wi' fuzzy-white hair
Wha kens his business.
Aince past Tutti, you check your hat
In a quiet soft-lit anteroom,
Syne the haill place is yours.   (pp 426-7)

The atmosphere of soft menace (e.g., the understated "Wha kens his business") is similar to a light Pinter, and the laughter that it evokes has a nervous quality about it. Tutti-Frutti Forgle, whose name is as comic and sinister as his appearance, is a magnificent St Peter in this funeral-parlour eternity, with its pearl button (shades of the pearly gates), fluorescent lighting, and bullet-proof mirrors. The timing is perfect—the slow delicate way in which one detail is added to another, each increasing the suspense and the atmosphere of soft menace. Meanwhile the Scottish accent is a fine undercutting device that increases the humour of this sophisticated American eternity.

A more brutal irony also makes an occasional appearance, an irony that both holds back and reveals the agony caused by the gap between what could be and what is. For example, in "Reflections in a Slum," the rage of the speaker emerges *through* the bitterness of the irony, as in "In the Children's Hospital" of *Second Hymn*. The "old folk" of the slum remind the speaker of a "bolshie the 'whites' buried alive":

Watch them. You'll see what I mean. When found
His eyes had lost their former gay twinkle.
Ants had eaten *that* away; but there was still
Some life in him . . . his forehead *would* wrinkle!   (p 430)

The violence of emotion bursts through the control in a dramatically horrifying manner, all the more violent in contrast to the emotionless tenor of most of MacDiarmid's writing at this period. Significantly when he has control over the form, as in this poem, he is able to release emotion; and this combination makes for a much more satisfying, dramatic, and impressive poetry than the combination of lack of formal control and lack of emotion. There is a tension that lies at the centre of the poems that I have been discussing, a tension that is ultimately the tension between the two sides of the basic paradox, and this tension holds the reader as the catalogues fail to do.

"British Leftish Poetry" is another fine example of how irony and the tension that it creates make a paradoxical vision once more possible. MacDiarmid reverses the relationship of the two paradoxical components of "Glasgow 1960." The effect, however, is similar, the humour and the irony based ultimately on incongruity. Instead of expecting football matches and receiving a cultural treat, the speaker here expects a cultural treat and receives a football match:

> Auden, MacNeice, Day Lewis, I have read them all,
> Hoping against hope to hear the authentic call.
> "A tragical disappointment. There was I
> Hoping to hear old Aeschylus, when the Herald
> Called out, 'Theognis, bring your chorus forward.'
> Imagine what my feelings must have been!
> But then Dexitheus pleased me coming forward
> And singing his Boeotian melody:
> But next came Chaeris with his music truly
> That turned me sick and killed me very nearly.
> And never in my lifetime, man nor boy,
> Was I so vexed as at the present moment;
> To see the Pynx, at this time of the morning,
> Quite empty, when the Assembly should be full"
> And know the explanation I must pass is this
> —You cannot light a match on a crumbling wall.   (p 418)

The use of Aristophanes is brilliant: the rather fussy "tragical disappointment," "killed me very nearly," "so vexed," in contrast to the strength of the climactic "You cannot light a match upon a crumbling wall," where the speaker's disgust emerges purely. Meanwhile the structure represents the crumbling of the wall—in contrast to the solidity that is required to light the match. The "all" rhyme of the first, second, and final lines (a firm, monosyllabic, masculine rhyme) encloses the poem and represents the outline of the wall. Everything that happens in between these framing lines represents the gradual, inevitable crumbling. Nothing rhymes, although sometimes the reader thinks that a rhyme is coming. He is teased by the echo of "call" in "tragical" and "called out" into expecting more than is given, just as the speaker had expected Aeschylus and heard Theognis instead. The closest we get to rhyme is the repetition of "forward," the near miss of "melody," "truly," and "nearly" (all weakly feminine), and the tantalizing thread of "l"'s that run throughout the poem, reminding the reader of the expectation of the "authentic call" and the failure to realize this expectation: "tragical," "Aeschylus," "Herald," "Called," "feelings," "pleased," "melody," "Truly," "killed," "nearly," "lifetime," "full." The total emptiness of the Pynx is emphasized, too, by the total lack of "l"'s. And the vigour of the final lines, originating in the emotion of the speaker who has thrown aside the fussy mask, is increased by the concentration of "l"'s that lead, this time, to a satisfactory rhyme: "You cannot light a match on a crumbling wall." It is a magnificent climax, the "authentic call" of MacDiarmid's individual voice.

Meanwhile his use of scientific facts often results in a tedious lecture-like catalogue. Very occasionally is he able to fit it into his poem as a suggestive part of the paradox. The moments when this merging occurs are rare—"On the Ocean Floor" was one of the few times before this. Scientific facts presented as facts *per se* do not guarantee poetry of a high quality, and often in MacDiarmid's work they accompany a lack of emotion, a loss of formal control, and a poetry of low quality. Sometimes, however, as in "On the Ocean Floor," the leap of imagination takes place through the language of science. Another fine example of a scientific epiphany takes place in "The Glen of Silence" in *Lucky Poet*. The paradox here is tragical. The silence, like the silence of the concluding lyric of *A Drunk Man*, is a silence that is more than a silence, a silence that can be heard. But, unlike the silence of *A Drunk Man*, this is the silence of death rather than the silence of life:

> *By this cold shuddering fit of fear*
> *My heart divines a presence here,*
> *Goddess or ghost yclept;*
> *Wrecker of homes. . . .*
>
> Where have I heard a silence before
> Like this that only a lone bird's cries
> And the sound of a brawling burn to-day
> Serve in this wide empty glen to emphasize?

Every doctor knows it—the stillness of foetal death,
The indescribable silence over the abdomen then!
A silence literally "heard" because of the way
It stands out in the auscultation of the abdomen.

Here is an identical silence, picked out
By a bickering burn and a lone bird's wheeple
—The foetal death in this great "cleared" glen
Where the *fear-tholladh nan tighem* [*sic*] has done   destroyer
  his foul work   of homes
—The tragedy of an unevolved people.   (pp 344-5)

The first stanza prepares us for the paradox. The archaic "yclept" resurrects memories of ballads, and the "goddess or ghost" reinforces the atmosphere of a terrifying supernatural presence. The three stanzas that follow contain the paradox, the silence that can be heard. At the centre lies the medical metaphor, precise, focused, and clinically exact, yet "indescribable" at the same time. This is an empty and a dead silence, surrounded by the two stanzas that show the relationship of this silence to the Highland glen, cleared of its people through the greed and inhumanity of the landlords, the all-powerful "*fear-tholladh nan tighem.*" The central stanza structurally fulfils the role of the dead foetus, surrounded by the mother's body, and the burn and the bird are like the auscultation of the doctor's fingers, sounds that reveal the silence. Meanwhile the sounds of the poem itself provide part of the meaning. The "fit of fear" in the first stanza is linked alliteratively with the "foetal death," the "*fear-tholladh nan tighem,*" and the "foul work." The "b"s of the "bird," "brawling burn," and "bickering burn" are like the tapping of the doctor's fingers. But the most important sound is "s," an "s" that runs threadlike through the poem: the sound of the silence, almost deafening in the central stanza that describes the dead foetus:

> Every doctor knows it—the stillness of foetal death,
> The indescribable silence over the abdomen then!
> A silence literally heard because of the way
> It stands out in the auscultation of the abdomen.

A poem such as this makes the tedious experiments of the "poetry of fact" well worthwhile.

Strangely enough another of the scientific passages that has earned special praise also deals with silence, and once again a paradoxical silence, one that can be heard. Buthlay calls it a "wonderful interpolation of a piece of scientific information as an analogy,"[9] and once again the structure seems to give tangible form to the sound at the heart of the silence. This section of *In Memoriam James Joyce* is enclosed by paragraph-stanzas taken from an article in the *Times Literary Supplement* that deals with Hölderlin's poetry and with his ability to find "the word with which silence speaks / Its own silence without breaking it." Even the space separating the scientific analogy from the rest, and the brackets that surround it set this section off structurally:

> (Silence supervening at poetry's height,
> Like the haemolytic streptococcus
> In the sore throat preceding rheumatic fever
> But which, at the height of the sickness,
> Is no longer there, but has been and gone!
> Or as "laughter is representative of tragedy
> When tragedy is away.")
>
> (p 410)

The analogy has a similar function to that of the intense illustrative lyrics in *A Drunk Man,* and it moves subtly from the paradox of the word that silence speaks, to the medical analogy, to the paradoxical relationship between comedy and tragedy. The brackets seem to enclose the mystery, and the entire stanza is really one long sentence that details the mystery, climaxing at its central point, at the "height of the sickness," with the old MacDiarmid trick of the two suspense-filled pauses that lead into the moving and simple statement: "Is no longer there, but has been and gone!" Once again the "s" is an important sound, the silence that is finally manifest in the "sickness," after the ear has become accustomed to associating it with "r": "supervening," "streptococcus," "sore," "preceding." In a section such as this, as in "The Glen of Silence," MacDiarmid is able to make science an integral part of the poetry, rather than the barrier it so often becomes in the rest of his later writing. The precision of the medical metaphor is a magnificent focus here, drawing the two sides of the paradox together and making them one.

It seems more than a coincidence that two of the most effective scientific metaphors should deal with the "word that silence speaks." Inevitably these call to mind the conclusion of *A Drunk Man* and the silence *"wha's deed owre often and has seen owre much,"* the redeeming silence that cast a pure and quiet tone of affirmation over the entire sequence. When MacDiarmid is able to face the pain of the paradox (for example, the tragedy of the "unevolved people"), the words and the rhythm and the control come to him; and then it doesn't matter whether he is using the language of science, or English with a Scottish accent, or standard English with a Gaelic phrase here and there. The "divided bird" becomes whole, and the sadness of its song is paradoxically part of its beauty. In these poems MacDiarmid has "come through," has risen "whole from the vortex of his unbeing," and the acceptance of the pain and of the vulnerability becomes a quiet kind of affirmation and confidence.

One other section of the later poetry attests to this. In *The Battle Continues* (1957), an abysmally poor volume aimed at the destruction of Roy Campbell and his *Flowering Rifle* (a poem written in support of the Fascists in Spain), MacDiarmid includes four lines that link suffering to a purifying and redeeming power:

> Ah, Spain, already your tragic landscapes
> And the agony of your War to my mind appear
> As tears may come into the eyes of a woman very slowly,
> So slowly as to leave them CLEAR! (p 417)

The climactic "CLEAR" rings out purely and cleanly, with quiet triumph, as "War" leads to "appear," "tears," "leave," and finally "CLEAR." The image is beautiful, the slow gentle movement of the tears, "very slowly, / So slowly," that builds without haste to the climactic clarity. The paradox has formed itself, and when MacDiarmid moves into a "scientific" analogy, it is appropriate and closely linked to the image of the tears in the woman's eyes. The speaker claims that it seems as if "the pressure of a loving hand had gone":

> The touch under which my close-pressed fingers seemed to thrill,
> And the skin to divide up into little zones
> Of heat and cold whose position continually changed,
> So that the whole of my hand, held in that clasp,
> Was in a state of internal movement.
> My eyes that were full of pride,
> My hands that were full of love,
> Are empty again . . . for a while
> For a little while! (p 417)

MacDiarmid is providing another version of the paradox (the same technique as in "The Glen of Silence" and the section dealing with the "word that silence speaks"). The entire hand is held still, but is full of "internal movement," with the "little zones" of heat and cold continually changing places. This detail of the paradox, the internal movement from one side of the paradox to the other, is the detail that provides for the leap of imagination at the end of the section, with its movement from full to empty, and confidently back to full: "empty again . . . for a while." It is a lovely climax, painfully and quietly beautiful, with the parallel between the eyes and the hands: "My eyes that were full of pride, / My hands that were full of love." And once again MacDiarmid gives proof that when he can face the pain that makes the paradox possible, the "divided bird" can still reach "that deep throb."

These moments are rare. No other section of *The Battle Continues* comes close to the quality of this. Much of *In Memoriam James Joyce* is almost unreadable. The various ways in which MacDiarmid tries to bolster his poetry after the *Drunk Man* (language, quantity, Cornish background, scientific details, catalogues) are unsuccessful unless the paradox takes shape, either through irony, or humorous incongruity, or, in its most moving manifestation, in a painful and quiet acceptance of suffering.

When this happens, the epiphany is once more possible, all the more treasured because of its rarity and because of the enormous amount of courage required to face and to accept the pain, to move slowly through darkness towards light.

Postscript

On 17 June 1978, Grieve wrote to William K. Malcolm about his coming death. A diagnosis of rectal cancer had been made two days before, and the doctor had put a six-month limit on his life.

> I have had a long and most interesting life and have no desire to prolong it. I have done, I think, the work I was born to do and even if I live a few years longer I doubt if I could add to that. [1]

The bright courage of this letter (combining, as it does, bravado and humility) was typical of MacDiarmid. The characteristic movement of his mind has always been one that attempts to pass through darkness into light. The work before his adoption of Lallans created the eternal fires of "Consummation" and "A Moment in Eternity." In *Sangschaw* and *Penny Wheep,* Lallans made possible the "chitterin' licht" of the paradoxical vision and helped MacDiarmid to "come fully alive." *A Drunk Man,* the meeting place of contraries and the turning point in his poetry, held darkness and light together in dynamic balance. After *A Drunk Man* the powers of darkness threatened to overwhelm the light, and only rarely was MacDiarmid able to hold the paradox together. While the journey through the darkness has been painful and difficult, the instinctual thrust towards light has remained as a guiding force.

Buthlay has pointed out several instances of MacDiarmid's earliest work influencing his latest: the interest in a "new beginning"; the advance handout being presented as literature; the packing of one parenthesis inside another; the mosaic technique described in *Annals* and used in sections of *In Memoriam James Joyce.* [2] In many ways (and more important ways than those of which Buthlay is aware) MacDiarmid's poetry has indeed come full circle. Most important of all, the central paradoxical vision remains, the guiding thread through all his work. As he indicates in the interview with Glen, "Change itself is necessarily unchanging by definition," and "the beginning is the end." [3]

Ouspensky remains—present not only in the insistence upon "higher logic," the logic of paradox, but also in MacDiarmid's tendency to push always towards the extreme in order to extend human consciousness, and in the search for a new language, one that Ouspensky claimed would be "without verbs."[4] While the polyglot catalogues of MacDiarmid's later poetry fulfil this qualification, the earlier experiments with language (and the most fruitful experiment of all—Lallans) probably originated in this same theory. It has given us some of the best of MacDiarmid's poetry, and some of the worst. Also, the exquisite paradoxes involving the sound of silence find a source in *Tertium Organum* where Ouspensky had claimed that the poet "hears *'the voice of the silence,'* understands the psychological difference between silences, knows that *one silence can differ from another.*"[5]

While Ouspensky may be a major ingredient, MacDiarmid has convincingly made Ouspensky's vision his own. The "chitterin' licht" and the silence *"wha's deed owre often and has seen owre much"* belong uniquely to MacDiarmid. Ouspensky has become part of the vision, and thus remains through all the twists and turns of the poetry, linked inexorably to Langholm and to the boy known as Christopher Grieve. The Langholm laddie who lived under the town library and carried washing baskets full of books downstairs is responsible for the "strong solution of books" in all of MacDiarmid's work. As a result, we are faced with an astonishingly well self-educated man who has taken upon himself the task of educating not only Andy and his mother, but a Scotland full of Philistines, and a world even more full of them. The "strong solution of books" has been responsible not only for the exciting combination of Lallans with an intellectual frame of reference, but also for the most tedious sections of the "poetry of fact." And the word "solution" also indicates the extent to which MacDiarmid, once he had read something, thought of it as *his*. From this "solution" the plagiarism problems have arisen.

Just as insecurity and arrogance come together in the whole plagiarism question, so insecurity and arrogance come together in MacDiarmid's lack of ability to judge the quality of his own work. In the years before his death he published many poems that had been written years earlier and that, for one reason or another, had been excluded from the *Collected Poems*. MacDiarmid claimed that the only reason for their exclusion was financial, and he heralded each new volume by emphasizing how incomplete was his *Collected Poems* volume. Very little of *A Lap of Honour* (1967), *A Clyack-Sheaf (1969), and More Collected Poems* (1970), however, merits inclusion in the *Collected Poems,* and

MacDiarmid would have been much wiser to have left most of these poems in obscurity.

In the *Complete Poems,* MacDiarmid was at last able to indulge his desire to shut nothing out. The result is an expensive and all-inclusive work—of enormous interest to the MacDiarmid scholar, but of much less interest to anyone else. ("Perfect," the subject of the *Times Literary Supplement* debate, has been boldly reinstated, while "Beyond Desire"—lifted straight from Hart Crane and substituted, by a stroke of clumsy genius, for "Perfect" in the second *Collected Poems*—has quietly disappeared. Nothing else has quietly disappeared; it is all there).

MacDiarmid's reluctance to admit that some of his work is of a lesser quality and his determination to let nothing perish in obscurity must have felt happily at home in the *Complete Poems* project.

One of the rare moments in which he recognized his inability to judge his own work is to be found in the early *Annals,* in the description of the mind of the narrator (much like MacDiarmid's own). At one moment it produces "the shooting of frost crystals on a window pane," and at another, "an ant-heap stirred."[6] MacDiarmid's later poetry, with the fatal division between the "thin high call" and "that deep throb," reveals that his mind is still that of the narrator of *Annals:* "Change itself is necessarily unchanging, by definition." The young Christopher Grieve of Langholm with all his uncertainties, frustrations, and hopes, remains as the most important ingredient in the poetry of Hugh MacDiarmid.

Similarly Christopher Grieve's frustrated desire to reach his father parallels MacDiarmid's movement towards "the whole, the general balance of things." The urge towards synthesis manifests itself in the desire to merge with God, the wish to create a society where class would be bound to class "in the treasure of the one life," the need to find a "moment in eternity,"[7] and, most important of all, in the formation of the paradox that reconciles all contraries.

In his poetry MacDiarmid has shown unique courage in standing between the worlds of vision and reality. Painfully he has faced the full horror of what it means to be a human being, has accepted it, and has been able, throughout the pain and the acceptance, to maintain a conviction that there is an Eden and a paradise, a world where man can achieve more than he has already achieved.

His subject from his earliest work to his latest has been man: the thistle and the rose that form one plant. Throughout the various stages of his poetry, this theme has remained constant. The balance of the paradox has been anything but steady. While light has emerged from darkness, darkness has threatened to engulf light. While Lallans has helped in the formation of the paradox, polyglot and catalogues have threatened to tear it apart. While Marxism has contributed to its balance, both Scotland and Christianity have shaped its nature.

It has produced the "irritating cuckoo" and the "deep throb" of the nightingale. It has lacked consistency, but it has gathered to itself "a' beasts." And it has made out of the various ingredients a poetry that is unique in the twentieth century, a poetry that in itself manifests all the failures and all the hopes of man, all his ugliness and all his beauty:

> The munelicht that owre clear defines
> The thistle's shrill cantankerous lines
> E'en noo whiles insubstantialises
> Its grisly form and 'stead devises
> A maze o' licht, a siller-frame. . . .

We cannot choose the rose and refuse the thistle.

Notes

CHAPTER ONE: THISTLE AND ROSE

1. For example, John Hughes, "Humanism and the Orphic Voice," *Saturday Review* (22 May 1971), pp 31-33; Karl Miller, "Scotch on the Rocks," *The New York Review of Books* (2 Dec. 1971), pp 13-16; Peter Jay, "Introduction," *Triquarterly,* 21 (Spring 1971), xi-xx; and my own "Language and Vision in the Early Poetry of Hugh MacDiarmid," *Contemporary Literature,* 12 (Autumn 1971), 495-508.

2. Lallans, "Braid Scots," or "synthetic" or "plastic" Scots, will refer in this book to the poetic language used by MacDiarmid and other modern Scottish writers. MacDiarmid feels free to use Scottish words from any dialect or century, provided they suit his purpose.

3. David Daiches, "Hugh MacDiarmid: The Early Poems," *Hugh MacDiarmid: a festschrift,* ed. K. D. Duval and Sydney Goodsir Smith (Edinburgh: Duval, 1962), p 47.

4. *The Modern Poets: A Critical Introduction* (New York: Oxford University Press, 1960), p 132.

5. *Lucky Poet* (London: Methuen, 1943), pp xxi-xxii.

6. "The Word Which Silence Speaks," *Akros,* 4 (Jan. 1970), pp 63-64.

7. "Talking with Five Thousand People in Edinburgh," *Poetry Scotland,* 2 (1945), p 50.

8. *Lucky Poet,* p 2 and p 8.

9. *Lucky Poet,* p 8.

10. *Lucky Poet,* pp 8-9.

11. *Lucky Poet,* p 219.

12. *Lucky Poet,* p 3.

13. *Lucky Poet,* p 19.

14. *Lucky Poet,* pp 76-77, p 225.

15. *Lucky Poet,* p 219.

16. *Lucky Poet,* p 230.

17. *The Uncanny Scot: A Selection of Prose by Hugh MacDiarmid,* ed. Kenneth Buthlay (London: MacGibbon and Kee, 1968), p 57.

18. *Uncanny Scot,* p 48.

19. *Lucky Poet,* p 225.

20. *Uncanny Scot,* p 60.

21. *Uncanny Scot,* p 74 and p 58.

22. *Uncanny Scot,* p 59.

23. *Lucky Poet,* p 228, p 2, and p 224.

24. *Lucky Poet,* p 40 and p 226.

25. *Lucky Poet,* p 227.

26. *The Company I've Kept* (London: Hutchinson, 1966), p 16.

27. *Lucky Poet,* p 230.

28. *Lucky Poet,* p 227.

29. *Early Lyrics by Hugh MacDiarmid,* ed. J. K. Annand (Preston: Akros, 1968), pp 6-7.

30. *Lucky Poet,* p 228.

31. *Lucky Poet,* p 18; *Company,* p 24.

32. *Lucky Poet,* p 19; *Collected Poems of Hugh MacDiarmid,* ed. John C. Weston, revised edition (New York: Macmillan, 1967), p 7 and p 289. Subsequent references to this edition will appear in the text.

33. *Uncanny Scot,* p 58.

34. *Uncanny Scot,* p 58.

CHAPTER TWO: "TREMBLING SUNBEAMS"

1. *Selected Essays of Hugh MacDiarmid,* ed. Duncan Glen (London: Jonathan Cape, 1969), p 44.

2. Duncan Glen, *Hugh MacDiarmid and the Scottish Renaissance* (Edinburgh and London: Chambers, 1964); Kenneth Buthlay, *Hugh MacDiarmid* (Edinburgh and London: Oliver and Boyd, 1964).

3. *Selected Essays,* p 44.

4. "The Word Which Silence Speaks," p 58.

5. *Selected Essays,* p 39.

6. *Selected Essays,* p 40.

7. *Uncanny Scot,* p 161.

8. See J. K. Annand's evidence for this date in *Early Lyrics of Hugh MacDiarmid,* p 10.

9. P. D. Ouspensky, *Tertium Organum: The Third Canon of Thought: A Key to the Enigmas of the World,* second American edition, authorized and revised (New York: Knopf, 1922), p 262.

10. *Selected Essays,* p 44.

11. *Tertium Organum,* p 83 and p 86.

12. *Tertium Organum,* p 161.

13. *Tertium Organum,* p 97.

14. *Tertium Organum,* p 228.

15. *Tertium Organum,* p 319.

16. *Tertium Organum,* p 134, p 265, p 158, p 161, p 171, p 199.

17. *Tertium Organum,* p 122.

18. *Tertium Organum,* p 162.

19. *The Scottish Chapbook,* 1 (Feb. 1923), p 183.

20. *Uncanny Scot,* p 97.

21. *Lucky Poet,* p xiii.

22. *Uncanny Scot,* p 15.

23. *Uncanny Scot,* p 67.

24. See Blake's *The Marriage of Heaven and Hell.*

25. *Uncanny Scot,* p 23.

26. *Triquarterly,* 21 (Spring 1971), p xv.

27. I. C. Smith, *The Golden Lyric* (Preston: Akros, 1967), p 17.

28. *Tertium Organum,* p 166 and p 170.

29. G. Gregory Smith, *Scottish Literature* (London: Macmillan, 1919), p 60.

30. Glen, p 40.

31. *Albyn* (London: Kegan Paul, Trench, Trubner, 1927), p 42.

32. Gregory Smith, p 33.

33. Gregory Smith, p 20.

34. Gregory Smith, p 20.

35. Norman Fruman, *Coleridge, The Damaged Archangel* (New York: Braziller, 1971).

36. "The Caledonian Antisyzygy and the Gaelic Idea," *Selected Essays,* pp 56-74.

37. *Tertium Organum,* p 244.

38. *Selected Essays,* p 58.

39. *At the Sign of the Thistle* (London: Nott, [1934]), pp 58-59.

40. For example, the accusation made by Karl Miller that "The Little White Rose" was improvised on a political platform by Compton MacKenzie.

41. *Annals of the Five Senses* (Montrose: C. M. Grieve, 1923), acknowledgement page, unnumbered.

42. *Uncanny Scot,* p 72.

CHAPTER THREE: "CHITTERIN' LICHT"

1. *Early Lyrics,* p 7.

2. *Early Lyrics,* p 7.

3. *Company,* p 184.

4. *Company,* p 104.

5. *Lucky Poet,* p 229.

6. *Annals,* dedication page.

7. *Annals,* p 84.

8. *Annals,* p 86.

9. *Annals,* p 194.

10. *Annals,* p 192.

11. *Annals,* p 183.

12. *Lucky Poet,* p 268; *Tertium Organum,* p 281.

13. *Tertium Organum,* p 281.

14. *Tertium Organum,* p 312.

15. *The Scottish Chapbook,* 1 (August, 1922), p iii.

16. *The Scottish Chapbook,* 1 (Mar. 1923), p 210.

17. See Glen, p 75.

18. Sir James Wilson, *Lowland Scotch as Spoken in the Lower Strathearn District of Perthshire* (London: Oxford University Press, 1915), p 169, p 190.

19. *Lucky Poet,* pp 18-19.

20. *Lucky Poet,* p 35.

21. Norman MacCaig, in conversation, January 1965.

22. *The Scottish Chapbook,* 1 (Oct. 1922), p 63.

23. *The Scottish Chapbook,* 1 (Feb. 1923), p 182.

24. *Penny Wheep* (Edinburgh: Blackwood, 1926), p 4.

25. *The Scottish Chapbook,* 2 (Nov.-Dec. 1923), p 63.

26. *The Scottish Chapbook,* 2 (Nov.-Dec. 1923), p 69.

27. *The Scottish Chapbook,* 2 (Nov.-Dec. 1923), p 70.

CHAPTER FOUR: "A ROUTH O' CONTRARIES"

1. *A Drunk Man Looks at the Thistle*, ed. John C. Weston (Amherst: University of Massachusetts Press, 1971), p 115. Hereafter, "Weston."

2. "Letter to Hugh MacDiarmid, 1940," *Poetry Scotland,* 2 (1945), p 27.

3. *Glasgow Herald,* 13 February 1926. See Weston, p 116.

4. *A Drunk Man* (Edinburgh: 200 Burns Club, 1962), p xiii. Hereafter, "Daiches."

5. Gregory Smith, p 4.

6. Gregory Smith, p 20.

7. Weston, pp 3-4.

8. *Times Literary Supplement,* 22 September 1927, pp 650-51.

9. *Early Lyrics,* p 15.

10. Daiches, p xvi.

11. Daiches, pp xix-xx.

12. Buthlay, p 49.

13. Buthlay, pp 50-51.

14. Weston edition of *A Drunk Man*.

15. Weston, pp 121-22.

16. Weston, p 116.

17. *Glasgow Herald*, 17 Dec. 1925, and 13 Feb. 1926. See Weston, pp 115-16.

18. Weston, p 115.

19. Weston, p 51.

20. "Talking with F. G. Scott," *The Saltire Review*, 1 (Winter 1954), p 53.

21. *Francis George Scott* (Edinburgh: Macdonald, 1955), p 24.

22. "The Poetry of Hugh MacDiarmid," *The Free Man*, 7 April 1934, p 9.

23. Daiches, p xv.

24. *Collected Poems*, p xix.

25. "Hugh MacDiarmid: *Sangschaw* and *A Drunk Man Looks at the Thistle*," *Studies in Scottish Literature*, 7 (Jan. 1970), p 179.

26. "Hugh MacDiarmid: *Sangschaw* and *A Drunk Man*," p 177.

27. *The Scottish Chapbook*, 1 (Feb. 1923), p 182.

28. Wilson, pp 139-40.

29. *Festschrift*, p 35.

30. Buthlay, p 74.

31. *Modern Russian Poetry* (New York: Harcourt Brace, 1921), pp 128-30.

32. *Modern Russian Poetry*, p vi.

33. "And this dead thing, this loathsome black impurity, / This horror that I shrink from—is my soul." *Modern Russian Poetry*, p 70.

34. *Tertium Organum*, pp 243-44.

35. "Hugh MacDiarmid: *Sangschaw* and *A Drunk Man*," p 179.

36. *Tertium Organum*, p 171.

37. Weston, p 122.

38. *Early Lyrics*, p 15.

39. *A Drunk Man* (1953), p xx; Weston, p 122.

CHAPTER FIVE: "SHADOWS THAT FEED ON THE LIGHT"

1. *Scots Observer*, 17 December 1931, p 15. See Glen, p 98.

2. *Scots Independent*, 3 (June 1929), p 106. See Glen, p 102.

3. *Company*, pp 192-93; *Burns Today and Tomorrow* (Edinburgh: Castle Wynd, 1959), p 50.

4. *Albyn*, p 13.

5. *Scots Independent*, 3 (May 1929), p 89. See Glen, p 149.

6. *Criterion,* 10 (July 1931), pp 612-13.

7. Glen, p 148.

8. *Hugh MacDiarmid: National Library Catalogue* (Edinburgh: National Library, 1967), p 13.

9. Glen, p 133.

10. *Lucky Poet,* pp 41 and 44.

11. "MacDiarmid—the Man," *Jabberwock,* 5 (1958), p 15. See Glen, p 135.

12. *Francis George Scott,* p 42.

13. *Lucky Poet,* p 19.

14. *Selected Essays,* p 53.

15. *Selected Essays,* p 55.

16. *Lucky Poet,* p 218.

17. *Lucky Poet,* p 219.

CHAPTER SIX: "LABRADORITE CRYSTALS"

1. *A Drunk Man* (Glasgow: Caledonian, 1953), p x.

2. *A Lap of Honour* (London: Macgibbon and Kee, 1967), p 11.

3. *Stony Limits and Scots Unbound* (Edinburgh: Castle Wynd, 1956), p v.

4. *The Scottish Chapbook,* 1 (Mar. 1923), p 210.

5. *Stony Limits and Scots Unbound,* p 151.

6. *Stony Limits* (London: Gollancz, 1934), p 66.

7. *Stony Limits,* p 65.

8. *At the Sign of the Thistle,* p 92.

9. *Stony Limits and Scots Unbound,* p 50.

10. *Stony Limits,* p 62.

11. *Stony Limits,* p 22.

12. *Stony Limits,* p 23.

13. *Stony Limits and Scots Unbound,* pp 44, 48, 49, 50, 54, 46.

14. *Stony Limits and Scots Unbound,* p 56.

15. *Stony Limits and Scots Unbound,* pp 48, 43.

16. *Stony Limits,* p 57.

17. Buthlay, p 82.

18. Buthlay, p 83.

19. *Stony Limits,* p 66.

20. *Stony Limits and Scots Unbound,* pp 100, 101.

21. *Stony Limits and Scots Unbound,* p 108.

22. *Stony Limits and Scots Unbound,* p 111.

23. *Stony Limits and Scots Unbound,* p 118.

24. *Stony Limits and Scots Unbound,* p 92.
25. *Stony Limits and Scots Unbound,* p 92.

CHAPTER SEVEN: "POLITICS IS BAIRNS' PLAY"

1. *Annals,* pp 191-92.
2. See Glen, p 126. "Why I Rejoined," *Daily Worker,* 28 March 1957, p 2.
3. See Glen, p 126.
4. *Selected Essays,* p 142.
5. *The Scots Literary Tradition* (London: Faber, 1962), p 158.
6. Buthlay, p 92.
7. Buthlay, p 91; *Second Hymn to Lenin* (London: Nott, 1935), p 65.

CHAPTER EIGHT: "DIFFERENT BIRDS IN DIFFERENT PLACES"

1. *In Memoriam James Joyce* (Glasgow: Maclellan, 1955), pp 12-13.
2. *Early Lyrics,* p 15.
3. *In Memoriam,* p 16.
4. Edwin Morgan's "Poetry and Knowledge in MacDiarmid's Later Work" (*Festschrift,* pp 129-39) is one of the rare examples.
5. Buthlay, p 105.
6. *Selected Essays,* pp 75-76.
7. See *Collected Poems,* pp 418-32. According to Buthlay (p 110), other passages were broadcast on the B.B.C. Third Programme on 19 December 1956.
8. *Complete Poems: 1920-1976,* edited by Michael Grieve and W. R. Aitken, 2 vols. (London: Martin Brian & O'Keeffe, 1978), p vi.
9. Buthlay, p 106.

POSTSCRIPT

1. *The Scotsman,* 13 September 1978.
2. Buthlay, pp 100-03.
3. "The Word that Silence Speaks," *Akros,* 4 (Jan. 1970), pp 63, 64.
4. *Tertium Organum,* p 122.
5. *Tertium Organum,* p 161.
6. *Annals,* p 86 and p 84.
7. *Annals,* p 192, p 27.

Glossary

a', *all*
abaw, *to abash*
abies, *except*
aboond, *to abound*
abune, *above*
aff, *off*
afore: *before*
agley, *astray*
ahint, *behind*
aiblins, *perhaps*
aidle, *slop*
ain, *own*
aince, *once*
airel, *note*
alane, *alone*
allemand, *formal procession*
allevolie, *at random*
alunt, *alight*
amang, *among*
amna, *am not*
ana', *also*
aneth, *beneath*
antrin, *strange*
arrachin', *going astray*
ashypet, *employed in lowest kitchen work*
aside, *beside*
atween, *between*
auld, *old*
ava', *at all*
awa', *away*
awn, *own*
ayont, *beyond*

ba', *ball*
bairn, *child*
bane, *bone*
baudron, *cat*
bauld, *(a) bold; (b) to make bold*
bawaw, *look of contempt*
bear-meal-raik, *fruitless errand; finding barley, not oatmeal*
bellwaver, *to struggle*

bellythraws, *colic*
benmaist, *lowest, inmost*
bensil o' a bleeze, *big fire*
beschact, *tattered*
bide, *to stay*
bield, *shelter*
biggin', *building*
bike, *nest*
birssy, *bristly*
bladder, *babble*
blae, *blue*
blate, *shy*
bleeze, *blaze*
blethers, *nonsense*
blinter, *to gleam*
bluid, *blood*
bonnie, *beautiful*
borneheid, *impetuous*
boss, *front of body from breast to loins*
boutgate, *circuitous road*
braid, *broad*
brak, *to break*
braw, *fine*
breenge, *to hurtle*
breist, *breast*
brenn, *to burn*
brent, *high, straight*
bricht, *bright*
brither, *brother*
broukit, *deserted*
burn, *stream*
buss, *bush*
byous, *wonderful*

cairney, *little cairn*
Cairngorm, *yellow semi-precious stone found in Cairngorm mountains*
camsteerie, *perverse*
canna, *cannot*
cauld, *cold*
chafts, *jaws*

cheenge, *to change*
chiel, *man*
Chinee, *Chinese*
chitterin', *shivering*
chow, *to chew*
chowl, *to twist*
chun, *sprout*
clanjamfrie, *shebang*
clapt, *shrunken*
cleiks, *merest shadow*
cleuch, *ravine*
clytach, *nonsense*
cod, *pillow*
coft, *bought*
coor, *to cower*
coorse, *course*
coort, *court*
coup, *to raise (a glass)*
courage-bag, *scrotum*
couthless, *cold*
cowd, *to float slowly*
crammasy, *scarlet*
cranglin', *winding*
cratur, *creature*
creesh, *fat*
crine, *to shrivel*
croodit, *crowded*
croon, *crown*
crowdle, *to crawl*
cude, *barrel*
cull, *testicle*
cuttedly, *tartly*

dainty-davie, *fastidious person*
daised, *discoloured, rotten*
daith, *death*
datchie, *secret*
daur, *to dare*
daurk, *dark*
dawin', *dawn*
dee, *to die*
deef, *deaf*
deid, *dead*
deil, *devil*
deltit, *spoiled*
derk, *dark*
dern, *to hide*

din, *done*
dinna, *do not*
dirl, *do not*
dirl, *rattle*
dod, *God!* (euphemism)
dog-hank, *inability of male dog to withdraw during mating*
doited, *mad*
doonsin', *dazzling*
doot, *doubt*
doun, *down*
doup, *empty shell*
dour, *sullen, stubborn*
dowf, *unfeeling, gloomy*
dozent, *stupid*
dree, *to suffer*
dreid, *dread*
drob, *to prick*
drochlin', *puny*
droun, *to drown*
drucken, *drunken*
drulie, *muddy*
drutlin', *piddling*
dry-gair-flow, *place where two hills meet*
dub, *puddle*
duffie, *spongy*
dune, *done*
dung, *dashed*
durty, *dirty*

eelyin', *vanishing*
eemis, *variable, uncertain, precarious*
een, *eyes*
e'en, *even*
efter, *after*
eident, *busy, eager*
eisenin', *lusting*
elbuck, *elbow*
Embro, *Edinburgh*
emeraud, *emerald*
ettle, *to try*

fa', *to fall*
faddom, *to fathom*
faem, *foam*
fain, *eager, longing*

fanerels, *flapping parts*
fank, *coil, tangle*
fankle, *to tangle*
farles, *filaments of ash*
faur, *far*
fecht, *fight*
feck, *plenty*
fegs, *faith!*
ferlie, *wonder, miracle, marvel*
fike-ma-fuss, *fastidious person*
fiky, *troublesome*
flauchter, *to flutter*
flee, *a fly; to fly*
fleer, *to flare*
floo'er, *flower*
forbye, *moreover*
forenenst, *in front of*
forenicht, *late afternoon*
forhooied, *deserted*
fork in the wa', *couvade, folk custom
    to transfer labour pains to husband*
fou, *drunk*
fousome, *disgusting*
frae, *from*
fraucht, *cargo*
freaths, *foam*
fu', *full*
fug, *moss*
fule, *fool*
fullyery, *foliage*

gaadie, *howler, rod*
gallimaufry, *hotch-potch*
gallus, *indifferent*
gane, *gone*
gang, *to go*
gangrel, *wanderer*
gant, *to yawn*
gar, *to compel, to make*
gausty, *ghostly*
gaw, *hold*
gean, *cherry tree*
geg, *deception*
get, *child, bastard*
gey, *very*
ghaist, *ghost*
gi'e, *to give*

gin, *if*
gird, *hoop*
glead, *ember, spark*
gleg, *eager*
glit, *slime, semen*
gloffs and gowls, *dark and light*
gorded, *frosted*
gorlin', *fledgling*
goun, *gown*
gowd, *gold*
greet, *to weep*
grieshuckle, *glowing embers*
gudeman, *husband*
guid, *good*
gurly, *savage*
gy, *spectacle*

ha', *hall*
ha'e, *to have*
haik, *to lift up*
haill, *(a) whole; (b) hail*
hain, *to keep, preserve*
hairst, *autumn*
hank, *to fasten*
harns, *brain*
haud, *to hold*
hauf, *half*
hauflin', *lad*
hazelraw, *lichen*
heicht, *height*
heid, *head*
hert, *heart*
hes, *has*
het, *hot*
hing, *to hang*
hizzie, *hussie*
hoo, *how*
hoose, *house*
how-dumb-deid, *midnight*
howe, *(a) hollow; (b) to hollow*
howff, *pub*
hunner, *hundred*

i', *in*
ilka, *every*
ingangs, *entrails*
ingle, *hearth*

intil, *inside*
ither, *other*

jouk, *to evade*

kaa, *to trap*
kailyaird, *kitchen garden
(disparaging term used to describe
excessively homely and sentimental Lallans writers)*
keek, *to peer*
keethin', *circles on water that
indicate the presence of fish*
ken, *to know*
kennin' haund, *sympathetic hand*
kip, *brothel*
kittle, *to tickle*
kyth, *to appear*

laich, *low*
lair, *learning*
laith, *loath*
Lallans, *"Braid Scots," or "synthetic" or "Plastic" Scots, the poetic
language used by MacDiarmid and
other modern Scottish poets*
lamoo, *lamb's wool*
lang, *long*
langsyne, *long ago*
lassie, *girl*
lauch, *laugh*
lave, *rest*
laverock, *lark*
leez me, *my blessings on*
let dab, *let on*
licht, *light*
lichtnin', *lightning*
lift, *air, sky*
lig, *to lie*
lint, *flax*
lochan, *small lake*
lo'e, *to love*
lood, *loud*
loon, *boy*
loppert, *clotted*
loup, *to leap, jump*
lowe, *flame*
lowse, *to set free*

lug, *ear*
lyart, *grey*

mair, *more*
maist, *most*
mapamound, *map of the world*
maun, *must*
mauna, *must not*
mebbe, *maybe*
mell, *to mix*
midge, *gnat*
mither, *mother*
mochiness, *closeness*
monoplies, *intestines*
mony, *many*
muckle, *large*
muffin-mouit, *muffin-mouthed*
mummle, *mumble*
mune, *moon*
mureburn, *annual burning of the
moor*

nae, *no*
nane, *none*
neebor, *neighbour*
neist, *next*
nesh, *nervous, anxious*
nicht, *night*
no', *not*
nocht, *nothing*
noo, *now*

ocht, *anything*
on-ding, *heavily falling rain*
ony, *any*
oor, *our*
'oor, *hour*
oot, *out*
ootour, *all over*
ootrie, *outré*
or, *before*
orra, *worthless, nondescript*
owre, *over, too*

paddle-doo, *frog*
pang, *to cram*
pap o' his hass, *uvula*
paspey, *dance*

pavane, *dance*
pavvy, *bustle*
peerieweerie, *the faintest sound, the smallest thing*
penny wheep, *beer bought for a penny*
plicht, *plight*
ploomen, *ploughmen*
plumm, *deep pool*
pooder, *powder*
pooer, *power*

querty, *lively*
quhile, *while*
quither, *beam*

radgie, *ready*
raff o' rain, *streaks of rain*
railya, *striped satin*
raim-pig, *basin of cream*
rashimill, *toy mill made of rushes*
ratch, *wrenching*
raw, *row*
reek, *smoke*
reenge, *to range*
reid, *red*
reishle, *to rustle*
reistit, *dried*
richt, *right*
rin, *to run*
ripe, *to plunder*
ripples, *diarrhea*
rive, *tearing*
riz, *rose (to rise)*
roond, *round*
routh, *abundance*
row, *to wrap; to roar*

sae, *so*
sair, *sore*
sall, *shall*
samyn, *ship's deck*
sang, *song*
saul, *soul*
saut, *salt*
saxpence, *sixpence*
scanse, *to glint*

scaut-heid, *scrofulous*
scoogie, *apron*
scunner, *disgust*
scunnersome, *disgusting*
seam, *semen*
seely, *happy, blessed*
sel', *self*
ser', *to serve*
shaddaw, *shadow*
shair, *sure*
shak, *to shake*
sheckle, *wrist*
sheepeik, *sheep grease*
shirrel, *turf*
sib, *blood relative*
sic, *such*
sicht, *sight*
siller, *silver*
sin', *since*
sinnen, *sinew*
skinkle, *to shine, gleam*
skrymmorie, *terrible*
slee, *sly*
sliggy, *cunning*
slorp, *to slobber*
sly, *green slime*
sma-bookit, *shrunken*
smeddum, *spirit*
snaw, *snow*
socht, *sought*
sonsy, *fat and happy*
soon', *sound*
souple, *supple; to bend*
spale, *to run down*
spatril, *note*
spauld, *backbone*
speil, *to run, play*
spelder, *to sprawl*
sperk, *spark*
spirt, *spurt*
splairgin', *splashing*
spleet-new, *brand new*
splore, *frolic, revel*
spreit, *spirit*
stairch, *starch*
stan', *to stand*
stane, *stone*

stang, *sting, prick*
starn, *star*
stented, *appointed*
stert, *to start*
sticket, *stuck*
stot, *(a) to bounce; (b) ox*
stound, *to throb*
stramash, *uproar*
strang, *strong*
strauchten, *to straighten*
s'ud, *should*
swee, *to sway, to move*
swelth, *whirlpool*
syne, *then*

tae, *to*
ta'en, *taken*
talla, *tallow, wax*
tap, *top*
tent, *heed*
tew, *to toil*
thegither, *together*
thocht, *thought*
thole, *to bear, suffer*
thorter-ill, *palsy*
thow, *to thaw*
thrang, *busy*
thrapple, *gullet*
thraw, *to throw*
threep, *to assert continually*
threid, *thread*
thieveless, *profligate*
thring, *to shrug*
thunner, *thunder*
till, *to*
tine, *to lose*
tint, *lost*
toom, *empty*
toon, *town*
tousie, *dishevelled*
tow, *rope*
twa, *two*
twal', *twelve*

'ud, *would*
ugsome, *disgusting*
unco, *strange*

vieve, *vivid*

wa', *wall*
wad, *would*
waesome, *sad*
waesucks, *also*
wame, *belly*
wan, *one*
wan-shoggin', *pale-shaking*
wark, *work*
warld, *world*
watergaw, *indistinct rainbow*
waur, *worse*
wean, *child*
wecht, *weight*
wede awa', *destroyed*
wee, *small*
weel, *well*
weet, *wet*
weird, *fate*
wha, *who*
wha's, *(a) who is; (b) whose*
whatna, *what sort of*
whaur, *where*
wheen, *few*
whud, *to thud, flit by*
whummle, *to overturn*
whuram, *crotchet*
wi', *with*
widna, *would not*
winnock, *window*
wi'oot, *without*
wir, *small crabbed person*
worm-i'-the-cheek, *toothache*
wrocht, *wrought*
wud, *mad*
wudden, *wooden*
wumman, *woman*
wun, *to win*
wund, *wind*

yech, *exclamation of disgust*
yin, *one*
yird, *to bury*
yirdly, *earthly*
yon, *that*
youky, *itchy*
yowdendrift, *counterswirl of snow*
yow-trummle, *cold weather in July
after the sheep shearing*

List of Works Consulted

I. WORKS BY MACDIARMID *(arranged chronologically)*

PROSE AND VERSE:

Annals of the Five Senses. (By C. M. Grieve). Montrose: C. M. Grieve, 1923.

The Islands of Scotland: Hebrides, Orkneys, and Shetlands. New York: Scribner's, 1939.

Lucky Poet. A Self-Study in Literature and Political Ideas. London: Methuen, 1943.

VERSE:

Sangschaw. Edinburgh: Blackwood, 1925.

Penny Wheep. Edinburgh: Blackwood, 1926.

A Drunk Man Looks at the Thistle. Edinburgh: Blackwood, 1926.

The Lucky Bag. Edinburgh: Porpoise, 1927.

To Circumjack Cencrastus or The Curly Snake. Edinburgh: Blackwood, 1930.

First Hymn to Lenin and Other Poems. London: Unicorn, 1931.

Scots Unbound and Other Poems. Stirling: Eneas Mackay, 1932.

Selected Poems. London: Macmillan, 1934.

Stony Limits and Other Poems. London: Gollancz, 1934.

Second Hymn to Lenin and Other Poems. London: Nott, 1935.

Speaking for Scotland. Selected Poems. Baltimore: Contemporary Poetry, 1946.

A Kist of Whistles. Glasgow: Maclellan, [1947].

A Drunk Man Looks at the Thistle. 2nd edition with introduction by David Daiches. Glasgow: Caledonian Press, 1953.

Selected Poems of Hugh MacDiarmid. Edited by Oliver Brown. Glasgow: Maclellan, 1954.

In Memoriam James Joyce. From A Vision of World Language. Glasgow: Maclellan, 1955.

A Drunk Man Looks at the Thistle. 3rd ed. Edinburgh: Castle Wynd, 1956.

Stony Limits and Scots Unbound and Other Poems. Edinburgh: Castle Wynd, 1956.

The Battle Continues. Edinburgh: Castle Wynd, 1957.

Three Hymns to Lenin. Edinburgh: Castle Wynd, 1957.

The Kind of Poetry I Want. Edinburgh: K. D. Duval, 1961.

Collected Poems of Hugh MacDiarmid. New York: Macmillan, 1962.

A Drunk Man Looks at the Thistle. 4th ed. Edinburgh: The 200 Burns Club, 1962.

The Ministry of Water. Glasgow: Duncan Glen, 1964.

The Terrible Crystal: A Vision of Scotland. Skelmorlie, Ayrshire: Duncan Glen, 1964.

The Fire of the Spirit. Glasgow: Duncan Glen, 1965.

Wuchulls. Preston: Akros, 1966.

Collected Poems of Hugh MacDiarmid. Revised edition, edited by John C. Weston. New York: Macmillan, 1967.

A Lap of Honour. London: MacGibbon and Kee, 1967.

Early Lyrics by Hugh MacDiarmid recently discovered among letters to his schoolmaster and friend George Ogilvie, with an appreciation of Ogilvie by Hugh MacDiarmid. Edited by J. K. Annand. Preston: Akros, 1968.

A Clyack-Sheaf. London: MacGibbon and Kee, 1969.

More Collected Poems. London: MacGibbon and Kee, 1970.

Selected Poems. Edited by David Craig and John Manson. Harmondsworth: Penguin, 1970.

A Drunk Man Looks at the Thistle. Edited by John C. Weston. Amherst: Univ. of Mass., 1971.

The Hugh MacDiarmid Anthology: Poems in Scots and English. Edited by Michael Grieve and Alexander Scott. London: Routledge and Kegan Paul, 1972.

Song of the Seraphim. London: Covent Garden Press, 1973.

Direadh, I, II, III. Frenich, Foss: Kulgin Duval and Colin H. Hamilton, 1974.

The Socialist Poems of Hugh MacDiarmid. Edited by T. S. Law and Thurso Berwick. London: Routledge and Kegan Paul, 1978.

Complete Poems: 1920-1976. 2 vols. Edited by Michael Grieve and W. R. Aitken. London: Martin Brian & O'Keeffe, 1978.

PROSE

Contemporary Scottish Studies: First Series. (By C. M. Grieve). London: Leonard Parsons, 1926.

Albyn; or Scotland and the Future. (By C. M. Grieve). London: Kegan Paul, 1927.

At the Sign of the Thistle: A Collection of Essays. London: Nott, [1934].

Scottish Eccentrics. London: Routledge, 1936.

Francis George Scott. An Essay on the Occasion of His Seventy-fifth Birthday, 25th January 1955. Edinburgh: Macdonald, 1955.

Burns Today and Tomorrow. Edinburgh: Castle Wynd, 1959.

The Man of (almost) Independent Mind. Edinburgh: Giles Gordon, 1962.

The Ugly Birds without Wings. Edinburgh: Donaldson, 1962.

Sydney Goodsir Smith. Edinburgh: Hamilton, 1963.

The Company I've Kept. Essays in Autobiography. London: Hutchison, 1966.

The Uncanny Scot: A Selection of Prose by Hugh MacDiarmid. Edited by Kenneth Buthlay. London: MacGibbon and Kee, 1968.

Selected Essays of Hugh MacDiarmid. Edited by Duncan Glen. London: Jonathan Cape, 1969.

BOOKS AND MAGAZINES EDITED BY MACDIARMID:

Northern Numbers, being representative selections from certain living Scottish poets. Unsigned. Edinburgh: T. N. Foulis, 1920.

Northern Numbers, being representative selections from certain living Scottish poets. Second Series. Edited by C. M. Grieve. Edinburgh: T. N. Foulis, 1921.

Northern Numbers, being representative selections from certain living Scottish poets. Third Series. Edited by C. M. Grieve. Montrose: C. M. Grieve, 1922.

The Scottish Chapbook. Edited by C. M. Grieve. I, 1 (Aug. 1922)—II, 3 (Nov.-Dec. 1923).

The Scottish Nation. Edited by C. M. Grieve. I, 1 (May 1923)—II, 8 (Dec. 1923).

The Northern Review. Edited by C. M. Grieve. I, 1 (May 1924)—4 (Sept. 1924).

Living Scottish Poets. Edited by C. M. Grieve. London: Benn [1931].

The Voice of Scotland: a Quarterly Magazine of Scottish Arts and Affairs. I, 1 (June-Aug. 1938)—IX, 2 (Aug. 1958).

The Golden Treasury of Scottish Poetry. London: Macmillan, 1940.

Robert Burns: Poems. London: Grey Walls Press, 1949.

Poetry Scotland. No. 4. Edinburgh: Serif Books, 1949.

Scottish Art and Letters. P.E.N. Congress number, Edinburgh Festival, 1950. Glasgow: Maclellan, 1950.

Selections from the Poems of William Dunbar. Edinburgh: Oliver and Boyd, 1952.

MISCELLANEOUS:

"To a Young Poet." *The Saltire Review*, 6 (Spring 1959), 75-77.

"Bracken Hills in Autumn." *New Saltire*, 5 (Autumn 1962), 30-31.

"The Return of the Long Poem." In *Ezra Pound: Perspectives: Essays in Honor of His Eightieth Birthday*. Edited by Noel Stock. Chicago: Regnery, 1965.

II.   WORKS ABOUT MACDIARMID AND RELATED WORKS

Abercrombie, Lascelles, ed. *New English Poems: A Miscellany of Contemporary Verse Never Before Published.* London: Gollancz, 1931.

Aitken, Mary Baird. "The Poetry of Hugh MacDiarmid." *Scottish Art and Letters* 4 (1949): 5-25.

Blaeser, Rolf. *New Scots Renascence; literarhistorische und liguistische Einfuhrüng in das Wesen der Dichtung MacDiarmids und seiner Schule.* Dillingen, Saar: Univ. Frankfurt, 1958.

Bold, Alan, ed. *The Penguin Book of Socialist Verse.* Harmondsworth: Penguin, 1970.

Bruce, George, ed. *The Scottish Literary Revival.* London: Collier-Macmillan, 1968.

Burgess, Anthony. "His Ain Folk." *Spectator,* 11 Nov. 1966, p 621.

Burns, Robert. *A Choice of Burns's Poems and Songs.* Edited by Sydney Goodsir Smith. London: Faber and Faber, 1966.

Buthlay, Kenneth. *Hugh MacDiarmid (C. M. Grieve).* Edinburgh: Oliver and Boyd, 1964.

Daiches, David. "Hugh MacDiarmid and Scottish Poetry." *Poetry* 72 (July 1948): 203-15.

————*Poetry and the Modern World: A Study of Poetry in England between 1900 and 1939.* Chicago: Univ. of Chicago Press, 1940.

————*The Present Age in British Literature.* Bloomington: Univ. of Indiana Press, 1958.

Davidson, John. *A Selection of His Poems.* Edited by Maurice Lindsay. London: Hutchison, 1961.

Davie, Donald. "A'e Gowden Lyric." *New Statesman,* 10 Aug. 1962, pp 174-75.

Deutsch, Babette. *Poetry in Our Time.* New York: Henry Holt, 1952.

————*This Modern Poetry.* New York: Norton, 1935.

Deutsch, Babette, and Yarmolinsky, Avrahm, trans. and eds. *Modern Russian Poetry.* New York: Harcourt Brace, 1921.

Dunbar, William. *Poems.* Edited by James Kinsley. Oxford: Clarendon Press, 1958.

Duval, K. D., ed. *First Editions of the Modern Scottish Renaissance 1920-1960.* Edinburgh: Duval, 1960.

Duval, K. D., and Smith, Sydney Goodsir, eds. *Hugh MacDiarmid: a festschrift.* Edinburgh: Duval, 1962.

Frost, A. C. "Hugh MacDiarmid: Scotland's Vortex Maker." *Bookman* 86 (Sept. 1934): 287-88.

Fruman, Norman. *Coleridge, the Damaged Archangel.* New York: Braziller, 1971.

Gibson, Morgan. "Three Scottish Poets." *Arts in Society* 3 (Summer 1966): 524-41.

Glen, Duncan. *Hugh MacDiarmid (C. M. Grieve) and the Scottish Renaissance.* Edinburgh: W. and R. Chambers, 1964.

————*Hugh MacDiarmid: Rebel Poet and Prophet.* Hemel Hempstead: The Drumalban Press, 1962.

————*The Individual and the Twentieth-Century Scottish Literary Tradition.* Preston: Akros, 1971.

————*The MacDiarmids: A Conversation.* Preston: Akros, 1970.

————*A Small Press and Hugh MacDiarmid, with a Checklist of Akros Publications, 1962-70.* Preston: Akros, 1970.

————"The Word Which Silence Speaks." *Akros* 4 (Jan. 1970): 53-64.

————Ed. *Hugh MacDiarmid: A Critical Survey.* Edinburgh: Scottish Academic Press, 1972.

Gordon, Ian A. "Modern Scots Poetry." In *Essays on Scots Literature.* Edinburgh: Oliver and Boyd, 1933.

Habart, Michel. "Hugh MacDiarmid: Visionnaire du Language." *Critique* 13 (Dec. 1955): 1056-63.

Hamilton, Ian. *A Poetry Chronicle.* London: Faber and Faber, 1973.

"Hugh MacDiarmid." Special issue. *Akros* 7 (Aug. 1972).

"Hugh MacDiarmid and Scottish Poetry." Special double issue. *Agenda* 5-6 (Autumn-Winter 1967-8).

Hughes, John. "Humanism and the Orphic Voice." *Saturday Review,* 22 May 1971, pp 31-33.

"Is Lallans a Unique Phenomenon?" *Times Literary Supplement,* 9 Sept. 1960, p 22.

Jamieson, John, ed. *An Etymological Dictionary of the Scottish Language.* New edition. Paisley: Alexander Gardner. Vol. I, 1879. Vol. II, 1880. Vol. III, 1880. Vol. IV, 1882.

Jay, Peter. "Introduction." *Triquarterly* 21 (Spring 1971): xi-xx.

Keir, Walter. "Post-War Poetry in Scots." *The Saltire Review* 4 (Spring 1957): 61-64.

Kinsley, James, ed. *Scottish Poetry: A Critical Survey.* London: Cassell, 1955.

Leavis, F. R. "Hugh MacDiarmid." *Scrutiny* 4 (Dec. 1935): 305.

Lindsay, Maurice. *History of Scottish Literature.* London: Robert Hale, 1977.

————*The Scottish Renaissance.* Edinburgh: Serif, 1948.

————"Talking with F. G. Scott." *The Saltire Review* 1 (Winter 1954): 48-55.

————Ed. *Modern Scottish Poetry.* London: Faber and Faber, 1966.

MacCaig, Norman, Ed. *Honour'd Shade.* Edinburgh: Chambers, 1959.

MacQueen, John, and Tom Scott, ed. *Oxford Book of Scottish Verse.* Oxford: Clarendon Press, 1966.

Miller, Karl. "Scotch on the Rocks." *The New York Review of Books,* 2 Dec. 1971, pp 13-16.

————Ed. *Memoirs of Modern Scotland.* London: Faber and Faber, 1970.

Milner, Ian. "The Poetic Vision of Hugh MacDiarmid." *Landfall* 16 (Dec. 1962): 362-71.

Morgan, Edwin. *Essays*. Cheadle: Carcanet, 1974.

———*Hugh MacDiarmid*. Harlow, Essex: Longman Group, 1976.

———"Jujitsu for the Educated: Reflections on Hugh MacDiarmid's Poem *In Memoriam James Joyce*." *The Twentieth Century* 160 (Sept. 1956): 223-31.

Muir, Edwin. "Letter to Hugh MacDiarmid 1940." *Poetry Scotland* 2 (1945): 27.

———*The Present Age from 1914 (Introductions to English Literature,* ed. Bonamy Dobree, vol. V). London: Cresset Press, 1939.

———*Scott and Scotland: The Predicament of the Scottish Writer*. London: Routledge, 1936.

———*Transition*. London: L. and V. Wolff, 1926.

National Library of Scotland. *Hugh MacDiarmid*. Catalogue number 7. Edinburgh, 1967.

O'Casey, Sean. *Sunset and Evening Star*. New York: Macmillan, 1954.

Ouspensky, P. D. *Tertium Organum: The Third Canon of Thought: A Key to the Enigmas of the World*. Translated by Nicholas Bessaraboff and Claude Bragdon. 2nd American edition. New York: Knopf, 1922.

Pacey, Philip. *Hugh MacDiarmid and David Jones: Celtic Wonder Voyagers*. Preston: Akros, 1977.

Paulin, Dorothy Margaret. "The Position of Poetry in Scotland Today." *The Poetry Review* 28 (Sept.-Oct. 1937): 361-72.

Power, William. *Literature and Oatmeal*. London: Routledge, 1935.

Reid, J. M. *Modern Scottish Literature*. Edinburgh: Oliver and Boyd, 1945.

Rexroth, Kenneth. *The New British Poets*. New York: New Directions, 1948.

Rodger, Ian. "Hugh MacDiarmid's 70th Birthday Report." *New Saltire* 5 (Aug. 1962): 24-29.

Rosenthal, M. L. *The Modern Poets*. New York: Oxford University Press, 1960.

Saunders, R. Crombie. "The Thistle in the Lion's Mouth." *Life and Letters Today* 44 (Mar. 1945): 147-55.

Scott, Alexander. "The Thistle and the Drunk Man." *The Saltire Review* 5 (Spring 1958): 48-50.

Scott, Tom, ed. *The Penguin Book of Scottish Verse*. Harmondsworth: Penguin, 1970.

Sealy, Douglas. "The Poetry of Hugh MacDiarmid." *The Dubliner* 3 (Autumn 1964): 23-35.

Shestov, Leo. *All Things Are Possible*. Translated by S. S. Koteliansky. New York: Robert McBride, 1920.

Singer, Burns. "Scarlet Eminence: A Study of the Poetry of Hugh MacDiarmid." *Encounter* 8 (Mar. 1957): 49-62.

Smith, G. Gregory. *Scottish Literature: Character and Influence*. London: Macmillan, 1919.

Smith, Iain Crichton. *The Golden Lyric*. Preston: Akros, 1967.

———"Hugh MacDiarmid: *Sangschaw* and *A Drunk Man Looks at The Thistle.*" *Studies in Scottish Literature* 7 (Jan. 1970): 169-179.

Smith, Peter McCallum. "A Scottish Revivalist." *The Poetry Review* 27 (Nov.-Dec. 1936): 443-50.

Smith, Sydney Goodsir. "In Defence of Lallans." *The New Alliance and Scots Review* 8 (May 1948): 23.

———"The Last Word." *The Saltire Review* 4 (Autumn 1957): 62-66.

———*A Short Introduction to Scottish Literature*. Edinburgh: Serif, 1951.

Soloviev, Vladimir. *La Russie et l'Eglise Universelle*. Paris: Librairie Stock, 1922.

Soutar, William. "The Poetry of Hugh MacDiarmid." *The Free Man,* 7 April 1934, pp 8-9.

Speirs, John. *The Scots Literary Tradition*. Revised edition. London: Faber and Faber, 1962.

"Summits and Spoil-Heaps." *Times Literary Supplement,* 14 May 1970, p 528.

Tindall, William York. *Forces in Modern British Literature*. New York: Knopf, 1947.

Tschumi, Raymond. *Thought in Twentieth-Century English Poetry*. London: Routledge, 1951.

Wagner, Geoffrey. "Contemporary 'Synthetic Scots'." *University of Toronto Quarterly* 23 (July 1954): 410-20.

Weber, Brom. *Hart Crane: A Biographical and Critical Study*. New York: Bodley Press, 1948.

Weston, J. C. *Hugh MacDiarmid's "A Drunk Man Looks at the Thistle": An Essay*. Preston: Akros, 1970.

Wilson, James. *Lowland Scotch as Spoken in the Lower Strathearn District of Perthshire*. London: Oxford University, 1915.

Wittig, Kurt. *The Scottish Tradition in Literature*. Edinburgh: Oliver and Boyd, 1958.

Wright, Gordon. *MacDiarmid: An Illustrated Biography*. Edinburgh: Gordon Wright, 1977.

Young, Douglas. *Plastic Scots and the Scottish Literary Tradition*. Glasgow: Maclellan, 1948.

Indexes

à Kempis, Thomas, 107

Ballad, 58-60, 64, 69, 74, 122
Biggar, 9, 212
Blake, William, 11, 27, 28, 34, 35, 36, 47, 48, 56, 62, 73, 82, 98, 102, 181
Blok, Alexander, 110
Boehme, Jacob, 46
Broughton Magazine, 42
Burns, Robert, 9, 10, 32, 33, 71, 97, 102, 103, 107, 119, 126, 127, 128, 133, 146, 160, 199, 201. "Holy Fair," 66; "Jolly Beggars," 128; *Merry Muses of Caledonia*, 119, 158; "Tam o' Shanter," 32, 53, 67, 86, 105, 128
Buthlay, Kenneth, 10, 23, 85, 89, 91, 92, 110, 189, 204, 205, 206, 215, 226, 229

Campbell, Roy, 227
Chaucer, Geoffrey, 82
Chesterton, G. K., 107
Christ-figure, 22, 56, 59-60, 62-63, 73, 74, 97, 98, 102, 103, 116, 134, 140, 141, 144, 146, 157, 199
Christianity, 13, 232
Coleridge, Samuel Taylor, 58, 186. "Ancient Mariner," 58, 60
Communist Party, 12, 197, 211, 212
Craig, John, 136
Crane, Hart, 35, 36, 37, 63, 65, 147, 187, 188, 231. "North Labrador," 188; "Voyages," 63

Daiches, David, 81, 85-87, 91, 92, 153
Deutsch, Babette, 91, 110, 112, 113, 114. *Contemporary German Poetry*, 91
Dionysian spirit, 32, 33, 67, 95, 96, 98, 128, 141
Donne, John, 36, 39, 132, 133
Dostoevski, Fedor Mikhailovich, 38, 89, 146, 148, 159
Douglas, C. H., 36, 158, 196
Drunken speaker, 86, 89, 137
Dunbar, William, 10, 32, 34, 53, 73, 75, 77, 127, 132, 133, 160. "The Tua Mariit Wemen and the Wedo," 32, 86

Eden theme, 13, 14, 50, 58, 77, 98, 115, 116, 129, 130, 154, 159, 167, 168, 170, 181, 185, 187, 231
Eliot, T. S., 20, 30, 37, 107, 114. *Four Quartets*, 30; "Hysteria," 70; "Sweeney among the Nightingales," 70; *The Waste Land*, 30, 36, 81, 107, 114
Elliot, Jean, 107

Gaelic culture, 169, 170, 181
Gaelic language, 20, 31, 36, 49, 159, 160, 161, 167, 186
Glasgow Herald, 80, 90
Glen, Duncan, 10, 12, 23, 24, 30, 33, 85, 160, 229
Grieve, Andrew Graham (brother), 16-18, 20
Grieve, Christine (daughter by Margaret Skinner Grieve), 167
Grieve, Christopher Murray [pseud. Hugh MacDiarmid]: birth, 13; break-up of marriage, 162-63, 165, 167; childhood, 14-20; death, 9, 229; and Edwin Muir, 31, 39, 53, 78, 90; and father's death, 21-22, 167, 184, 200-01; and First World War, 19, 41-42; and George Ogilvie, 21, 41-43, 91; marriage to Margaret Skinner, 42; marriage to Valda Trevlyn, 162; and mother, 16-19, 22; name-changing to Hugh Mac-Diarmid, 12, 49; political activities, 12, 156, 197-98, 212; psychological crisis of divorce, 155, 161-63, 173, 174, 191, 199; rivalry with brother, 16-17, 19, 20, 22. Works: see separate indexes
Grieve, Elizabeth Graham (mother), 13, 16-19
Grieve, John (ancestor), 13
Grieve, John (father), 13; death of, 21-22, 184, 200-01
Grieve, Margaret Skinner (first wife) 42, 162
Grieve, Michael (son by Valda Trevlyn Grieve), 9, 163, 184
Grieve, Valda Trevlyn (second wife), 162, 163, 184

INDEX TO MACDIARMID'S WORKS

(**Boldface** indicates detailed treatment)

(*a*) BOOKS

(*b*) MISCELLANEOUS SHORT WORKS

(*c*) INDIVIDUAL POEMS